DATE DUE

D0558144

JUST

Enter Justinian

Exit Justinian

HOC OPVS
GVLIELMO
GARTHWAITIO
DVNELMIAE
BARONETTO
EQVITI COR-
ONAE BELGICAE
INSCRIPTVM EST
QVI VT GRATIAS PATRIAE
SVAE AGAT SALVTEMQVE
COMMVNEM CIVITATIS
ADIUVET STVDIA HISTORIAE
GVBERNATIONIS ORIGINIS-
QVE ET AVCTVS DIGNITATIS
REGIAE FOVET.

Theodora

Justinian

JUSTINIAN

THE LAST ROMAN EMPEROR

By

G. P. BAKER

ILLUSTRATED

Cooper Square Press

First Cooper Square Press edition 2002

This Cooper Square Press paperback edition of *Justinian* is a
unabridged republication of the edition first published in New York i
1931.

Published by Cooper Square Press
A Member of the Rowman & Littlefield Publishing Group
200 Park Avenue South, Suite 1109
New York, New York 10003-1503
www.coopersquarepress.com

Distributed by National Book Network

Library of Congress Cataloging-in-Publication Data Available.

ISBN 0-8154-1217-7 (pbk. : alk. paper)

♾™ The paper used in this publication meets the minimum requiremen
of American National Standard for Information Sciences—Permanenc
of Paper for Printed Library Materials, ANSI/NISO Z39.48–1992.
Manufactured in the United States of America.

CONTENTS

ILLUSTRATIONS, MAPS AND DIAGRAMS

PREFACE

The name Justinian has become proverbial, like Joseph, and Judas, and Julius Cæsar: and (as in their cases) it grew proverbial for one typical reason which has obscured the variety and immensity of its possessor's claims to our interest. Every lawyer knows the magnitude of Justinian in the history of law: but any one who prefers to walk at large in the vast fields of human life and human character, where most things look dwarfed, will find him bulking huger as a man and a husband than as a legislator. He was a great personality, whose story may enlarge our conceptions of the ideals which men may entertain, and the programmes to which they may elect to work. Even during his own life-time, there were people who believed that he was not a man at all, but a fiend and a limb of Satan. A man must take a very large size in characters before his enemies will pay him this kind of compliment. Because he was first of all a great man, Justinian was a good many other things also.

He possessed to a quite extraordinary degree a gift in which only Alexander the Great can have excelled him —the power of forming a point of contact and reconciliation for other strong personalities. His wife, whom he picked off the stage—and some said out of the gutter—was one of the most remarkable women who ever lived. He found and made one of the greatest soldiers—Belisarius, a man whose genius approximated with uncommon closeness to that of Hannibal; and one of the most famous architects—Anthemius of Tralles, who built the church of Sancta Sophia; and one of the most expert jurists—Tribunian, the chairman of the commission which drew up the Code and the Digest. Paul the Silentiary and Romanus were poets whose fame does not reach beyond the language in which they wrote; but in Procopius of Cæsarea, Justinian had a historian of the first rank to record his reign—a man whose work is an enchanting romance of adventure and scandal. All these found their opportunity and their aim in Justinian's grand idea of an imperial civilization.

The pages of Procopius, though by no means the only, are by far the most vivid and entertaining of all our sources of information concerning Justinian and his reign. Part of the value of Procopius is that, being a Greek, in the Greek intellectual tradition, he is no bald annalist, nor bare describer of events. He has the Greek ideal of style, which turns language into a full-ranged organ of expression; he sees the human agent and he appreciates the human motive; he can render to us accurately the character and mentality and idiosyncrasy through which the motive arrives. . . . And he was himself a human agent with a human motive and idiosyncrasy. One of the most fascinating of historical recreations is to pursue Procopius himself through his own history, employing his own testimony when possible to eliminate the distortion produced by his own prejudices, and to extract the truth pure. That it is not an easy task is a large part of its interest.

In the early years of the seventeenth century a remarkable thing happened. A new and until then barely suspected work of Procopius—his *Anecdota,* or Secret History—was discovered, and in due course edited and printed. It purported to be the ninth book of his History, written, but never during his life-time published by Procopius. The reasons why he should have held it back are obvious. It contains a whole series of statements of the most sensational nature concerning the empress Theodora and other persons—with details which would have made Chaucer or Rabelais jump. This book has ever since been a bone of contention among historians: and not unjustly, for it is a very readable book, which raises more than one problem of the first importance. The general reader, therefore, is apt to find, scattered through some books treating of Justinian and Theodora, vague allegations against the moral character of the latter, for which no confirmatory details are given. All these allegations are derived from the *Anecdota,* and the details are not supplied because they are of a kind which in the past has not usually been printed for general circulation. But we are all psychologists now: and it is very probable that the scandals of the *Anecdota* would make much less impression upon modern youth than upon its Victorian grandparents. In any case, for fifty years past belief in these allegations has steadily faded until today it may be regarded as extinguished. They have been questioned and finally dismissed on two independent grounds. On the one hand, the whole experience of mankind, ancient and modern, is conclusive that a woman of the type and temperament depicted by Procopius in his *Anecdota* could not have developed into the Theodora of history. It is as impossible as the allegation would be that Immanuel Kant spent his youth as a race-course card-sharper. On the other hand, a student of Procopius soon becomes aware of characteristics in that historian which help him to understand both why the allegations were made, and why they should be false.

The secret of Procopius is that he was an impressionist. That is to say, he could set down with perfect truth and admirable vividness anything which he saw with his own eyes and experienced in his own person: but he did not know a lie when he heard it. He had no gift of intellectual judgment; no power of recognising truth or falsehood by their intrinsic qualities or internal structure. That instant intuition into the truth of a statement which some men possess, he had not at all. He listened with wide-eyed surprise to the ingenious gentlemen who, over a bottle of wine, told him what they alleged to be the truth. He was not present at the orgies of Theodora, or the strange proceedings of Justinian's head. These were tales *told* to him. He swallowed them, just as he swallowed that yarn, related by some keen-eyed Sindbad from the Persian Gulf, of the Swimming Oyster and the Admiring Shark. How many drinks Sindbad got out of Procopius while he was putting it over, or how much money he borrowed upon the strength of it, we do not know; but one thing is certain. Sindbad was a liar. So was the gay old dog who divulged to Procopius the horrid truth about Theodora.[1]

Theodora and Justinian were not the only people who suffered at the hands of Procopius. He drew an almost

---

[1] Procopius, *History*, I, iv, 1–31. The angel-faced English and cynical Franks whom Procopius met in Italy also seem to have recognised this characteristic in the historian, for they were successful in impressing upon him a number of stories concerning Britain which were worthy of the ancestors of Captain Kearney and Baron Munchausen. *History*, VIII, xx, 6–58.

equally false picture of Khosru, the great Persian king. But with all his faults, Procopius conveys to us with amazing richness the tremendous pageant of politics and war—not in a dry, dehumanised way, but with all the dazzling richness of human personality embodying and carrying on the story. Even his absurdities and his scandals are heartening: we feel that the world cannot be really a bad place when even its wickedness and folly are so interesting. And when he forgets his prejudices and his hatreds and himself, and simply depicts the story unreeling itself before his eyes, he makes the world in which he lived a place of extraordinary interest, and conveys to us a vicarious experience which we could not otherwise enjoy. . . . To this world he is almost the only window. While British history is plunged into the irritating twilight of the period between the battle of Mount Badon and the rise of Ceawlin of Wessex, Procopius sets picturesque in a blaze of sunshine the life and adventure and romance of Italy and Africa and the Persian frontier.

In days when history is often narrated on a sort of mechanistic hypothesis, as if human action could be adequately calculated with graphic curves on blue squared paper, it is worth any one's while to study the story of an age in which the element of human personality is particularly striking. The trouble is not that human action cannot be described on blue squared paper. It can be—but only after the fact. The practical difference between mechanism and personality is that mechanical movements can be demonstrated mathematically before the event, but personal actions only after the event. Personality is a force which continually demonstrates a new law. Some men, it is true, are good judges of character; but their gift is based more upon telepathy than upon experience.

In the history of Justinian and Theodora no one can get away from the overwhelming fact of personality. Every step of the story is determined by human motive, and influenced by the quality of human character. Everything could have been different; everything very nearly was. When Demetrius sailed for Rome rather than for Naples, and when Isaac the Armenian made his raid upon Ostia, they did things as trifling as throwing a cigarette away to the right hand rather than to the left, or buying one newspaper rather than another at the bookstall: but their decisions changed the course of history. And this extraordinary sense of hazard in common things is half the interest of the story.

It is particularly good for the modern man to study it, just because he himself lives in an age in which personality seems to cancel out. It does not seem as if individual action could change the course of history. . . . But just to think so, changes the course of history. Whatsoever we do, we are changing it: though most of us will not live to see the figures chalked up at the far end of things.

Justinian and Theodora constituted the first notable man-and-woman partnership in history. They still remain perhaps the most striking example of what is possible through the combination of a first rate masculine mind with a first rate feminine mind. All who knew them recognised that this fact of partnership was the chief and decisive fact about them. Even a modern reader may find it interesting and helpful to see a working model of the dual machine in operation. Theodora was the first feminist in modern history. If she had faults, it may be said of her with some confidence that the Lord made her to match the men.

They were difficult men to match. . . . And after all, even if we accepted the worst that Procopius said of her, we could only deduce that whatsoever she did, she did with all her might. He admitted her beauty, her charm, her infinite cleverness and firmness of heart. If he gave rein to his imagination merely over her private character, it was possibly the form of calumny which, of all others, would be least wounding to the feelings of its victim.

From all that has just been said it naturally follows that the present book has been based mainly upon Procopius, as the only possible foundation for a vivid narrative of the times, and that it has followed the principle of giving his *Anecdota* full credit for the same historical value and the same virtues and faults which mark the rest of his works. If the tale of Theodora and the forty young men is decisively rejected, the case is otherwise with the much more serious story of Theodora's share in the death of Amalasuntha. The former is mere embroidery: the letter is an essential link in constructing the history of the age.

While Procopius, like Herodotus, Xenophon or Thucydides, is an author for the ordinary cultivated reader, most of the other sources of contemporaneous Byzantine history are material only for the professional scholar or the special student. In correcting and supplementing Procopius notice has been taken of many works, some of which, when it seemed helpful to the general reader, are named in footnotes. The learned reader naturally will not need such guidance. But particular heed throughout has been paid to the views of the late Professor J. B. Bury, especially as expressed in his *History of the Later Roman Empire* (1923). That work—which includes and summarises the results of Dahn, Haury, Panchenko, and a whole host of scholars—is critical and cyclopaedic rather than narrative. From such a point of view it is probably superior to any other single work: but it does not (and never was intended to) convey a coherent picture of the age and the interworking of its forces. He himself recognised, in his preface, the loss of perspective which is inevitable in the cyclopaedic method. It is just this perspective which we recapture from Procopius; and to combine some such values and perspective as we find in Procopius, with the more essential of the details so laboriously sought out and established by modern scholarship, is one of the aims of this present book.

There should be no need to add that it has another aim to condition its method. While it endeavours to preserve the correct values and perspective in relation to Justinian and his times, it seeks to preserve a similarly correct perspective in relation to the whole process of evolution of which Justinian's life and work form a part. The development of political civilization from the stage of the city state to modern times is one continuous and unbroken process which can be described in one definite formula. We can see, in the careers of Hannibal and of Sulla, the process by which separate city-states were collected into one multiplex state, and the problems which were involved by the change. We can see, in the lives of Tiberius and Constantine, the influences which created a particular type of monarchy for that multiplex state, and destroyed all other types. So, in a life of Justinian, it is possible to illustrate with unusual clearness the contest between the old, mature imperial system and the young immature system of national states which was beginning its career in western Europe. Some of the influences which vitally affected European history for many centuries afterwards are already visible—the difficulty which north Europeans found in maintaining themselves in Africa; the only slightly smaller difficulty which they found in holding Italy. Even in Justinian's reign we can see the first sign of political facts which time has only hardened and sharpened. We can see the system of national states settling with its centre somewhere in northern Gaul—where it remains to this day.

This book, therefore, like its predecessors, is not an encyclopaedia of the known facts respecting its subject, but an attempt to place him in true position in relation to a much larger process of evolution the programme of which will be found briefly indicated in *Sulla the Fortunate*. It is an attempt, not so much to discuss or establish particular details concerning Justinian as to utilise profitably for its purpose those facts which have been already, with reasonable certitude, established.

G. P. B.

Elmer, Sussex.

1931.

CHAPTER I

CHOOSING PARTNERS

I

THREE small and frightened girls, crowned with garlands which did not interest them and which tended to slip off; a vast open space before them, full of light and air; the immense ring of faces, and the perpetual sound of voices that constituted the Hippodrome of Constantinople. . . . The sea-like murmur rises to a terrifying note of surprise and enquiry as the three small girls fall on their knees in the midst of the light and air, and hold out beseeching hands. In the Hippodrome

Their mother, who has pushed them out, is standing back in the shadow waiting.

The mandator walks up, and turning to the ring of faces begins to speak across the Hippodrome. Not every man's voice can carry over that vast space.

These are the three children of Acacius the Bear-Keeper, of the Green party. Their mother has married again; but her new husband has not been kept on as Bear-Keeper. The children pray the Green party that he may have the job.

The sound grows in volume; it rolls round the Hippodrome, and increases awfully, terrifyingly, appallingly; the three small girls tremble to the heart's core to hear the thunder. The Green party have been canvassed by the enemy; they say NO. The Blues and the Greens

A bland person strolls across the sand to the mandator,

and speaks to him in an ordinary voice, while the three cower and tremble.

The mandator lifts up his voice again, till it carries across the Hippodrome. The Blue party need a Bear-Keeper. These three children pray that their new father may have the job.

The Blues have watched. The mere fact that the Greens have refused the petition arouses their interest in the proceedings. A new sound arises and grows: a thunder even more awful and soul-shattering than the last. But now a large number of thumbs are turned up; and a large number of faces lean over to look at the three small girls. It is YES.

They hurry away back into the shade, but now to the left hand. Here is the portico of the Blues: a long, columned and covered space where the Blue committee-men and staff preside over various activities. Across that portico, many years later, Belisarius is to hasten followed by his crowd of steel-clad slaughtermen. But Belisarius at this moment is still a boy at Germania in Thrace.

The three small girls were Comito, Theodora and **The girls become Blues** Anastasia. Theodora was to become the empress Theodora, and Comito was to be the mother of the empress Sophia.

This was the way in which they first became Blues.

II

A life of Justinian naturally begins with Theodora. The historian has described her as she was in her prime, as empress: a little woman, with the face we see upon ancient Greek vases—pale, soft, large-eyed, with long

sweeping lashes and blue-black wavy hair. But her physical beauty was the least thing about her. Over and
above that, she shared to the full those characteristics we
can still detect in the women of the Greek vases—a mischievous and imp-like brilliance, a quickness and cleverness and charm, of the kind which will hypnotize men
into swearing that even a plain woman is the loveliest
thing God made. She had a sense of humour, and she was
as quick on the nail as most women are, who have to fight
their way in the world.

It is perhaps in Paris, rather than in any other modern
capital, that we could learn by observation something of
the child and woman Theodora was. The children of
Acacius the Bear-Keeper were born into the theatrical
world, and grew up in it. The theatrical world in all ages
has had its faults. It does not always cultivate an ascetic
view of morals. But in all ages it has been a cheerful,
clever, and stimulating world, and to do well in it, professionally, a young girl needs to have all her wits about
her. No one ever accused Theodora of being wanting in
this respect. Her deadliest enemies admitted her triumphant art. All they said was . . . but we will consider this a little later on in the narrative; and besides,
Theodora (at any rate in her younger days) would
probably have replied that Procopius the historian must
have been there himself if he knew so much about it.
And as we shall see, it probably was not true.

An age which has seen and appreciated some famous
modern artists of the theatre can easily find an appropriate pigeon-hole in which to "place" Theodora. Her
speciality was impishness. Procopius himself describes
the way in which she could convulse an audience of

Theodora

hardened Byzantine Greeks. She could make very amusing faces. She was no dancer, and never excelled in any form of "serious" art.[1] She was very popular—Procopius, of course, says that she was far too popular. . . . It was more than *he* ever was!

III

The daughter of Acacius seems from the first to have determined to be a lady. One way of getting out of a profession is to get out at the top. The first important enterprise of Theodora, so far as we have any record, was when she went to Egypt with Hecebolius, the governor of Pentapolis. It was a considerable rise in the world from being the daughter of a Bear-Keeper: but Theodora's career as an unofficial wife was short. What went wrong we are not told. Possibly Hecebolius was one of those men who want to keep other people back, instead of pushing them on; or Egypt may have been a dull place to live in . . . It still is . . . In any event, the menage broke up; and either Hecebolius turned Theodora out, or she shook the dust of his accursed house off her shoes— for she went back to Alexandria, and began to work her way home.

Her tour through the east seems to have been a profitable one; for by the time she arrived again at Constantinople she had enough money to live upon, and she had changed her mind about some things. She took a house, and with an inspired instinct set up a loom and began to

Early career of Theodora

---

[1] Procopius, *Anecdota*, Θ′, δ′. Even Dr. Hodgkin persists that Theodora was a dancer, although Procopius explicitly states that she was not. But probably Dr. Hodgkin, as a Quaker, was far too shocked at the awful things he was reading to pay careful attention to details.

play the part of Penelope waiting for her Odysseus. Who her Odysseus would be, probably she could not guess; but, like Penelope, she wove and waited until her Odysseus should arrive.

The romance of Theodora began with the day when he did arrive. And his name was one which is still a fame and proverb throughout the western world—he was Petrus Sabbatius Justinianus, the future emperor Justinian Justinian.

Her new friend was no highbrow. He was a stalwart, energetic Thracian peasant, round faced, fresh complexioned,[1] and inclined to be serious, as country-bred men frequently are: a man who was apt to fidget, and a hard worker. He was, of course, rich. Theodora had a natural sympathy with the deserving poor, but no personal taste for the hardships of poverty. The friendship grew. It was largely based upon the fact that Providence, in its infinite wisdom, had seldom made a prettier or more perfect complementary pair than those two. She liked his solid reliability, his gift for finality. He was a man who did not take his money back, or argue over change; and he kept his appointments. There was very little of the gay young spark about him. When he was a boy, he must have stayed where his mother put him, for he still preserved the same trait. It is one that most women find rather endearing.

Justinian, for his own part, never lost his taste for

[1] The author's thanks are due to Mr. Harold Mattingly for kindly selecting the coins which have been used to illustrate the personal appearance of Justinian. The frontispiece (enlarged from a gold solidus in the British Museum) shows the emperor as he was in middle age, younger, probably, than the 57 years he counted in A. D. 539, round about which date the coin was struck. The two silhouettes, printed at the beginning and end of the book, show the profile, which is more aquiline than might be expected from the full-face view.

the fiery little imp with the long dark lashes and the quick tongue. He paid her the greatest compliment a man can pay a woman—an unwavering life-long devotion. It was not an empty compliment. Most peasant-bred men like to get sixteen ounces to the pound; and if Justinian paid in a coinage very much stamped with his own image, we may be sure that he thought he was obtaining his money's worth.

The bond of unity

All their later life showed that the bond which grew up between them was very far from being superficial or evanescent. It was not the infatuation of a gilded youth for a chorus girl.[1] He was capable of appreciating the whole of her charm; but even the more external clevernesses of Theodora do not seem to have mattered so much to Justinian as the deep intelligence and high-tempered character he detected beneath them. . . . Theodora seems to have responded wonderfully to this form of appreciation. The more he valued her for such gifts, the more they grew and blossomed. She had been amusing, when amusingness was wanted; she could be great, when greatness was asked. He had only to name the part, and she would play it.

IV

Justinian was not the kind of man who kept a mistress in a hidden rose-bower. That element of solidity in him which gave him his strength made him also resolve

---

[1] Justinian made public references to her which, although no one today would notice them as peculiar, were of some originality in his own age. "Our most *pius* consort given us by God" shows us that we are out of the classical period, and entering the age of Christian theories of the relation of the sexes.

to marry Theodora. Those elements of ingenuity and resolution which made him great enabled him successfully to carry through a task on which a weaker man might have suffered wreck.

His task was to get the daughter of Acacius, the famous imp of the Greek comic stage, into the great palace of Constantinople as the revered wife of its future ruler. The first person to be consulted was of course, the emperor. Problems

The awe with which Theodora looked up to the figure of Autocrator Cæsar Justinus, the pious, the victorious, the august, was not shared by Justinian, who knew the old gentleman as his uncle Justin. The old fellow, who was a man of the world, and could scarcely scrawl his name, would probably not have bucked very seriously if Justinian had proposed to set up even a mistress in the imperial palace. But in the case of a wife he would have pointed out that it was necessary to consult the empress Euphemia.

Many years earlier—before the birth of Theodora—old Justin (who was then young Justin) had set out with two companions from the village of Bederiana, near Uskub. It was the usual course for younger sons to follow, for whom there was no land available. With their bags slung over their shoulders, they walked the four hundred or so miles of mountain and plain to the golden city of Constantinople. Men of their type were wanted in the imperial guard. For thirty years or so Justin stood erect in silver and steel in the imperial presence chambers, and lounged and played quiet games of dice with others of his kind in the ante-rooms. He rose to be commander of the guard, and became a senator. But all his fingers were still thumbs, and he was no use when any one wanted advice on spelling.

The emperor Justin

Although he had never had education himself, Justin had become well aware of its advantages. He was not so foolish as to waste his time in attempting to acquire gifts which he was now too old to enjoy. He had a better plan. His sister Vigilantia had married a man named Sabbatius, who belonged to the neighbouring Dardanian village of Tauresium: and she had two children, Petrus Sabbatius and Vigilantia. Justin sent for the boy Petrus. The old guardsman, now Count and Senator, had plenty of money. Petrus received the education which Justin might have given a son of his own. The best that money could buy and Constantinople could produce—and that was probably the best then available in the world—went to form the mind and temper of Petrus: and never did education shape better human material.

Petrus and Justin got on well together, and the nephew seems to have been in his way fond of, and at all times faithful to the handsome, curly-haired old uncle, and his aunt Euphemia. He owed his advantages to the accident that Euphemia was childless. In her time she had been a prisoner of war, booked to be put on the market as a slave. Justin had taken a fancy to her, and

Euphemia

had married her, and renamed her Euphemia. Their relations were prosaic and happy; much like those of a successful building contractor who has married his cook.

Justin expressed his satisfaction with Petrus by legally adopting his nephew, who, according to Roman custom, took, at his adoption, the name of Justinian, in compliment to his new father. We shall see, a little later on, the peculiar circumstances in which Justin became emperor. The old fellow was quite content to be a majestic figure-head, while Justinian and a party of educated friends ran all the business for him. But they were all of them men, and Euphemia was no doubt sufficiently experienced to know that men seldom criticise an elderly woman adversely, if she is decently polite to them. . . . The really serious question would only arise when Justinian broke to his aunt the awful news that he was importing into the quiet precincts of the imperial palace the smartest imp in Constantinople, the darling of the stage, a long-lashed beauty whose wicked eyes would see in a moment all that was wrong with poor Euphemia. . . . How could Euphemia bear it?

v

Justinian did not press his wishes. Not until Euphemia was dead did he carry out his plan of marrying Theodora. The emperor seems to have raised no objection. After all, he was quite the kind of man who would have liked her—though not as a wife. His private ideal of domesticity ran more to the washerwoman type.

No one troubled to chronicle the details of Justinian's wedding. When and where [1] it took place we are equally in the dark. But the details which survive concerning the marriage settlements and the home of Theodora throw an interesting light upon some of the ideas and feelings with which the two were engrossed.

Marriage of Justinian and Theodora

Economic independence was one of the points which they sought to secure for her. Before their marriage,

---

[1] The year 526, about a year or less before the death of Justin, is a likely date.

Justinian had already given her considerable sums of money; but he contemplated that, as soon as she became his wife, she should receive an endowment in the more permanent form of land. The reason for this was a very solid and well-calculated one. If she were to be kept as a pet, one income would be quite enough for them both; but if their marriage were to be an alliance, a partnership, in which both were to be free agents and active participants, then it was necessary that both should have independent resources legally secured to them.[1]

That they discussed in principle, and planned in practice, some such idea as this, is fairly certain from the nature of what they did. The marriage settlements of Theodora were far more than was necessary for pin money or a dress allowance, even for the wife of the heir to the imperial throne. They were plainly intended to be more. They were, by their amount and nature, meant to equip Theodora with power to be an active and independent agent, who could at need intervene in great affairs with resources adequate to the possible magnitude of the task. This was a new idea. No woman before—at any rate, no prospective empress—had ever been provided for on such a scale or according to such a principle.

The settlements

The principle so introduced by Justinian to suit the case of Theodora would have had some remarkable effects if applied universally to marriage endowments. Not until quite recent times has such an idea been gener-

---

[1] Procopius refers to this spirit of partnership, *Anecdota* I´, θ´–ιβ´ and again in B´, ι´, where he purports to quote a remark of Theodora herself that "my husband never does anything without consulting me." The slight inconsistency and incoherence of Procopius on this subject may be due to the fact that he could not conceive an equal partnership between a man and a woman.

ally accepted even in principle. The marriage settlement of Theodora was the first model for the economic endowment of marriage as an equal partnership.

VI

Previous to his marriage, Justinian had occupied a house known as the House of Hormisdas, which stood near the sea, between the southern end of the Hippodrome and the waters of Propontis. Here, apparently, their married life began. This house was destined to become much more famous later on, as the House of Theodora, and we shall find it mentioned again and again. Justinian must have intended from the first that it should be Theodora's peculiar preserve. In addition to being a strong and well-protected building, it was situated close to the harbour of Boucoleon, which gave direct access to the sea.

While the marriage endowments, and this house of Hormisdas, together marked that Theodora came to Justinian as a partner and helper who intended to face great risks in his company, it would not have been altogether advisable to underline this conception too much. To introduce her into the imperial circle was like introducing a new member into a firm. It was necessary to conciliate, and to enlist the sympathy of a considerable number of important people whose support was indispensable to Justinian. He therefore walked very prudently at least until the death of Justin and his own election to the throne. Once this was secure, he would be able to make his own arrangements.

There were two forces that expressly needed conciliat-

Partnership

ing. One was the army. It was not, in these days, so dangerous a force as the earlier army which had made and unmade emperors at its will; but it still exercised great influence upon the course of events. The Excubitors would not have worried too much over Theodora's youthful morals, but they might have shied at any hint of petticoat government. Justinian, not being a soldier himself,[1] needed to exercise prudence in this quarter. A civilian emperor almost inevitably attracted a certain amount of criticism from the military.

Powers to be conciliated

The other force was the Church: and this was, if anything, even more important than the army. The bishops exercised legal powers of restraint upon the provincial governors and rights of criticizing and reporting their action. As the governors were more or less isolated individuals, while the bishops settled the general policy of the Church in synod, the bishops were infinitely the more useful allies and the more dangerous opponents. As we shall see, Justinian rested a large part of his hopes upon their support. If the bishops once took against Theodora, the mischief would be irreparable. Hence it was highly necessary to see that nothing which was done jarred upon their consciences. . . . Fortunately, Theodora had theological views. They were, it is true, Monophysite, whereas Justinian's were Catholic; but this did not very much matter. Monophysite views were sufficiently fashionable for the purpose. The bishops of this prejudice were charmed at a woman accom-

---

[1] He was Count of the Domestici, Commander of the Imperial Guard and also Master of Soldiers "in praesenti," an office which made him all that a Minister of War today would be. But he probably could not have drilled a squad of recruits. He was more usually known as "the Patrician."

plished enough to appreciate the profound truths for which they contended. If any objections to her past were raised, they ignored them. The enemies of the Church have always exhorted her to tolerance; it is hard to blame the bishops if they exercised a virtue so often demanded of them.

When the critical moment came, therefore, and Justin died, neither the army nor the Church considered the existence of Theodora any obstacle to the claims of Justinian; [1] neither, for that matter, was any objection raised by ordinary public opinion, which apparently had not heard of any of those scandals long afterwards recorded in secret by Theodora's enemies. They had plenty of opportunity for lodging at least an objection. Justinian had governed the empire ever since his uncle's accession, so he was pretty well known. For six months before Justin's death he was regent with full imperial power. When Justin's last illness began, in the spring of 527, the senate formally applied to him to name his successor. He nominated Justinian as his colleague, and on April 4, in the great hall of the palace, the patriarch of Constantinople solemnly placed the imperial diadem on Justinian's head. In the Delphax the imperial guard were paraded, and here the solemn ceremony of accepting and acclaiming the new Augustus was gone through. . . . It was usual to have this ceremony in the Hippodrome, where the Man in the Street could express his view. If this part were slurred, nobody, on the other hand, registered any dissatisfaction.

For four months the new emperor and his empress

Theodora is accepted

---

[1] Procopius, *Anecdota,* I', s'–ζ'.

were before the world for its inspection. On the first of August Justin died. The old soldier did not die of any civilian disease, but of the results of a long-standing arrow wound in his foot which had imperfectly healed. With his death the daughter of Acacius the Bear-Keeper, the admired star of the comic stage, became the first woman in the empire.

Theodora
becomes
empress

VII

Once the bar was safely crossed, Justinian took a more independent line. Although men may sometimes pretend to the contrary, the possession of formal and legal power, according to the accepted ritual of the State, is a great advance even for one who has long governed in secret. Justinian had for many years controlled vast revenues. Now he no longer needed to render account to any man; and the change was visible.

There were imperial estates which by long custom were earmarked for the empress. The Augusta's household was a department of state with very rich revenues of its own. These now became Theodora's, and by Justinian's arrangement they were augmented a good deal beyond the customary. She became a very rich woman in her own right. The House of Hormisdas was allotted now to her sole personal use. Extensive changes adapted it to the new era; the wall of the imperial palace was extended to enclose it; and Justinian may have been thinking of himself and Theodora when he approved the designs for the pair of churches with a single connecting court, which belonged to the new Hormisdas. One was a basilica of the old type; but the other was an octagonal domed building planned in the new style by (probably) Her house Anthemius of Tralles, who decorated it with the monograms of the emperor and empress, and joined their names in an inscription which still exists. . . . The basilica descends from old Rome; the octagonal domed church looks forward to the new Byzantium that was to come; the change is marked and symbolized by the names of Justinian and Theodora, and the work is done by Anthemius of Tralles. The basilica has disappeared; but the octagonal church still remains.

Had Theodora been the descendant of a hundred kings, she might have worn old clothes and cultivated democracy. But the daughter of Acacius could take no risks. Her court etiquette was exceptionally strict, and contained no opportunity for smiling at ex-favourites of the stage. Respect in all forms of reference to the imperial person was rigidly enforced, and prostration was an invariable rule for all who entered the imperial presence. . . . Theodora's household was under a discipline which was never, to our knowledge, broken by rebellion or treachery. Theodora possessed, in fact, a much greater gift for discipline than Justinian, who, although he approved in principle of a strict etiquette, had at the back of his mind some of the instincts of the villager who is in the habit of meeting his neighbours on informal terms. . . . Her servants are scarcely known Her household to us by name. They remain impressive and reticent, as they were to their contemporaries; but that they were capable and efficient, all their acts show. Owing to this gift which Theodora possessed, of strict and effective organization, she became, and she remained to the end of her life, her husband's intelligence department and his detective bureau. . . . She knew everything. All the news came to her; she had her finger on every thread of intrigue; she had her agents in every place. . . . Justinian must have been quite aware that she did not always tell him everything. Sometimes she thought she knew better than he did. He had no power to prevent this independence; and it is probable that such an independence was part of their bargain together. A good husband who has a good wife has no hesitation in shutting his eyes when told to do so.

VIII

She lived the life which she preferred, and to which she was accustomed—a sleek, silken, cat-like life; but the cat is a fierce and hardy animal, and so was she. She was a great sleeper: or at any rate, she kept her room a good deal. Some people think best in bed. She rose late, and spent long in bathing and dressing. Her toilette was of that curious and elaborate type which sometimes goes out of fashion in favour of a judicious naturalism and simplicity; but the power possessed by such arts of creating an astounding and miraculous aura, a real and fascinating addition to the personality of a woman, always brings them back. She did not diet herself. She ate and drank what she liked. Possibly she was of too nervous a type to put on flesh.

Her life

If, however, the insinuations of the historian are to go for anything, these were not the only tastes of Theodora. She liked the sea, and for several months of the year passed her time at the sea-side. . . . As her household complained of hardship at these places, we may safely infer that it led a healthy and arduous life. Justinian built a house at Pythia, where the hot springs were; and to these she went at due seasons.

Her life was by no means one of selfish luxury. Theodora was one of the first women to take an active interest in social questions; and she must have been the first who ever gave that interest a distinctly feminist turn. Her general attitude towards the male sex was unmistakably critical. She very obviously did not like all the ways and habits of thought which distinguished the lord of creation in her own days; and very probably she would not think that our own age had greatly improved on the old model. She amazed and scandalized her contemporaries by starting a Rescue Home for girls. More than this, she secured the passing of a law which prohibited the traffic in women, and provided for the expulsion of persons convicted of it. The compensation which was rendered necessary by the passage of this law she paid out of her own resources.

Her activities

She was the general champion of women; and every woman with a grievance, who could do so, laid it before Theodora. If husbands and other deluded persons did not always appreciate her interference, she was ready to repay their hostility with interest. Most of them found it safer to leave her alone.

It was impossible that Theodora, being what she was, should not make many and bitter enemies. But she neither apologised to them nor placated them: she confined herself to the task of hitting them back.

IX

The genius of Theodora was for organization and discipline: but that of Justinian was a genius for recognizing genius in others. He was himself a man of ability: no man can appreciate in others what is not in himself: but the greatness of his reign and the fame of his personality is founded upon the deeds of men whom he chose and lifted out of obscurity. He showed this gift in picking his wife. He showed it in the astonishing galaxy of various talent with which he surrounded himself: John "the Cappadocian," his prime minister; Tribunian, his chancellor, the real author of the Corpus Juris Civilis; Belisarius, his commander-in-chief; Anthemius of Tralles, his architect; Paul, his poet; and Procopius, his historian. All these were men of strong individuality as well as of high intelligence. Tribunian was a Hellenist—a believer in the old religion; the sort of man who, if tackled upon the subject, would have had a complete allegorical and symbolical explanation to offer: not the sort of man who would have believed in the objective reality of the manifestation if Pan had spoken to him out of a thicket in the twilight. It does not seem to have mattered much. He was a quiet man who will enter the scene very seldom in the course of this book. Most of the time presumably he was busy in his office, examining and arranging material for the Corpus.

Anthemius came of a clever family, and had brothers as brilliant and original as himself. If the famous interiors he designed had, as is probable, any resemblance to the interior of his own mind, it was a beautiful, golden, sun-litten mind, large and majestic

Justinian's
mighty
men

and enchanting, lined with wonderful pictures. He began the second great period of Greek architecture, and he did as much as most men to imprint upon later Byzantine civilization that rare and strange and austere beauty which distinguished it. He might have lived and **Anthemius** died in comparative obscurity. Justinian was the man who found him the opportunities and the places and above all the money. So the dreams arose at the word of Anthemius; and some of them are still there.

Of all his flock, though some died before him, Justinian lost only one—and that was John: but this was because John could not be headed off from getting across Theodora, and he suffered the consequences. John—as he himself would have been the first to point out—was the man who provided the money. Other people might be decorative and romantic, and might accomplish those works which attract the eye, or read well in a book, or sound imposing in a speech—the lust of the eye and the pride of life—but John was Number One, who, by hard and unpleasant work, rendered all these pretty things possible. He supplied the funds—the Needful.[1]

X

Justinian discovered John very early in his reign, when the Cappadocian was working as a subordinate clerk in the war office. A brief accidental word or two caught Justinian's attention. The treasury was in a bad state: a man was very much wanted who had the force and determination to reorganize and reawaken the whole

---

[1] Chrêmata—a word employed by Procopius.

system of collecting the revenue, and who had the mind of an administrative reformer. Justinian had further conversation with John. . . . John went up several steps to an important official post. . . . He justified the advance. He received rank and dignity, to enable him to deal on equal terms with great men. Three years after Justinian's accession, John became Praetorian prefect— Prime Minister, as we should call the post. His job was to make things hum.

John the Cappadocian

Although some strong bond of sympathy connected them there can seldom have been two men more dissimilar than John and Justinian. The emperor was a cool, somewhat ascetic man, highly educated in the learning of his age, and not merely of religious views, but of religious temperament. John was a big, massive, rough, quarrelsome fellow, with the constitution of a navvy, the temper of a sea captain, and no book-learning to speak of. He never faltered: but—and in the Constantinople of that age, it was a weakness—he had a natural incapacity for retreat. He had a one-way mind, and his one way was forward.

XI

When Justinian let loose John the Cappadocian upon the department of revenue, he did something for which many of his subjects never forgave him. John grabbed the system, shook it violently, and proceeded to make it walk. Any system, from a Byzantine tax office to a modern steel rolling mills, would have walked when a man like John held it by the ear. He instituted reforms

according to his own notions of what was called for—
not according to the wishes of the persons concerned.
Believing that the imperial Post no longer paid for itself,
he abolished it, and a wail of horror went up from the
people who had enjoyed its benefits. Fabulous legends
circulated about him. Wealthy and influential tax-
dodgers, who in the past had got off with far less than
their correct assessments, were now invited to call at
the prefecture. An interview with John was evidently
a memorable experience. It was reported that he had
underground dungeons where the tax-dodgers, loaded
with fetters, were cast by brutal myrmidons of the prefecture: but it is very probable that a glance at these
was enough in the majority of cases. The officials of the
revenue entertained sentiments concerning their chief
scarcely calmer than those of his victims. "Phalaris,"
"Cyclops" and "Briareus" are among the names applied
to him. He apparently did not mind. . . . And if some
of the tax dodgers, after having been under-assessed so
long, were now in the excitement of the moment somewhat over-assessed—well, John did not care.

As nearly all our information concerning John comes
from his enemies, it is naturally of a sombre hue. His
friends might have told a different story. He retained the
confidence and friendship of Justinian for many years.
His reforms were often necessary and advisable; he did
not always spare himself or his own official privileges.
We need not pay too much attention to the stories of his
illiteracy. He would not be the only good business-man
who "could hardly read or write." Had he lived today,
he would no doubt have done his round of golf, and

driven a high-powered car with any of his contemporaries; with a dictaphone and a good stenographer he would not have needed to worry about those nasty things, pen and ink: and no one would ever have thought of alluding to his difficulties with these articles. . . . Even as it was, John and his secretaries no doubt got through more work by dictation than all the grave old gentlemen in Constantinople with their decorous script. . . . And probably John said so.

John's enemies had other things to say of him. It was (they alleged) his custom to hurry through his work so that he could devote his leisure to wallowing in debauchery. Here the rebutting evidence is weaker. That John was a formidable trencherman is likely enough; and men of his type are not uncommonly drinkers. That he was a profound admirer of the female sex is probable. If his tastes in this direction were old-fashioned, and even oriental, we have the natural starting-point for that feud with Theodora which was destined to have such remarkable results.

XII

Justinian
and his
ministers

    This fierce, this powerful and Rabelaisian type of man, driving his way with energy through all opposition, does not seem quite the type with which Justinian would have naturally formed links of friendship. And yet there is no doubt that the emperor liked John. A hint of the tastes which drew them together is contained in a speech which Procopius put into John's mouth. Although the speech is probably the composition of the historian himself, it has characteristics which suggest that he is decorating a theme the substance of which was really John's: for he does not attribute similar sentiments to other men. According to Procopius, John said to Justinian:

"The good faith which you show towards your subjects enables us to speak frankly on all matters of public interest, even if you do not personally agree with our remarks. You exercise authority with good sense, and do not necessarily approve of the man who tells you what you want to hear, nor disapprove of the man who argues against your views; you can sum up all sides fairly, and we are all satisfied with your judgment. Knowing that this is so, I am about to advocate a policy which you may not like at the moment, but later on you will bear witness to the loyalty with which I speak." [1]

Procopius was an open enemy of John, and a secret enemy of Justinian; but these words are enlightening as to the large and tolerant temper in which their relations were conducted. The historian bears witness more than once to this characteristic of Justinian. The emperor was an easy man to speak to; no one who wished to see him was turned away. He did not trouble about informal behaviour on the part of people unacquainted with the technicalities of court etiquette. One would think, the historian bitterly comments, that he was a sheep. . . . John Malalas tells of the man who was tried for treasonable slander. Justinian had the offender before him, scanned the report of the trial, and tearing it up, said: "You are pardoned for your offence against me. Pray that you may be pardoned for your offence against God." . . . This was the kind of man who could appreciate John.

Justinian's temperament

[1] Procopius, *History*, III. x. 8–11.

We shall gain some light upon the characters of John and Justinian, as well as a closer insight into the story, if we carefully note the extent to which this tolerance was carried. John did not like Theodora, and did not approve of her: and he frankly said so, and argued his case to her husband. He was not a man to hide his feelings nor to hold his tongue: and he never went out of his way to placate the empress nor to get upon friendly terms with her. Theodora knew at least the substance of what he said to Justinian, and she was deeply incensed. For years Justinian managed to keep his lion and his tigress from one another's throats. As we shall see, they ended by getting at each other at last, with devastating results: but for long he maintained peace, without letting either of them prejudice his mind against the other.

John and Theodora

XIII

What these slanders of John the Cappadocian may have been, Procopius does not inform us; but since he elsewhere relates, in another connection, a considerable amount of scandal about Theodora's past, it does not seem altogether unreasonable to suggest that these famous stories are nothing less than the slanders set going by John. As Praetorian prefect, John had ample opportunities for looking up Theodora's earlier history; he had equal opportunities for inventing anything he could not discover; he was a good deal of a rake himself, and probably conversant with quite a library of Rabelaisian stories; and (as Procopius tells us) he meant mischief against the empress, and therefore had a strong motive.

The truth of these scandalous stories has exercised the minds of historical students ever since the *Anecdota* of Procopius were first printed. Our view of them might be a little altered if we believed them originally to have been factors in the political game, employed by John to destroy the influence of Theodora over her husband. The history of John's downfall, when it came, if read in the light of such an idea as this, takes on a new aspect. . . . On such a view, these stories were no hole-and-corner whispers, but charges made direct to Justinian himself: and Justinian, far from removing his friendship, continued to trust and protect John.[1]

Conflict of forces

The belief of Theodora was that John's aim was the imperial throne. He wanted her out of the way, so that he could do what he liked with Justinian. Procopius put this also down in his history. Whether it was true or not, we are in no position to judge: but it is easy to believe that John consulted mediums and spiritualistic counsellors, who (always fair and false) reported favourably of his chances. He should, they said, wear the mantle of Augustus. Poor old John!

He had no illusions about Theodora. The head of John, taking his last apprehensive look round before locking his bedroom door at night, is one of the vivid memories a reader takes away from the pages of Procopius. She would get him some day! Meanwhile, John did not fail to glance under his bed.

[1] Were John the originator of these stories, we should have a complete explanation why they were known to Procopius, a man in close contact with the imperial circle, and why they should be unknown to other historians.

XIV

But in the head of Justinian himself was an Idea to which all these things and people were subservient. Theodora and John and Tribunian and Anthemius possessed meaning and significance only in so far as they subserved this idea. He needed them all; he conciliated and restrained, for all fulfilled some essential function and he could dispense with none of them.

The plan of campaign

Let us consider the nature of this idea, this programme, policy or plan of campaign; for in it and by it was worked the drama, half tragedy and half comedy, which men know as the Reign of Justinian. Human beings, with their human motives, were the agents; but they acted parts in a play larger than most of them knew.

CHAPTER II

THE PLAN OF CAMPAIGN

I

JUST as Theodora learnt, from her early experience of the stage, those principles which she embodied in her policy as empress, so young Petrus Sabbatius, leaving his native mountains for the lecture rooms and libraries of Constantinople, was impresed with certain notions which remained firmly fixed in his mind. His study of Roman law and Roman history only strengthened the impression which he gained in riding from Tauresium to the capital—a route which his uncle had walked—that the grandeur he gazed upon was civilization itself.

There was nothing in the experience of any young man of the age to suggest that civilization was multiplex, or possessed more than one valid tradition. The age had no nationalistic experience to offer. To come from the life of Tauresium to that of Constantinople was to be deeply and ineffaceably impressed by the overwhelming moral supremacy of civilization. To study the history and nature of civilization was to perceive that it was a unity. There was no other. "Rome" was a name for the whole tradition of civilized life.

To this truth Roman law bore unmistakable witness. Only one such system of jurisprudence existed: only one could exist. If another were possible, the human mind was quite unable to imagine what it could be like. There was one truth, one logic, one mathematic; and on the same principle there was one law and therefore one civilization.

Such a fact placed upon the man who perceived it a real compulsion. If he honoured peace, the reign of law, orderly government, impartial justice, enlightened religion, wise education, the enjoyment of the artistic heritage of man—then it was an obligation upon him to restore the rule of the Roman empire. Other men doubtless had felt this, and had submitted to a helpless sense that they could do nothing against the adverse current of events. But Petrus came at a happy moment; time and place and opportunity were with him; his way had been prepared, the word passed to him, and Destiny stood off to see him begin.

II

Italy had ceased, six years before Petrus was born, to be the home of a Roman emperor. Eadwaeccer the Rugian chief had deposed Romulus Augustulus, and reigned as king in Italy: since when the emperor at Constantinople had been the only Roman emperor.

This curious result had come about through a somewhat interesting process. The great wars and migrations which had taken place through the westward movement of the Huns had scattered the north European peoples all over southern Europe. A similar inundation had taken place more than once before, and southern Europe had absorbed or destroyed the invaders. But during the hundred years or so before the birth of Petrus Sabbatius, she had been obliged to confront a new condition of affairs which greatly modified her power of absorption. The new factor was the rise of the northern kingships.

The
problem

When the Gothic King Irminric transformed the tribal monarchy of the Goths into a political monarchy, he carried through a revolution which enabled the Goths first of all to conquer a large part of northern Europe and then to retain their existence unimpaired through a century of war and change and migration. His example was imitated: and the north became the home of a score of similar monarchies based upon the same model. Their history had varied a good deal, and was destined to vary yet more in the future which was still to come; but when Petrus Sabbatius was a boy, the existence of these kingships had enabled the northern peoples, driven before the Huns, to retain their identity and coherence. The Goths had settled in Spain and Dacia without being destroyed or absorbed. The English settling in Britain, and the Franks in Gaul, had proved their social organization to be stronger than the Roman provincial system. In Africa, the Vandals, instead of a helpless band of refugees, were a conquering power. In every quarter, the existence of these kingships had enabled the immigrants to defy the Roman government. A modern onlooker, glancing over the state of western Europe as it was in the youth of Petrus, would have seen the Roman empire as merely one monarchy amongst many. . . . To the Roman citizen, such a conception was impossible. These kingships, exercising power within the frontiers of the empire, were in his view intrusive, illegal and destructive forces, which had no right to be where they were, and had not the slightest claim to regard themselves as civilized governments.

The kingships and the empire

The difficulty was to give this view any practical force. In actual fact, the Gothic and Vandal kings were persons to be treated with the utmost respect. Anything resembling impoliteness towards them might have very unpleasant results. The Roman emperors of the west became more and more restricted in their real power. At last they became very little more than the rulers of Italy.

Worse than this, their situation was rendered all the more difficult by the consequences which flowed from the policy of the emperor Theodosius the Great. Theodosius had welcomed into the Roman army the flower of the northern tribesmen. In the days of his grandsons, these Germans had become more powerful than the Italians in the government of Italy. Not only was the emperor gradually ousted from the provinces of Britain, Gaul, Spain and Africa, but the Germans commanded a majority within the imperial government itself.

Although the emperors at Constantinople were much more free from the proximity of these northern kingships, they were in equal danger from the German penetration of the imperial government. Emperors began to be mere nominees of powerful German ministers. It needed no great genius to foresee the inevitable result. One day the German ministers would grow tired of nominating emperors, and both in Italy and at Constantinople the long tradition of Roman government would die out, and northern kings would reign in its stead.

The
German
ministers

III

When the emperor Marcian died, it would have needed a bold man to predict any other end to the Roman empire. But just at that moment a man made a mistake. The man was Aspar, the leader of the German party at Constantinople, and the mistake he made was a misjudgment of character. He thought one of his officers, a Dacian named Leo, a suitable person to nominate as the new puppet emperor. He nominated him: and Leo turned out to be a stronger man than Aspar. This mistake diverted the stream of history into a new channel.

Coming into office at the time when Roman power was at its lowest ebb, Leo dodged the inevitable, forestalled his masters and rivals, and refounded the strength of the imperial military guild. He built up a new power independent of the Germans. The material he used consisted of the Isaurian tribesmen of Asia Minor, determined desperadoes who were thoroughly at home in the gentle arts of fighting and intrigue. These he welded into the famous "Excubitors." An Italian emperor might tremble in the presence of his master. With a few Isaurians throwing dice in his ante-room, Leo found no necessity to tremble.

Leo I (A. D. 457–474)

Leo did more than refound his own position: he intervened in Italy to restore the strength of the western emperors. He went further even than this. He made an attempt to smash the power of the new kingships. The point of attack he chose was the Vandal kingdom in north Africa.

His reason for this choice was that the Vandals, like the Carthaginians before them and the Moors after them, made Africa the base of a dangerous naval power, which dominated the western Mediterranean, excluded the eastern merchants from western markets, and even harried the eastern Mediterranean. The new kingships showed little sympathy with the commercial classes of the empire, and looked with suspicion on the cosmopoli-

Leo's policy

tan spirit of trade. The mercantile influence was on the side of Leo, and Leo recognized its claims to consideration.[1]

Had Leo been successful in his Vandal war, the western empire would never have fallen. But a number of serious difficulties stood in his way. His organization was not yet sufficient for so great a task: Gaiseric, the Vandal king, was a man with a touch of genius: and there was treason behind the scenes. . . . According to the story, Aspar fully realized the results which would follow the victory of Leo, and determined to prevent them. He offered the reversion of the imperial throne to Basiliscus, the brother-in-law of Leo. He then employed the influence which he so gained over Basiliscus to impress upon the mind of the latter the extreme difficulty and probable failure of the African expedition, and the desirability that it should fail. Having done this, he engaged the assistance of the empress in persuading Leo to appoint her brother Basiliscus to the command of the expedition.

Whether this story be true or not, in any case Basiliscus did command the expedition. It was one of the greatest and best organized armaments ever fitted out by a Roman government. The western emperor Anthemius co-operated. Failure seemed impossible: and up to a certain point every step was successful. But the Vandal kingdom did not fall. Beaten on the sea, and feeling disaster close at hand, Gaiseric obtained from Basiliscus five days' truce. He used the five days to fit out a fleet of fire-ships, with which he made a last attack on the Roman fleet: and the

Leo and the Vandals

[1] Practically all the remaining commerce of the Mediterranean at this time, was in the hands of easterners—particularly Greeks. The supremacy of the imperial coinage would indicate as much, even if other evidence were lacking.

great expedition collapsed in defeat and ruin. . . . The prestige of the Vandals was heightened, and the power of the German party in Italy was assured. The defeat of Basiliscus enabled them to counteract every effort of Leo to restore the power of the Italian element. . . . Leo himself was brought to the verge of bankruptcy. . . . But three years later he assassinated Aspar.

IV

After Leo's grandson had reigned a few months, he was followed by his son-in-law, the Isaurian chief Tarasikodissa, the commander of the new Isaurian Excubitors, who had adopted the civilized Greek name of Zeno. The accession of Zeno meant that as far as the eastern empire was concerned, the Germans were thrown out, and could remove their baggage. An Isaurian who got his teeth into the imperial dignity was not likely to let go. The contest now was shifted to Italy. Here the Germans, moving from one success to another, at last felt strong enough to carry through the great revolution. Eadwaeccer, after deposing Romulus Augustulus, and terminating the line of Roman emperors in Italy, sent the imperial insignia to Constantinople. It was not his intention to be himself an emperor; he did not intend even to be an independent sovereign ruler. His plan was to reign as an under-king, a sub-regulus, with the Roman titles of Magister Militum and Patrician, under the suzerainty of the emperor at Constantinople.

End of the western empire

Zeno probably spent many quiet hours in thinking this over. The conception of Eadwaeccer, that he should have all the advantages and none of the responsibilities of independent sovereignty, pocketing ninety nine per cent or so of the revenue, and warning off enterprising Franks and Alamanni because he was merely a vassal of the emperor—this conception had a beauty that Zeno must have noticed. After thinking it over for several years, and quietly trying, without success, one expedient after another, the emperor hit upon a good reply. The Ostrogoths settled in Illyricum were an unmitigated nuisance and worry to the government. Zeno commissioned their young King Theuderic to invade Italy, turn out Eadwaeccer, and hold Italy on the same terms—without prejudice to imperial rights. If he failed, no harm would be done. If he succeeded, Zeno would have a vassal connected with him on terms of his own dictation. And in any case the two barbarian powers would help to weaken one another.

The plan succeeded. Theuderic was a remarkable man who has gone down to history, not exactly as a famous pacifist and philanthropist, but at any rate as one of the **The Goths** best of those early northern kings who founded the na-
overthrow
Eadwaeccer tional states of Europe. The teaching of the Sermon on the Mount was imperfectly represented among the means he employed against Eadwaeccer; and his career hints that his acquaintance with this portion of the scriptures was limited. After a stern struggle, the Goths took possession of Italy. When, however, the envoys of Theuderic arrived in Constantinople to acquaint the emperor officially with his success, they found Zeno no longer there, and a new Augustus reigned in his stead.

Ariadne, the daughter of Leo I, had married Tarasikodissa to please her father. When Zeno died, she married again to please herself; and this time she chose a tall,

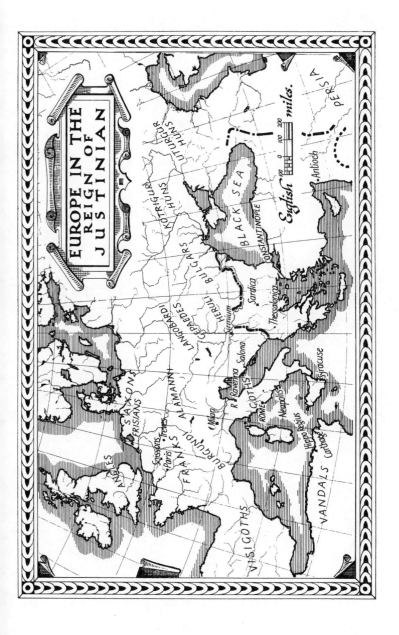

EUROPE IN THE
REIGN OF
JUSTINIAN

handsome and dignified official of the palace, named Anastasius. Her choice, though one that most women would have endorsed, did not escape criticism in some quarters. The virtue of Tarasikodissa had been that he represented the new anti-German military guild—the Excubitors. In religion, he had been neutral. But the new emperor was a Monophysite in religion. This fact threw into relief a number of truths which illustrate the nature of the struggle which was being waged.

V

Petrus Sabbatius was nine years old when Anastasius succeeded to the imperial throne. He was quite old enough to realize the meaning of the story which began to unfold itself before his eyes.

Rome "comes back"

While Leo and Zeno had been engaged in the task of eradicating the German element at Constantinople, and fighting it in Italy, they had not sufficiently taken note of the total nature of the process at work in Italy. Rome, superseded as a political capital, was making a remarkable "come back" as a religious one. The more the Germans groped for the power of governing the details of men's conduct, the more the patriarch of Rome grasped the power of governing the principles which determined it. As long as there was an emperor in Italy, the pope could never be the first man in the land: but he was rising to power as fast as the emperor, in the hands of the German party, declined. The western emperors at last faded and vanished; and with the reign of Anastasius the surprising truth became evident that the secular head of the empire lived at Constantinople, and the spiritual head lived at Rome. The empire had begun by possessing a single focus, or centre. Then it developed two foci. Finally, the foci had become of different kinds. What would happen next?

Relation-
ship of
Rome and
Constan-
tinople

What actually happened was, of course, that the public opinion of the empire began to take a great interest in the question of reconciling these two centres of power. Rome—even in her great republican days, at the height of her military success—had always had a hankering after spiritual authority: she had always wanted the pleasure of laying down the law, more than the privilege of enforcing it. The Greeks, almost from the beginning, had noticed this Roman characteristic. Now that the power to enforce law had passed into other hands, the Roman instinct for directing the world into the strait and narrow way became unmistakable.

There was ample scope for its operation. Had Rome not grasped at power, there were others ready and willing to snatch it. . . . This is not the place in which to state—much less to argue—the theological questions at issue. Every one of these questions involved a political as well as a religious problem.[1] When Nestorius, the patriarch of Constantinople, laid down the Nestorian doctrine, he made a bid for spiritual supremacy on behalf of Constantinople. When Cyril of Alexandria forced the condemnation of Nestorius, he was attempting to establish the spiritual supremacy of Alexandria: and his successor, Dioscurus, very nearly succeeded in achieving it when he vindicated the orthodoxy of Abbot

[1] This has never been more tersely and neatly stated than in Diehl's *History of the Byzantine Empire*, pp. 9–12. Broadly speaking, Arianism was the doctrine of the new northern kingships settled in the Roman empire. Monophysitism was Syro-Egyptian Nationalism. Catholicism was Roman Imperialism.

Eutyches, the champion of Monophysitism, at the "Robber Council" of Ephesus. Pope Leo I entered the fray with a doctrinal theory which commended itself to the judgment of western Christians. The emperor Marcian, who sympathized with the Roman doctrine, allied himself with the pope. At the Council of Chalcedon Eutyches and Monophysitism were condemned, Dioscurus was deposed, and Rome demonstrated her ability to find a formula upon which the majority of Christians could agree. That her interpretation was sound we may judge from the fact that it has been accepted by the majority of Christians ever since.

Council of Chalcedon A. D. 451

The triumph at Chalcedon went far to make the pope a great ecclesiastical monarch, the leader of Christian opinion. No one could doubt that his relations with Anastasius were those of one great potentate with another. The simple fact that Anastasius was heterodox in religion brought into activity papal powers which otherwise might have slumbered unused.

One thing was certain—and that was, that discord between the two centres of civilization would hardly further the cause of civilized man. Anti-Civilization would advance with giant strides if the two centres were mutually antagonistic.

VI

The whole of the youth and early manhood of Petrus was passed under the reign of Anastasius. In order to derive the full benefit from a good education, it is necessary to start fairly young: and the journey of Petrus to Constantinople, and the beginning of his life there, must

The
moulding
of Justinian

have taken place hardly later than the year 500. He was thirty-six and had long been Justinian when Anastasius died: that is to say, all the formative period of his life was over by then.

Justin was never a brainy nor a specially enterprising man. The strong probability is that the whole of the circumstances which finally brought him to the imperial throne were the work of Justinian. The old uncle might have died comfortably as prefect of the Excubitors: but the nephew had heard the call, and laid his own path to empire through his uncle. The first step was to secure the election of Justin. The next step would be to make himself Justin's successor.

The principle which lay behind the whole life and activity of Justinian was the doctrine of the unity of civilization, and its identity with the Roman empire. He was therefore orthodox in religion: that is to say, he accepted in full those statements of belief by which the Christian faith, under a succession of emperors and Councils from Constantine and Nicaea downwards, had been universalized and made at once the principle and the expression, the cause and the result, of one universal civilization. The Catholic faith was the theory of the Roman empire. It was this political reference which

Religion
and Politics

gave the emperors their interest in Christianity. Had it been exclusively a philosophy—a mere explanation— they are hardly likely to have troubled over it. None of them—save possibly Julian—was particularly interested in philosophy. None of them, for example, showed very much anxiety to legislate for Neo-Platonism. . . . What they were interested in was the quality of Christianity as a function of civilization—a principle and a control of human conduct. . . . Hence the conviction of the unity and universality of civilization implied a conviction of the unity and universality of the church: and this excluded such heretical and minority opinions as Monophysitism. By the nature of the case, young Justinian must have been opposed to the opinions of Anastasius: and we know that he was.

But he worked from within, not from without. When Count Vitalian led a Catholic revolt against Anastasius, Justin was far from associating himself with it. That Justin was the primary agent in the defeat of Vitalian and the survival of Anastasius implies that Justinian's advice to his uncle had been to stand with the legitimate emperor, Monophysite or not. A title to empire founded upon successful revolt was of no use whatever to Justinian. He needed a strictly legitimate title. His policy was to protect the Monophysite emperor for the sake of the legitimate title which he could transmit to properly elected successors.

The legitimate title

Anastasius died without children, and at his death no successor had been nominated by him. Whether or not he recognized that another Monophysite emperor might be a mistake, he left the ground clear for an election which should represent public opinion. Among the candidates Justin was not a conspicuous figure. He was not even an important one. His election was due to a series of well-planned manœuvres which he very certainly did not think of for himself. Step by step it was brought about that Justinian's uncle became emperor. That he was Justinian's uncle was an essential feature in the case: though at the time few men may have thought so.

VII

The candidates for the imperial throne included three nephews of Anastasius—Probus, Pompeius and Hypatius—who had a respectable backing of a not very energetic sort: as well as a person named Theocritus, who was the candidate run by the Grand Chamberlain Amantius. These were the original starters in the contest; but, as we shall see, none of them was in the concluding stages, when the actual election was made. The Grand Chamberlain, well aware that Justin was not a candidate, approached him with suggestions for a combination to secure the election of Theocritus. The Excubitors could sway the result; and Amantius placed a large sum of money in the hands of Justin, for judicious distribution. Apparently Justin raised no objection.

On July 9, 518, the election began. The Excubitors and the Scholarians, together with a large audience of the general public, collected in the Hippodrome, which was quite large enough to contain probably as many as desired to be present. Among the civilians were the armed body-guards (the "Partisans") of the Blue and the Green parties: the Blues being Justinian's men. Finally Justinian himself was personally present with his picked corps of the imperial guard—the Candidati. The senate, the imperial consistorium and the patriarch, dressed in grey, met in the great hall of the palace. Both these bodies of electors set to work, independently of one another, to discover a name on which all could agree. The door (the "Ivory Gate") between the Palace and the Hippodrome was locked and guarded by officials.

The conference in the palace was opened by the

Election
of a new
emperor

Magister Officiorum, the Secretary of State, the head of the general administration. He advised the meeting to agree upon a nomination as soon as possible, before their friends in another place (the Hippodrome) could suggest a name. The meeting accordingly began tentatively to put forward candidates. At first none of these gained enough general support to be nominated.

These decorous proceedings were pale beside the fun in the Hippodrome, where the inferior electors were gathered. Only a modern American political convention could show any approach to the amount of zeal and energy which were there displayed. The Excubitors had their candidate ready, an officer named John. They proceeded to elevate him upon a shield without waiting for such trifles as the general expression of the meeting, while some of them knocked at the Ivory Gate and called for the imperial purple to be produced. The Blue partisans took it upon themselves to express dissent; and a scuffle followed in which stones were thrown and swords drawn, and some loss of life occurred, before order could be restored. The Scholarians then suggested a candidate of their own and knocked at the Ivory Gate; but the objections expressed by the Excubitors were strong enough to make it necessary for Justinian to intervene to rescue him, and the officials in charge of the Gate blandly negatived all suggestions of fetching the imperial purple. As Justinian was upon the spot, the Excubitors seized him, and named him as their candidate. He declined the honour, however, and the Ivory Gate remained closed. Thus both the Excubitors and the Scholarians had proposed candidates, and one had been refused by each, and one objected to by the Blues. As

Proceedings in the Hippodrome

far as things went up to this point, honours were easy, and no one could make any complaint.

The proceedings in the Hippodrome, though invisible to the meeting in the palace, were probably very audible, and no one in the palace could be totally ignorant of the names which were being suggested. The problem before the grave and reverend seniors was to agree upon one of their own circle who would be acceptable to the majority in the Hippodrome. They were no doubt hastened in their decision by the fear that the Hippodrome would agree upon the name of some quite impossible person. In such cases the perversity of the human mind is well known. The conference agreed upon exactly the one name which had not hitherto been mentioned, but which would command the combined vote of the Excubitors and the Blue Party. This name was Justin's.

Justin is nominated

He was hurried along the Hippodrome. The meeting there, still engaged in objecting to everything, was startled at the sudden opening of the doors of the Kathisma, the great Imperial Box which overlooked the race-course. The person who was nominated by the senate stood before them: Justin.

The groans of the Scholarians were drowned by the cheers of the Excubitors and the Blues. The officials at the Ivory Gate now hastened with polite smiles to hand out the imperial robes and regalia. Justin was arrayed in the purple tunic and the scarlet shoes. The patriarch placed over his shoulders the imperial mantle, and crowned him with the imperial diadem, while the ministers paid the first official salutations to the new emperor. The lance and shield were handed to him, and with one voice the assembly chanted the electrical words of acclaim: "Justine Auguste, tu vincas!" He replied, in the words of the imperial coronation rite: "Since, by the decree and choice of Almighty God, and by your unanimous election and suffrage, I am called to undertake the empire, let us invoke the help of divine providence." They chanted: "Son of God, have compassion upon him. Thou hast chosen him: therefore have compassion upon him." Finally, after the solemn words of what now would be known technically as his Coronation Oath, he announced the gratuity. "To celebrate the beginning of my fortunate reign, I will give five pieces of gold and a silver pound to each shield." To this the answer was: "God save the Christian emperor. So say all of us." The new emperor then terminated the ceremony with the words: "God be with you!"—after which the procession was formed to conduct him to Sancta Sophia, and then back to the palace.[1]

Thus it came about that Justin became emperor by the nomination of the senate and the acceptance of the army and people: a title sound and constitutional.

VIII

The formal election of Justin was in fact and in substance the election of Justinian. The latter, while in name Count of the Domestici and Master of Soldiers, was in actual fact the ruler of the empire. The old gentleman, armed with his gold stencil plate through which to write his name, carefully signed the documents put

---

[1] Constantinus Porphyrogenitus, *De Cerimoniis*, ϟγ′ (I. 93, p. 426 Bonn): a full and interesting account.

before him by his nephew, and everything went off very well.

Justin and
Justinian
The first steps of the new reign betrayed the policy which for close upon fifty years to come Justinian was to pursue. In notifying the pope of his election, the emperor is made to attribute it, not only to the senate, the ministers and the army, but to the favour of the Indivisible Trinity—a phrase sufficient to class him as catholic and orthodox. Count Vitalian, whom Justin had fought on behalf of a Monophysite emperor, was now called to Constantinople to share in the new policy.

When, on August 1st., correspondence with Rome was begun, Justinian had the whole situation in hand. The emperor did everything he wished; the Patriarch was his faithful ally; the army was with him, and the Blue partisans controlled the expression of public opinion. The long negotiations which followed between the emperor and the pope represented a real attempt to establish an agreement between the dissevered parts of the empire. The important point to notice is that the initiative was on the part of the emperor. The pope was not prepared to worry himself unduly over the problems involved, still less to make any serious concessions for the sake of agreement. All the hard work of exploring avenues to peace had to be done by Justinian at Constantinople.

Seven months later—on March 25th, 519—the papal legates arrived. They did not bring an atmosphere of heartening enthusiasm with them. Their instructions were very strict, and very full. The enthusiasm was on the part of the imperial court. At the tenth milestone from the city, the legates found an impressive reception awaiting them. Justinian, Vitalian, and other important persons were there to receive them with honeyed words and flattering courtesies.

The plenary conference revealed that the legates had brought a form of submission with them. This was examined and agreed to. On March 27th the patriarch took the bitter pill with plentiful assistance of moral jam. He turned the bare formula of submission into a courteous personal letter with the necessary phrases embedded in the midst. Finally the names of five patriarchs of Constantinople, and two emperors, Zeno and Anastasius, were solemnly struck off the records of the Church of Constantinople.

Negotiations with Rome

Benevolent friends had cautioned the legates, somewhat to their alarm, that the streets of Constantinople would simply run with blood if these conditions were to be enforced; but as the legates recorded, with relief, nothing happened. It is a testimony to the genius of Justinian that he could shepherd his party to such lengths of conciliation.

These measures, the effects of which were confined to a comparatively small circle of people in Constantinople, were not all that was involved in a reconciliation with Italy. Everywhere, throughout the east, Monophysite bishops were ejected from their dioceses and monasteries of the heretical doctrine were closed. In Egypt, Palestine and Syria, where Monophysite opinion was prevalent, the new order of things was hated and loathed. It had to be endured. The government was sufficiently strong to be able to enforce its policy. Monophysitism was driven underground.

Imperialism in power

IX

Justinian's rise to power was not effected without careful attention to possible rivals and enemies. Early in Justin's reign Amantius and Theocritus were executed; Vitalian, who was a much more serious competitor, needed delicate handling. He had helped in the work of conciliation, and he was rewarded with the distinction of the consulship. Exactly what happened is obscure; but it is certain that after holding his consulship for seven months, Vitalian was killed in an affray within the palace. Even if Justinian neither ordered nor encouraged the deed, it is possible that it was committed by men who knew how useful it would be to him. Vitalian was one of those men who are capable of exerting power in its negative form. He could obstruct and prevent, and his weight as a counterbalance seems to have been considerable; but he contributed very little to the creation of policy. Justinian had some reasonable motives for destroying him.

Not only so, but he wiped out the memory and the prestige of Vitalian by himself taking his consulship in the year following. His year of office was one of extraordinary splendour. Not within living memory had such profusion and pageantry been exhibited. Vast sums, in the old imperial spirit, were spent on the shows; twenty lions and thirty panthers were exhibited simultaneously in the arena, as well as other beasts. Such was the excitement that the day ended in confusion, and the final race had to be cancelled.

This was the Justinian who became the friend of Theodora, and played Odysseus to her Penelope. He was

Justinian Consul A. D. 521

already at the height of his power and success; but not yet at the height of his fame or his greatness. He was ready to listen to any one who could open new roads to him.

X

One of the peculiarities of Theodora's position was that she was a converted Green. Her intense enthusiasm for the Blues, founded upon that childish experience in the Hippodrome, was a link with their chief. She seems indeed to have made him take rather more seriously his headship of the Blue party. There was just this difference between the relation of Justinian to his Blues, and that of an American boss to his organization, that the Blues were not a voluntary society, and were far from being unauthorized or illegal. They were a legally constituted body of old standing, bearing some resemblance to national volunteers or a civic guard; and their real use and intention would have become obvious, had Constantinople been threatened with a siege. The Blues, the Greens, the Reds and the Whites would then have been revealed as organizations of the four quarters of the city, by which the civil population was registered and enrolled for collective action in time of stress. Similar organizations, denoted in the same way by colours, existed in all the considerable cities of the empire. The immemorial custom of the sections was to treat themselves in peace time as sporting organizations. It kept their system alive and vigorous.

An active organization of any sort is almost certain to take some interest in the burning questions of the day.

Justinian
and the
Blues

The Blues and Greens, at least, if not the Reds and Whites, had associated themselves with political and religious tendencies. The Greens were Monophysite and nationalistic; the Blues were Catholic and imperialistic. Justinian, in becoming patron of the Blues, gave this connection a more vivid and determinate trend. Under his rule the Blues became a combatant organization not altogether unlike the modern Fascists. Their job was to **The Blue party** sway public opinion in favour of Justinian. His function was to get sound and reliable Blues into public posts, to feed the hungry and visit the sick, and to superintend that sometimes very necessary "underground railway" by which imprudent or over-enthusiastic Blues could be efficiently transported out of reach of the law. The system of the Greens followed suit.

Procopius has left on record a very vivid picture of the Partisans as he knew them; fierce, swaggering men who modelled themselves upon the Hun. Why they chose the Hun remains a mystery; but the fashion set that way, and Constantinople had become familiar with the man with the shaven forehead and long hair combed down behind, the fierce full beard and whiskers, and the balloon sleeves. Most of the active members carried concealed weapons, and knew how to use them.

Justinian's leadership of the Blues underwent a crisis at or just before the time when he met Theodora. In the year 524 he had a serious illness, and while he was hovering between life and death a number of disturbing events took place. Publicly and in broad daylight, a man of some consequence, named Hypatius, was assassinated by Blue partisans in the church of Santa Sophia. The affair created an extraordinary scandal, and was reported to the emperor. Very plainly, powerful influence, hostile to Justinian and the Blues, was brought to bear; and it had a very good case to work on. Justin accordingly issued a commission to the proper authorities to see that the danger to the public peace was terminated. Attempt to crush the Blues A. D. 524

Armed with this commission the city prefect, Theodotus, the governor of Constantinople, set about the task of rooting out the Blue partisans. An enquiry investigated the whole subject; some of the leading men were executed, while others had to go into hiding. When Justinian recovered, it was to find his Blue organization destroyed or dispersed. He did not, at the time, trouble over the original authors of the measure; he struck promptly at the agent. Confessions implicating Theodotus were extorted from some of his subordinates. It was shown that he had exceeded his instructions by executing, without legal authority, a person of senatorial rank. . . . The source of the attack upon the Blues can be surmised by the fact that Theodotus was warmly defended by Proclus, the quaestor, one of the imperial ministers. Proclus, however, could not withstand Justinian. The emperor banished Theodotus to Jerusalem; where the exile spent the rest of his life in hiding, dodging the watchful avengers of the Blue partisans.

The blow had its effect. From this time forward the activities of the Blue partisans were considerably modified, and no more scandals occurred. The change was not due to lack of power, for the fall of Theodotus paralysed all opposition, and the same protection as before was extended to Blue agents by Justinian; but the latter seems to have felt that matters had gone too far, and that a more decorous policy was expedient. Justinian's action

XI

All this will illustrate and be illustrated by the kind of influence exerted by Theodora, who, as a converted Green, brought into discussion an experience different from that of a normal member of the Blue party. She was still more or less of a Monophysite and a nationalist, who valued the Greek east far above any unknown and questionable Roman west. She reflected, probably, a view very prevalent in Constantinople if not at the moment in the ascendant. Justinian's education gave him a knowledge of, and a sympathy with, the great Roman imperial idea, the tradition of Augustus and Hadrian, which was only in small part shared by the ordinary man of his age in the eastern provinces. Like most women, Theodora based her own ideas upon experience. She had personally travelled through the south-eastern provinces, Egypt, Palestine and Syria, where Monophysitism was most prevalent; she had earned her living there, and realized by first-hand experience how widely the doctrine was spread, and by what kind of man it was held. She seems to have sympathized with that kind of man. But the chief thing she did was to induce Justinian to see that the policy of suppressing Monophysitism might be neither possible nor desirable.

Theodora's influence

He was not an easy man to influence, and he did not change his views readily; but from his first contact with Theodora the modification began. Gradually he acquired the idea that a much better course would be to establish a ground of agreement and union with the Monophysites. While Justin lived, Justinian made no overt change in the official policy of the government. He waited until his own accession before he made public overtures to the Monophysite bishops. He thought he could find a formula of reconciliation to which both parties might subscribe.

This new policy was hastened by a turn of events not, perhaps, included in the programme which Justinian had drawn up. This was the development of difficulties with Persia on the far-eastern—the Caucasian—border of the empire. Peace with Persia had lasted unbroken for some twenty years. The troubles which now threatened were due to the natural spread of both empires. As their respective civilizations gradually sank into the surrounding barbarian tribes, the borders of both empires extended, until, in the Caucasus, they were in awkward contact. Justinian did not want a Persian war. All his interests were Roman and western. His difficulty was that the Persians were not sympathetic with his projects. They did not want a restored Roman empire upon their western frontiers, and the Persian government was quite prepared to intervene to prevent such a consummation. It could do so quite easily. A threat to Lazica, the Colchian country between the Black Sea and the Caspian, was a simple and inexpensive way of distracting the attention of the Roman government, which dared not ignore it. Hence a Persian war was becoming a possibility. Whether it were allowed to drag on, or whether a finish were forced, in either event the sympathy of the inhabitants of the frontier districts was absolutely necessary to Justinian. Their loyalty and staunchness constituted the principal reliance of the government.[1]

The Persian problem

[1] On this head we see the remarks in J. B. Bury's *History of the Later Roman Empire*, II. 14–15.

But many of these inhabitants happened to be Monophysites in theology. To conciliate them became not only a preferable policy but a pressing necessity.

The Persian war began in the year of Justinian's marriage to Theodora, the year before Justin died and Justinian succeeded. The policies which Justinian had to apply and to guide, the events which he had to meet and control, were slowly but surely becoming more complex. Not only had he to achieve the reunion of an empire which had divided itself into two dissimilar halves, but he might have to do it while threatened by a dangerous attack from the east. At the very moment when he had at great cost reached a reconciliation with the papacy, he was forced to seek another with the Monophysites, and so to endanger both. . . . But the presence of Theodora by his side was a real help. They had mutually undertaken to maintain independence in their partnership. The first result of their plan was that Theodora was free to adopt a bolder policy of conciliation towards the Monophysites than would have been possible to Justinian. We shall see in due course how the plan answered.

Theodora and the east

CHAPTER III

THE FORGING OF THE INSTRUMENT: THE WORK OF BELISARIUS

I

THE approach of the Persian war found the empire unready to meet it. The old generation of soldiers, of the same age as Justin, was dying out. It had never been especially able; it had never produced any great man; it had merely carried on the established tradition of methods and tactics, without much originality or change. Justinian needed to look about him. In the year The new of his marriage he picked two very young men from his generation military household, and gave them a more or less independent joint command on the Persarmenian border. Of the two, one was Sittas, the husband of Theodora's elder sister Comito; and it is possible that Theodora suggested his name. The other was an unknown Thracian named Belisarius, who as far as we can tell had no claim or influence. Justinian first picked him out purely on his intuitive judgment of men.

Sittas and Belisarius conducted a raid into Persarmenia, and seem to have conducted themselves with good sense and discretion. The next spring came—the one in which Justin fell ill, and co-opted Justinian as his successor. The two young men, trying to repeat their modest success of the year before, were met by experienced Persian commanders, and defeated. They were not the only Roman officers to get into difficulties. On the Mesopotamian frontier the commander, after advancing into Persian territory, retired without adequate cause. Justinian—the new emperor—took totally different views of the two episodes. The commander in Mesopotamia was dismissed, and Belisarius was transferred from the Persarmenian front to replace him.

Belisarius
and
Procopius
(Spring
A. D. 527)

This was the first step of Belisarius on the ladder of promotion. It involved the command of the fortress and garrison of Daras, and was of sufficient importance to necessitate a political officer to advise him on questions of civil administration. The person sent him was the future historian Procopius. No supernatural portents are recorded at their meeting: no halo rested upon their heads—no lightning flashed or thunder pealed. Yet they were to make one another immortal. The deeds of Belisarius, as recounted by Procopius, make one of those great books of adventure the list of which begins with the Iliad, and ends, for the present, with the epic of the Arabian desert.

II

Daras had a short but important history. The town had been built by Anastasius as a check to the Persian city of Nisibis, just across the border. Nisibis was the Mesopotamian staple town—its market was the clearing house for the Perso-Roman trade, so that there was The
fortress
of Daras some excuse for its fortifications and garrisons. But Daras had not this excuse. The Persian government entered strong protests against the foundation of Daras, pointing out that it was a breach of the treaties. Anastasius, however, maintained the new military station,

and the offer of an indemnity induced the Persian king
to let the matter drop. Hence Daras had survived to become the first considerable command held by Belisarius.

Up to this point, the hostilities between Persia and the
empire had been desultory and trifling. It would have
been an easy matter to reach a fresh settlement. The orders which next reached Belisarius, however, involved a
serious breach with Persia. He was directed to build a
new fortress at Minduos, on the very edge of Roman
territory. It was almost certain that the Persians would
regard this as a declaration of war.

All these considerations, however, did not concern
Belisarius. His task was to execute the orders received.
The planning, the assembling of material and the collection of workmen must have taken time: but as soon as
all was ready, the stuff and the men were rushed to the
spot, and building was begun. The walls were already
rising, when a peremptory ultimatum came from the
Persians. If the work was not stopped, they would stop
it. Belisarius reported this threat. Justinian replied by
sending two armies from Syria, under the brothers
Coutzes and Bouzes. A fierce battle took place at Minduos, ending in the complete defeat of the Roman
forces. Two of the high officers were killed, and three
captured—one being Coutzes himself.

Trial and
error

The Persians were content with their success, and
after destroying the new fortress they retired. The rest
of the year was devoted by Justinian to the task of re-
organization. Fresh troops were brought up, and many
of the officers of the frontier fortresses were replaced.
The emperor was still working more or less in the dark.
He gave the command of the new army to Pompeius,

the nephew of Anastasius. A more uninspired appointment it would have been hard to make. Pompeius had neither brains nor energy, nor any power of exciting them in others.

The unfitness of Pompeius became visible when, after a hard winter, hostilities began again in the spring of 529. The Arab was quite as enterprising then as he is today. A powerful raiding force of Persians and Arabs, under Al Mundhir, king of Hira, came as suddenly and as swiftly as a sand-storm out of the desert, nearly reached Antioch, and was off again before Pompeius could bring it to action. Although reprisals were made, Pompeius was unable to organize and carry through a raid comparable to this of Mundhir. Justinian saw himself to be altogether on the wrong track. His next step showed that he had at last discovered the right one.

Belisarius made commander in-chief in the east A. D. 529

He made the daring experiment of lifting the obscure commandant of Daras right over the heads of a hundred officers senior to him in service and more experienced in war. At one step Belisarius was made Master of Soldiers throughout the East—the grand commander-in-chief on the eastern frontier. In order that the command of Belisarius should not be inconveniently large, Sittas was given a similar status in Armenia. Sittas had the mountain area; Belisarius the Mesopotamian plain.

While the government occupied the attention of the Persian king with negotiations and communications, Belisarius left Daras to begin the serious work of organizing his first great army. In the following spring he was back in Daras, where he was joined by Hermogenes, now the Magister Officiorum, but once the military assistant of Vitalian. Hermogenes was an able man, and a useful chief of staff. In case anything went wrong, Rufinus, a trusted representative of the emperor, took up his position at Hierapolis with power to open negotiations with the Persian government, if required.

III

It is evident enough that the imperial secret service had learnt of an impending Persian attack upon Daras. As soon as the information was verified by the approach of the Persian army, Belisarius and Hermogenes set to work to prepare a defensive field position outside the city. The idea—almost certainly evolved by Belisarius—was not to fight behind fortifications, but to face a field battle, employing chiefly cavalry and mounted troops. The function of Hermogenes was to see that this dangerous idea was carried out with prudence and good sense.

Policy of Belisarius

The method was dangerous, because the Persians were very nearly double the strength of the Romans: and to choose an open field battle with an enemy whose superiority in numbers is as nine to five argues either extraordinary folly or the confidence of genius. Justinian was gambling a little upon the possibility and hope that it might be genius. If so, all was well.

Belisarius began by several very unusual measures. He marked out and dug a long trench, cut in discontinuous sections, and with a bay in the centre of its length. This trench was a sufficiently original expedient; but Belisarius added to its peculiarity by the mode in which he distributed his troops. His left wing, which was of cavalry under Bouzes, and his right, which was of various cavalry units under different commanders, were stationed behind the trench, and outside the bay. His centre, with himself in command, was likewise behind the trench, but behind the bay, though overlapping it. But out beyond the trench, and inside the bay, he stationed four corps of Hun cavalry, Sunicas and Aigan on the left, Simmas and Ascan on the right. The effect of these very remarkable arrangements was to turn the old accustomed dispositions inside out. The flying reserve of Hun cavalry was advanced beyond the trench; the main body of infantry was reserved behind it.

Everything now took on a curious air of interest and excitement.

Perozes, the Persian commander, evidently thought that he had a soft thing on hand. He sent an amusing message to Belisarius, ordering a bath and a lunch in Daras for tomorrow. When, however, he had actually surveyed the position planned by Belisarius, he changed his mind. The day passed with nothing more than very light skirmishing. The troops were entertained during the idle hours of waiting by some spectacular feats on the part of the professional trainer and masseur attached to Bouzes' army. At evening, the armies separated with nothing done.

This was itself a victory for Belisarius. Next day, a fresh body of troops ten thousand strong arrived to reinforce the Persians. An exchange of ironic letters took place between the commanders; but Belisarius was not to be dodged out of his prepared position. It was pretty clear that if Perozes wished to break the Roman army, the prepared position would have to be attacked. He made his plans with this object in view; and probably

Prelimi-
naries to
the battle
of Daras

The
Persians
recognize
their diffi-
culties

the lack of activity on this second day arose from the conferences held by the Persian leaders in order to settle their method of attack.

On the third day, serious business began.

Perozes had decided to fight with a continuous front line, holding a reserve line in the rear with which to feed his fighting front. The famous Persian crack corps known as the "Immortals" was held as a special reserve, and stationed in its natural position, the rear. While these dispositions were being arranged, Pharas, the leader of the Herulian auxiliaries of Belisarius, came to him, and suggested that his men were not being properly utilized. There was, he pointed out, a hill on the left, beyond Bouzes' position; and he asked to be given a roving commission to go round the hill, and strike into the coming battle when he thought fit. Belisarius and Hermogenes agreed to this proposal. The Herulians were very warm stuff, but highly temperamental. The main thing was to keep them interested. If they would really enjoy hiding behind the hill and making a surprise attack, the best course was to let them do it. Belisarius would have hesitated very much to allow regular troops to do so dangerous a thing; but a Herulian had nine lives.

Final dispositions

Satisfied with the permission given, the Herulians set out to make their way unobtrusively to their new position. Perozes was unconscious of what was taking place.

IV

The battle of Daras opened just before noon. The object of Perozes was to begin immediately before the Roman dinner hour, so that the Romans should fight hungry. After a sharp exchange of arrow shot, in which the Persians had the disadvantage, owing to the wind being against them, the fighting opened in earnest. The Persian right wing, of formidable Cadiseni tribesmen, attacked Bouzes, crossed the trench, and drove the Roman corps before their triumphant onslaught. The Hun cavalry outside the trench at once charged the inside flank of the Cadiseni; but meanwhile the Herulians had come round the hill, and had evidently decided that any time was the properest time to fight, for at this point they waded into the outside flank of the Cadiseni with tremendous moral effect. Seeing the Hun mounted bowmen also moving against them, the Cadiseni broke and fled. They were received back into the Persian line, which closed behind them. Their losses, however, had been very severe: some three thousand had fallen.

First stage of the battle

While this had been attracting general attention, Perozes had quietly carried out a concentration upon his left, sending the Immortals also thither to be ready to take advantage of any favourable opportunity. To counter this, Belisarius and Hermogenes ordered the Hun corps of Simmas and Ascan to be prepared, and called upon Sunicas and Aigan to be ready to support them. Drafts from the centre were sent forward to back the Huns. The Persians, charging at the run, drove the Roman right wing before them. The mistake made by Perozes was that in organizing this manœuvre he allowed the junction between his left wing and his centre to be opened out and the shoulder of the wing to be exposed as it charged. This was the objective at which the Huns struck. The Hun charge cut the Persian advance from its supports, and penetrated to the Persian wing com-

mander who was directing the fighting from his position in the rear. Sunicas himself cut down the Persian
standard-bearer and threw everything into confusion.
The isolated Persian wing, in full pursuit of the fleeing
Romans, was called off and hastily returned. The Huns
now became the object of a rush from all parts. They
held their own with unflinching courage. Sunicas killed
the Persian commander, and threw him off his horse.
When the Roman wing, rallied and brought up to
counter-attack, fell upon the rear of their recent assail-
ants, the flight became general. Five thousand Persians
fell. Belisarius and Hermogenes at once cautiously
checked the pursuit.

Conclusion of the battle of Daras

The battle of Daras was epoch-making. It revealed
the fact that a great tactician had arisen—a commander
who could plan a battle as if it were a game of chess: a
military juggler of Hannibal's type. Justinian's gamble
had proved successful: he had backed a man of genius.
For the rest of the year the Persians avoided any general
action in Mesopotamia.

For Justinian, it was an exceedingly cheering and encouraging year. It looked as if he had really overcome
what had once seemed the hopeless difficulty of finding
adequate military direction. Sittas also, in Armenia, had
achieved considerable success, defeating superior forces
of Persians, and capturing two great fortresses.

Rufinus had been sent to Hierapolis in order to be
able to help the defeated Roman army by diplomatic
action if things went wrong. His services had been unnecessary. He was now despatched to the Persian court
in quite a different spirit to see if a satisfactory peace
could be arranged. Old Kobad, however, the King of

Kings, a man of strong character and great determination, was not the sort of man who made peace because he had been defeated. He would not hear any suggestion that his government was in the wrong. He stated his case in a most uncompromising form, pointing out the refusal of the Romans to contribute their share to the expense of guarding the Caucasian passes, although they profited as much as the Persians did from the security so established. Kobad reminded the ambassador, moreover, of the systematically provocative conduct of the Romans in building Daras, and in attempting to build a fortress at Minduos. He would not alter his views on these subjects: the only terms of peace he would consider included the dismantling of Daras, and the payment of a share in the expenses of protecting the Caucasian passes. He dropped a strong hint that a money settlement would satisfy him. This Rufinus reported to Justinian on his return to Constantinople. Justinian did not see the necessity of paying an indemnity to a defeated foe, and the matter stood over.

Justinian and peace *(margin note)*

v

More than one battle of Daras would be required to bring a power such as Persia to a different frame of mind. While Rufinus was negotiating with Kobad, a person of another stamp was advising the King of Kings on the military problem. Al Mundhir was intimately acquainted with the geography of Syria and the north Arabian desert. His plan was to cross the Euphrates at a point fairly low down in its course, and to strike across the desert north of Palmyra. By this means it would be possible to circumvent the line of Roman fortresses, and to reach a point where neither fortress nor field army existed to stop them. Antioch would easily fall to a surprise attack: and not improbably a return could be effected by the same route before any Roman army could arrive. As the desert passage was reputed to be dangerous, Al Mundhir offered the guarantee of his own personal guidance. Persia continues the war

Kobad was taken with this. The plan was agreed to. The next spring, accordingly, a Persian army crossed the Euphrates at Circesium and marched up the right (the western) bank to Callinicum, where it crossed the Roman frontier. Proceeding onwards the short distance to Sura, an expeditionary force was launched across the desert. By Barbalissus it reached the lake of Gabbala, some sixty miles or thereabouts from Antioch. Here it met its first check: but a startling one. Belisarius was twelve miles off at the city of Chalcis, with an army over twenty thousand strong! He had got wind of the whole affair, and had made a series of forced marches to intercept the Persian army. While the citizens of Antioch were fleeing from their city, Belisarius had thrust in between the city and the invaders.

There was a pause. Belisarius had shown that he could not only fight, but march. In spite of his reputation for brilliance, he was throughout his life a very sober and prosaic fellow; and now, at Chalcis, he had not the slightest intention of performing any military heroics. His aim was to clear the invaders out of the country at the cheapest possible rate per head. This attitude was incredible to an army brought up on heroics and inefficiency. Belisarius was generally supposed to be trem- Persian raid into Syria bling in his shoes. The Huns, in particular, who could not live without heroics, found themselves unable to take such a standpoint seriously. Sunicas disobeyed orders. The fact that he discovered the nature of the Persian plan of campaign, and that their aim was Antioch, did not excuse him in his commander's eyes. Belisarius probably knew all he needed to know of the Persian intentions. Even so influential a person as Hermogenes, acting as peacemaker, found difficulty in persuading Belisarius to overlook the military offence. Belisarius was at all times particular in disciplinary matters, because the enforcement of discipline was the hardest task he had, as well as the most necessary. He could not work his tactical methods with an all-nation army, unless it would obey him with exactitude.

When Belisarius slowly advanced, the Persians began their retirement to the Euphrates. The two armies retraversed the route by which the Persians had come: each night the Romans occupied the camp which the Persians had made the previous night. When the Persians left Sura, they made the short march to Callinicum and stopped. As their next step would be into the desert, they doubtless wished a little extra time for preparation. The Roman army, coming on as before, overtook them before they had started in the morning.

Persian retreat

Merely to issue commands was now useless. It was necessary to appeal to the army. Hermogenes agreed that an action was undesirable; it was the day before Easter, and many of the men, in accordance with their religious custom, were fasting, and would continue the fast into the following day. Belisarius accordingly summoned a general assembly, and addressed the troops. He pointed

out that they had nothing to gain by victory and much
to lose by defeat, and he asked them to have confidence
in his decision to avoid fighting. . . . His reception was
a bad one. Even some of the officers joined in demonstrations against him. Belisarius therefore gave them their
heads, and the order of the day was issued.

VI

He drew up his army quite simply: there was no time
for more, and perhaps he did not feel so confident in
the discipline of his men that he dared risk more. The
infantry, his weakest arm, he put on the left, close to
the river. The Saracen auxiliaries he stationed on rising
ground to the right, where they faced men armed and
trained like themselves, the tribesmen of Al Mundhir.
In the centre he massed his cavalry, including a body of
men of whom we shall hear in a moment: his own comitatus. These dispositions meant that he did not intend
to put his trust in tactics of manœuvre, but in the
superior training and armament of his men.

Battle of Sura or Callinicum April 19th A.D. 531

The struggle was a fierce one. The Persian bowmen
were the more numerous, and faster in handling their
weapons; but the Roman archers were bigger men drawing a stronger bow, and they shot clean through shields
and armour. No result could be foretold until the afternoon came; and then the Persians concentrated on their
left. Driving off the lightly armed Saracens, they exposed the Roman right. The result was a complete en-
velopment of the Roman army. The troops in that
section—many of them zealots from Asia Minor—were
exhausted with fighting and fasting. In spite of prodigies

of valour by the Huns, who fought like tigers when
driven to bay, and who died sword in hand,[1] the wing
was broken, and the survivors were driven into the river,
where some saved themselves by taking refuge on islands.
The men of Belisarius' own comitatus were next in order
of position. As soon as Belisarius saw that Ascan, the
Hun leader, was down, he knew what to expect. His
order was to dismount, and to cast loose the horses. This
diversion gave them time to crowd up with the infantry;
the shield-wall was formed, and massed shoulder to
shoulder they made an impenetrable hedge. Assault after
assault was ineffectual. The Roman archery was far more
deadly than the Persian, and the Persian horses could
not be brought up to face the arrow-storm, but reared
and threw the ranks into confusion. Night fell on an
indecisive battle. Nothing could be done in the dark,
and the Persians withdrew. Belisarius and some of his
men found a freight boat, in which they got across the
river to an island. Others swam.

The
Romans
enveloped

When daylight came, barges arrived from Callinicum,
and took off the fugitives. The Persians held possession
of the battlefield, and stripped the dead. The booty must
have been considerable; for the equipment of a Roman
horse-archer was an expensive one. The historian notes
that the Persians found their own dead quite as numerous
as the Roman.

---

[1] The ordinary modern notion of Huns is that they were barbaric nomads of
hideous aspect sweeping all before them by their uncountable numbers; and Englishmen have probably never really understood the German emperor's famous reference
which fixed "Hun" as a colloquial term for German during the war. A little study
of Procopius (e. g., I. xiv. 44–51; I. xviii. 38; II. xxvi. 26; III. xviii. 18, VI. i.
1–10 and 21–34.) might throw light upon the real status of the Hun as a fighting
man. Anything is useful which corrects mistaken notions concerning the powers
and qualities of Asiatics.

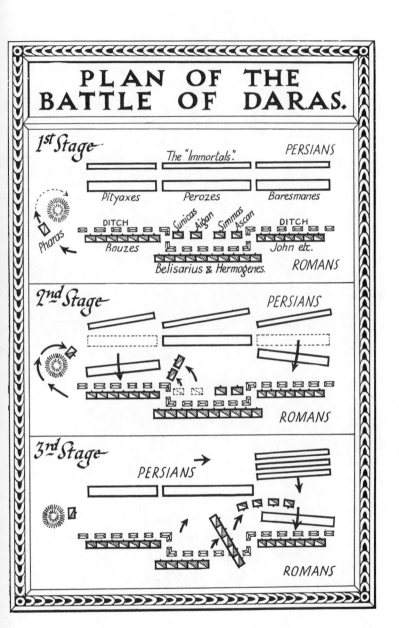

PLAN OF THE
BATTLE OF DARAS.

1st Stage

The "Immortals".   PERSIANS

Pityaxes   Perozes   Baresmanes

Pharas

DITCH   Cunicas   Aigan   Simmas   Ascan   DITCH

Bouzes   John etc.

Belisarius & Hermogenes.   ROMANS

2nd Stage

PERSIANS

ROMANS

3rd Stage

PERSIANS

ROMANS

No laurel crowns were handed to the Persian commander when he reached home. Kobad was furious at
the heavy losses incurred without practical reason or
substantial reward. He treated the occasion almost as if
it had been a Persian defeat.

VII

But the trouble at the Persian court was hardly worse
than that which broke out at the Roman headquarters.
Immediately after the battle Hermogenes transmitted to
the emperor a separate report, as, being a minister, he
was fully entitled to do. Justinian sent Constantiolus
post haste to conduct an investigation.

Charges
against
Belisarius

The reports of Hermogenes and Constantiolus have
long since perished, and no one now knows what was in
them: but the case against Belisarius is still preserved in
the pages of John Malalas, and his defence is contained
in those of Procopius, his friend and legal assistant.

Angry charges were brought against Belisarius, chiefly
by the Huns. They represented a continuation of the
dissensions which had broken out with Sunicas at Chalcis. Although he had then arbitrated, Hermogenes was
himself a Hun by race, and he was influenced by the
contentions made after the battle. It was alleged that it
had been within the power of Belisarius to come to the
rescue of the Huns on his right wing; that he had deliberately abandoned them, and had crossed over to the
island with the fugitives, leaving Sunicas and Simmas to
fight the Persians to a standstill. He had not honestly
exerted himself to make the battle a success.

Belisarius, as we have seen, contended that he had

been forced against his will and judgment into the engagement; he had not wanted it, and could not be responsible for the results. His officers and men had fancied that they knew better than he the right military policy to pursue; and after throwing away, by their insubordination, all the advantages he had gained over the Persian army, they tried to conceal the disastrous results of their own action by blaming him for adopting the only course open to him.

After hearing all sides, Constantiolus seems to have exonerated Belisarius, and to have accepted his statements, for no more was heard of the adverse charges, while Belisarius continued to possess the full and unwavering confidence of Justinian. Nevertheless, the disagreement with the Huns was destined to affect the whole career of Belisarius.

VIII

The dissensions after the battle of Callinicum, the results of the battle itself, and some of the causes which had contributed to those results, all combined to bring Justinian to a critical decision. He had been feeling his way towards it for some time past; now, as if for the first time he saw his way clear before him, he made up his mind. He recalled Belisarius, and transferred the command to Mundus. The latter carried on—quite adequately, although the best of men were liable to look a little commonplace when they took over a command from Belisarius. Mundus was not called upon to conduct any extensive operations.

For reasons of his own, the emperor meant to slow

down the war. When, on September 8th. 531, old Kobad
died—an event perhaps not wholly unforeseen—Justinian at once opened negotiations for peace. A mission
of his best and most trusted representatives went to
Persia with instructions that they might go to considerable lengths to obtain a cessation of the Persian war.
This being so, Belisarius was no longer indispensable on
the Mesopotamian front.

Death of
Kobad
Sept. 8th
A. D. 531

The rise of Belisarius had furnished Justinian with the
last indispensable element he needed to make possible the
reconquest of the empire. Belisarius had made his reputation not by ornamental methods, but by genuine military invention—real originality in his profession. He
had solved problems which up to this point had baffled
the best soldiers the empire could produce. No commander before him had been able to invent tactical
methods which would utilize to the full the advantages
that were to be found in the human material available.
The regular soldiers of the imperial army were reliable,
but uninspired. Most of them were Thracian, Illyrian
or Anatolian peasants—who to this very day possess the
same qualities of valour and steadiness, and lack of imagination. The so-called Fœderati, who were now re-
cruited indiscriminately from Roman subjects and from
non-Roman tribesmen, were most of them cavalry, and
were quite up to the old standards of Roman auxiliary
troops. The Allies—a term which covers the Huns,
Herulians and Saracens whom we have seen taking part
in the Persian war—were often magnificent soldiers;
but as they were tribesmen serving under their own
chiefs, their discipline was often doubtful and their
temperament difficult. Finally, there were the Bucel-

The Roman
army

larians—the military retainers in the private service of great men and high military commanders. Strictly speaking, they were illegal—but licences were issued in approved cases to permit their enrolment. They derived from a curiously complex origin. There was in them a strong reminiscence of the clients with whom an old Roman patrician was surrounded; a strong touch of the armed body-guard of the Greek tyrant, and more than a suggestion of the household of gladiators who often surrounded a Roman oligarch of the late republic. But the immediate pattern which gave them colour and shape as an institution was the comitatus of the northern kings. This, copied from the empire by the kings, was now copied back in its new form by Belisarius: and it is possible that the improvements he introduced set the wheel in motion again, and were recopied by the kings.

The new
tactics

The inspired invention of Belisarius was a mode of employing the comitatus of specially picked and trained men as the core round which to assemble all the other elements of the Roman military service. Where the military system had been weak was in its lack of an absolutely dependable core. In old days the legions had formed such a core. The disappearance of the ancient city-state and its citizens had extinguished the type of man who made a good legionary soldier. Till a substitute was provided, the Roman army remained weak and unsatisfactory. Belisarius did not attempt to revive the legionary soldier. He took the typical first-class fighting-man of his own day, and trained him to be a perfect instrument for the tactical improvisator. This typical soldier was the armoured cavalryman armed with spear, sword and bow. Belisarius trained him to be the most effective fighter of the day with all these weapons. We have seen how, at Callinicum, the Persian bowmen were dominated by the stronger Roman bow. At the battle of Daras, a year earlier, it was first made clear how the various elements of a Roman army, with their quaint diversity of training and temper, could be made to supplement one another, and subserve a scheme the basic idea of which was just this variety and diversity. Belisarius turned this very weakness, which had made the late Roman armies a somewhat comic-opera affair, into their chief source of strength. His recipe was a combination of all arms based upon the comitatus of armoured and mounted bowmen. The scheme not only worked, but worked miracles.

Effect of the new tactics

IX

It was in this first Persian war of Justinian that Belisarius founded his wonderful comitatus, which afterwards carried him to immortal fame in that little military pantheon where Alexander and Hannibal and Cæsar also dwell. In four years he had collected and trained a body of men who were never equalled by any similar body in their own age. Its members pass and repass perpetually across the pages of Procopius. Its senior members were the special officers, the picked deputies, whom Belisarius employed for missions of responsibility and danger. They were intended to think as well as to act.

The only bar to complete and unqualified admiration for this institution lay in some of its indirect implications. It was almost too great a force for a subject to pos-

The instru-
ment

sess and control. It was a royal household, an imperial
dignity. The members were not Roman soldiers, but a
private staff engaged by their employer, and paid by
him. They took no orders from any other man; and although the law required them to take the oath of allegiance to the emperor, it would not have been safe to
rely too much upon a guarantee so frail. Not all of them
were Roman subjects in the usual acceptance of the
term. Many were Goths or Huns; the one qualification
considered was military excellence.

It is certain, from the later course of events, that Justinian and his advisers realized this dangerous side. A
possible danger, however, is a very different thing from
an actual one, and the new military system of Belisarius
was far too useful at this stage to be questioned. Until
Belisarius appeared upon the scene Justinian had needed
to rely almost exclusively upon negotiation and diplomacy for the achievement of his dream of the re-
establishment of the empire—and we have seen some of
the results to which negotiation exposed him. But now a
new factor was introduced into the case. It was prac-

A new
factor

ticable—or it seemed practicable—to give just that fillip
to events which can be given by the judicious exercise
of military force.

The possibility was especially welcome to the emperor
at this juncture. Some of his projects had been begun
very much on faith that he would be able to carry them
through. Especially in the case of his negotiations with
the Vandal kingdom of Africa, he must often have won-
dered whether he really would be able to back his words
with actions. If the diplomatic contest came to a deadlock, could he depend upon conquering Africa, or even

in forcing upon the Vandals the necessity of a reconsideration of the case? Could men like Sittas or Bouzes reconquer the Roman empire? The discovery of Belisarius solved this problem. Justinian believed him to be adequate to such a task.

X

Justinian's negotiations with the Vandals had indeed been somewhat chequered. The peace which the emperor Zeno had made with Gaiseric, king of the Vandals, in A. D. 474,[1] had continued unbroken ever since. The sons and the grandsons of Gaiseric had ruled untroubled by old Rome or new Rome. Old Rome had dropped out, and the Gothic king reigned in Italy. New Rome had been, of late years, quite friendly; and the Monophysite Anastasius had lived on good terms with the Arian King Trasamund. The successor of Trasamund, who came to the throne in 523, during the reign of Justin, was a well-disposed man named Hilderic, who was half a Roman by blood—for he was the grandson of the emperor Valentinian III. on one side of his pedigree, as well as of Halt-foot Gaiseric on the other. A half-Roman mind, as well as the influence of Justin's example, perhaps affected his general policy. He suspended the religious persecution in Africa, and showed a disposition to regard Justinian as a brother and a friend.

It was one thing for a pure-bred Vandal such as Trasamund to be friendly with a Monophysite emperor. It was altogether another thing for a half-Roman, half-Vandal such as Hilderic to be friendly with an Orthodox

[1] Bury, *History of the Later Roman Empire*, I. 390.

and Catholic emperor, who had given such plain proofs of his views and tendencies as Justinian had. The relationship of the Vandal state to the government at Constantinople was not a problem to be solved by smiles and handshaking: and there were men among the Vandals who perfectly realized this fact. To suspend the persecution of Catholics implied endorsing their theology: and endorsing their theology implied acknowledging the existence and the legal claims of the Roman empire: and it looked as if the fourth and fifth moves of the game might involve "castling," and the reign of Justinian in Africa, and the occupation of a delightful house in Constantinople by Hilderic. . . . No one professed a false surprise when one day a strong deputation of Vandal leaders waited upon Hilderic; and the conversation was shortly followed by Hilderic's disappearance, and the accession of his cousin Geilamir to the rule of the Vandals.

Deposition of Hilderic May 19th A. D. 530

If Justinian seriously intended the things he was credited with intending, he could hardly submit to this rebuff. Since when had friendship with a Roman emperor become a crime? For the sake of his own dignity and prestige in the eyes of the world it was necessary for him to come to the help of the deposed Vandal king. But more than this: here was the providential opportunity for intervention in Africa. A reconquest of the Roman empire must begin there if anywhere, as Leo had perceived. To start on Spain or Italy with the Vandal fleet in command of the western Mediterranean was an impossibility. . . . Hence, now was the time, and here was the place. If Justinian really meant business, he must make his decision now.

XI

Justinian took up the case of his friend Hilderic. If he had loved Hilderic a little more, or if he had been interested in the Vandal kingdom of Africa a little less, he might have touched the diction of his correspondence with some of that mellifluous quality which does not injure those who employ it, and often goes down very well with proud and impatient recipients. As it was, his tone was imperial and authoritative.

Justinian supports Hilderic

He pointed out that neither the universal customs of civilized mankind nor the particular provisions of the testamentary settlement of Gaiseric justified the imprisonment, and the deprivation by violence, of an old man who was legally king of the Vandals. He reminded Geilamir that it was no very profitable exchange to obtain an invalid title a very short time sooner than the valid one which was waiting for him in the ordinary course of events. He requested that Hilderic should be allowed to remain nominally and outwardly king of the Vandals, while Geilamir could reserve to himself the decision of questions of policy. If this course were pursued, said Justinian calmly, the Almighty and We would both take up a favourable attitude.

This communication evidently annoyed the Vandals, for they dismissed the imperial messenger without a reply, and redoubled the strictness of Hilderic's imprisonment. They could not more perfectly have suited Justinian's hopes. He wrote again to Geilamir. He remarked that it had not occurred to him that his former request would not be granted. Since Geilamir had elected to seize the Vandal royal power, he might keep it for what

Negotiations between Justinian and the Vandals

it was worth. . . . Justinian then delivered his ultimatum, demanding the release of Hilderic and his passage to Constantinople; in the event of a refusal, matters would not be allowed to rest where they were. . . . He wound up by notifying Geilamir that the old treaty with Gaiseric was still in force, and that he, Justinian, proposed to act in pursuance of the testamentary dispositions made by Gaiseric, and in defence of Gaiseric's legitimate heir.

Such a clever and startling conclusion evidently frightened as well as enraged the Vandals. If they admitted Justinian's contention, they were placing the Vandal realm under the tutelage of the emperor, who evidently proposed to undertake the task of superintending its arrangements. Accordingly they took the trouble this time to reply: and their answer is interesting. They argued that nothing had been done contrary to the common custom of civilized nations. Hilderic had been accused of changing the policy of the kingdom, and had been deposed by the action of the Vandal people. They submitted that Justinian had no standing in the matter, and no right to intervene: and that any intervention by him would be a breach of the treaty between Gaiseric and Zeno. . . . They clinched this by the superscription with which they headed the letter: "The *Basileus* Geilamir to the *Basileus* Justinian." [1] . . . This amounted to the assertion of an absolutely sovereign and independent Vandal Kingdom, not in any way what-

The
Vandal
standpoint

---

[1] Procopius, *History*, III. ix. 20. While Procopius, writing in Greek, could hardly avoid using the word "basileus" fairly often, he marks something exceptional in this letter by quoting the superscription as well as the contention in the body of the letter. In the other letters quoted, he gives no superscription. Justinian was exceedingly angry.

soever subordinate to the Roman empire, but equal in standing. It was the careful denial of the whole assumption on which Justinian's policy was based.

After this it was time for all persons not connected with the quarrel to get out of the way.

XII

Such was the situation when Belisarius, with that famous comitatus of his, rode into Constantinople on his return from Mesopotamia.

Although Belisarius came back fresh from the disaster at Callinicum, Justinian paid no heed to trifles. The emperor was satisfied with the military competence shown in the two campaigns. The mere fact that ignorant and foolhardy subordinates had forced Belisarius to fight a battle against his wishes did not detract from the merit of the great intercepting march to Chalcis, and the prudent and skilful pursuit which escorted the Persians out of Roman territory. . . . Justinian had now something better to offer. On the Persian border there had been rival commanders, jealous seniors whose claims had been overlooked, and many other drawbacks. Belisarius should have an entirely free hand in Africa. On African soil, free from all entanglements and rivalries, his mind could employ its genius to the full.

Belisarius destined for Africa

It would need to do so; for once Belisarius set foot on Vandal soil, he could only leave it again either dead or victorious.

CHAPTER IV

NIKA: THE REVOLT OF THE BLUES AND GREENS

I

THE African policy of Justinian, although the natural continuation of the policy which he had adopted from the beginning, met with far more opposition. Reconciliation with the papacy, distasteful as some parts of the process had been, broke no bones and, above all, involved very little expense. An invasion of Africa was an altogether different proposition. It alarmed a large section of public opinion hitherto favourable to Justinian. How it must have affected the large masses of men who, in all ages, are inarticulate, we can see by noticing the reaction of some of the principal ministers and supporters of the emperor, whose opinions were recorded and have survived to enlighten us.

Belisarius, as a man of sobriety and intelligence, was not overwhelmed with gratitude at the offer of a field for his talents in Africa. It sounded a little too much (at any rate, on first hearing) like an order to go and get the moon. John the Cappadocian was vehemently opposed to the whole idea of an African campaign, and felt it his duty to say so in a loud voice and simple language. They all knew the history of recent expeditions to Africa. Every one had ended in disaster. Leo had thrown away a hundred thousand pounds bullion, with the only result that for thirty years the budget could

(margin note: Opposition to Justinian's African policy)

(margin note: John's contentions)

78

not be balanced. Every attempt to turn out the Vandals had been a complete failure. Besides (said John) suppose they were turned out: Africa could not be held unless the empire went on to reconquer Sicily and Italy. Did Justinian propose to face such a necessity as that? . . . John evidently had a picture in his mind of himself working overtime at bullying the tax-defaulters in order to fill a bottomless pit with money: and the sincerity of his opposition to the project was unmistakable.

Belisarius had signalized his return from the Persian war by getting married to a somewhat unexpected person named Antonina: a widow with a grown-up son. Procopius hints that the lady—who was connected with a family of eminent charioteers well known in racing circles—had bestowed her hand upon Belisarius in the spirit of her kinsmen who were accustomed to drive winners. It is probable that her influence encouraged him to contemplate with confidence the prospect of an advance in professional status. It is just possible also that the force of John's opposition had some share in modifying the feelings of Belisarius. After all, the prospects **Belisarius veers** were not quite so hopeless as John painted them. Belisarius was not altogether such a perfect fool that he could not look a Vandal in the face. A great deal would depend upon the amount of backing Justinian gave. It did not need to be enormous in amount; it needed only to be of the right kind, and given at the right moment. Here Justinian rose to the occasion. He meant to force an African war in the teeth of his ministers and the consistorium and the senate, and he was willing to place unusual and indeed unprecedented powers in the hands of Belisarius. That freedom of action and close support, for which Scipio Africanus had hoped in vain from a republican senate, should be given to Belisarius by an imperial monarch.

Belisarius was too much of a soldier at heart to stand out against the wishes of his emperor. He was prepared to leave his bones in Africa if positively ordered to go there. . . . John, though by no means ready to go to this length, was after all a friend and a minister. If Justinian positively insisted upon his insane policy, John could only shrug his shoulders with marked emphasis, and proceed to raise the money required. Where John gave way the consistorium was little likely to make a stand. The bishops, of course, were warmly in favour of rescuing their oppressed brethren from beneath the blood-stained hoof of the Arian tyrant. Only the senate was left.

Justinian
is firm

II

Justinian was not to carry his point so easily as all this. He had gone against nearly all his advisers—against soldiers, consistorium and senate—though not against church. The storm which had hovered and muttered uncertainly in the background now began to blow steadily —and it blew up for trouble.

The trouble started upon the eleventh of January, in a curious way. During the interlude between two races in the Hippodrome, a man stood up among the Greens, and began to call across the stadium to the imperial box.

Talking across the Hippodrome was not a job for amateurs. To do it effectively needed professional voice-production. Whosoever this man was, therefore, he was no accident. Innocent and casual as they might appear, it is pretty certain that the groups of spectators amongst whom he rose were an organized body-guard carrying concealed arms, and ready to deal with the first sign of interruption.

The first sign of trouble

The dialogue which then took place is famous, for it was the first episode of the Nika sedition. Back-chat with an emperor for one of the actors is not so common that we can afford to despise it.

The Green crier began by calling upon the name of Justinian. When he had attention, he began to voice the complaints of the Greens, and to demand justice from a powerful oppressor. He spoke as an individual petitioning Cæsar for equity.

Justinian himself replied; but his answers were chanted across the enormous space of the Hippodrome by the voice of his official mandator. He enquired with interest the name of the unknown person who was injuring the applicant.

The alleged petitioner replied guardedly that his oppressor was to be found in the Shoemakers' street.

Justinian observed that in such a case no single person was guilty.

The applicant lifted up his voice in sorrow and expostulation, insisting that he had really been wronged, and by a person. . . . Pressed to name the person, at last he let the cat out of the bag. The person was Calopodius.

Argument in the Hippodrome

This was sailing very close to the wind, for Calopodius was a member of the imperial circle; and after the men-tion of his name there could be no doubt that Justinian himself was the person really indicated. . . . The body-guard probably at this point looked brightly about it to see if any action was called for: but none was required. . . . The emperor merely replied that Calopodius had nothing to do with the applicant.

His oppressor, said the applicant hopefully, would perish like Judas.

That was it, returned Justinian; the whole thing was a put-up job.

Like Judas, said the applicant, dwelling on the theme.

A warm exchange of strong language followed, of a type not now fashionable. Justinian remarked that the people concerned were Monophysites (that is to say, opponents of the policy of a united empire, and supporters of the old party of Anastasius.) The Greens then collectively joined in, and represented themselves as a persecuted party, whose lives were not safe because of their party loyalty. This Justinian vehemently denied. They retorted that he was a murderer. The Blues rejoined that the Greens were the only party with murderers among them. . . . Quite so, returned the Greens; *your* murderers are not here because they have bolted for their

The Greens retire in protest lives. Who killed the woodseller down at the harbour bar? . . . *You* did!—said Justinian. (*Tumult.*) Amid shouts, violent epithets and general uproar the Green party proceeded to leave the Hippodrome, while the emperor and the Blues hurled after them remarks which, though now more or less obsolete, would have been considered hot stuff by contemporary judges of invective.[1]

---

[1] For the whole detail of this dialogue see Bury, *History of the Later Roman Empire*, II. 71-74.

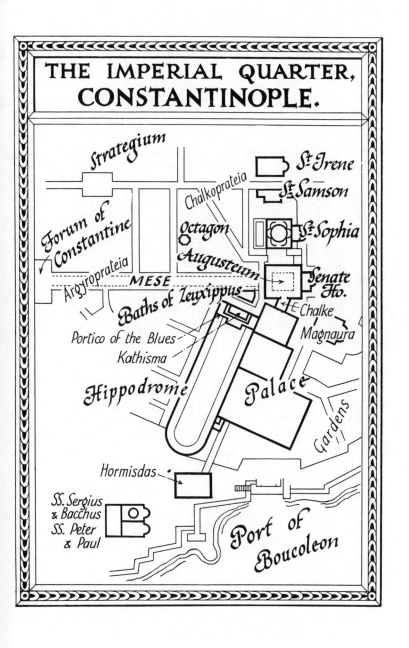

THE IMPERIAL QUARTER, CONSTANTINOPLE.

Strategium

St Irene

St Samson

Chalkoprateia

Forum of Constantine

Octagon

St Sophia

Augusteum

Argyroprateia

MESE

Senate Ho.

Baths of Zeuxippus

Chalke

Magnaura

Portico of the Blues

Kathisma

Hippodrome

Palace

Gardens

Hormisdas

SS. Sergius & Bacchus
SS. Peter & Paul

Port of Boucoleon

III

This took place in the morning. In the afternoon, more, and disturbing, news came. Seven of the partisans, condemned to death for rioting, had been executed over at Pera across the harbour. For some reason, the hangman bungled his work, and two of the condemned men were picked up alive. One was a Green, and one a Blue.

There is a widespread popular belief that a man who in this sort of way escapes the rope is morally exempt from any further attention on the part of the law. Before the true facts were realized, the neighbouring monks of St. Conon hurried the two half-hanged men into a boat, and rowed them up the harbour to the church of St. Laurence in the north-west corner of the city. There they were safe in sanctuary. The prefect at once despatched soldiers, who picketed the church.

The following day was Monday. It was a blank day (as it still is for butchers), and evidently a good deal of scene-shifting went on invisibly behind the curtain. Precisely what took place was only imperfectly known even to Justinian and his ministers; to us, it is not known at all. We can do no more than mark the course of events.

Monday Jan. 12th A. D. 532

Tuesday was the Ides of January—the thirteenth of the month. Justinian took his place in the Hippodrome according to the regular programme. It was an important day to the racing world: what we should call a Gold Cup day. The preliminary heats which had been run off on Sunday were now to be followed by the serious business, the finals: and what finals, in any form of sport, can sometimes be, we all know.

IV

It was a troublesome day from the first, with ominous
and threatening undercurrents. Whether some agreement had been come to between the parties was not at
first quite clear, but certainly there was a queer una-
nimity about them. During the intervals between the
races there was a systematic cry to the imperial box for
reprieve to the two half-hanged men at St. Laurence's
sanctuary. The appeal was a difficult one for a statesman
to answer. It was the kind of cry which can easily be
started by small organized groups, and is readily taken
up in perfect good faith by the ordinary spectator. But
the events of Sunday had made it very difficult for Justinian to grant the appeal. He had been taunted then
with judicial partiality. The two men had been fairly
tried and legally condemned according to the process of
law which was generally accepted by public opinion. No
one questioned that. What he was being asked to do was
not to reverse an injustice but to interfere, without
demonstrable reason, with the normal course of judicial
administration. He was very unwilling to do this. He
had moreover made it his aim to preserve absolute im-
partiality between the factions. The attack on his fairness made him all the more reluctant to intervene. It
seemed the safest course therefore to make no reply to
the appeals.

Whosoever had worked out the programme was no
mean strategist. Justinian's steadfast refusal was a lever
with which to raise to its height the agitation of the
Greens, and at the same time to stampede the Blues in
their company. The plans had quite evidently been laid

Tuesday
Jan. 13th
A. D. 532

beforehand. At the twenty-second race no longer was any appeal made to the imperial box. Instead arose the cry: "Long live the humane Blue-Greens!" It spread. When the last race was over, the concourse poured forth into the streets of Constantinople, enthusiastically celebrating the new-born party, the Blue-Greens.

The combined Blue-Greens

What this might signify remained to be seen. The programme and proceedings of a Blue-Green party were not mentioned in any work of reference accessible to Justinian.

V

He had not long to wait. The crowd began to set for the Praetorium, where a body of organized and determined men appeared, demanding the intentions of the government concerning the half-hanged refugees at St. Laurence's sanctuary. They received no reply from the prefect of the city. By this time the crowd was increasing; people were streaming up, and the vortex which was set going at the Praetorium gradually sucked in all the spectators and neutrals and loafers and hangers-on who surrounded it. Mr. Facing-both-Ways is often brave with Mr. Foolhardy to lead him. . . . The mob began by smashing in the doors of the Praetorium, and slugging the officials inside. They then let out all the prisoners, and made a bonfire of the building. After this auspicious beginning, the delighted and elated band of brethren, Blue-Greens, prisoners, loafers, general public and all, proceeded up the Mesê, the Broadway or Cheapside of Constantinople. At the end of the Mesê, where it entered that great colonnaded forum

Rioting begins

called the Augusteum, a whole world lay ready for their enjoyment.

Bonfires, and assaults upon representatives of the government, often have a strangely exhilarating effect upon the ordinary human being. In the gathering dusk a large part of the population of Constantinople started with energy about the task of celebrating the night after the races. They set fire to the "Chalkê," the so-called Bronze Gate, the great main entrance of the imperial palace. Round the Augusteum the flames drifted north to St. Sophia's; and the great church was presently burning to heaven. The senate house also caught fire, and added its humbler effort to the general illuminations. It was a glorious night. . . . Justinian's views upon the amount of authority possessed by absolute monarchs, and the amount of servility engrained in the populace of Constantinople, might have made interesting reading if some one had had an opportunity of collecting them.

The first con- flagration

VI

On Wednesday morning the government, marooned in the imperial palace, made an effort to get into touch with the rioters. Something had to be done. . . . A fair number of ministers, officials and other people, useful or decorative, were crowded into the palace, unable to get home. They had attended court on the Ides of January, to receive their various insignia of office, and the zone of fire had cut them off.

Wednesday Jan. 14th A. D. 532

That zone was not by any means diminishing, for the mob were now setting fire to the Baths of Zeuxippus, just outside the Augusteum, and the latter was involved

in the flames. The enthusiastic spectators were induced
to leave this new display of fireworks by the news that
Basilides, Mundus and Constantiolus were up in the imperial box. They poured into the Hippodrome; and, if
mobs are alike in all ages, they very probably began the
proceedings by a number of voluntary critical remarks
upon the personal appearance of those trusted officers of
Justinian.

No; they did not want any races. What did they
want? They said, Down with Eudaimon, the prefect!
Down with Tribunian! Down with John the Cappadocian! Basilides and his colleagues returned to the palace
to communicate these demands to Justinian.

The demand for the dismissal of the ministers was a
totally new element in the situation. No hint of any
such suggestion had been made before; and it indicated
the point at which the mob, now too deeply committed
to draw back, was openly made subject to political purposes. Justinian, however, thought it just as well to com-
ply with the demand. By doing so, he might partly dis-
arm the instigators who were inspiring the mob. But
both the demand and the compliance were equally un-
real; for not the retention or dismissal of subordinate
ministers, but the life of Justinian was now the issue at
stake.

And, in fact, the demand was forgotten before the
afternoon was far advanced. The insurrection was slipping out of the hands of the Blue-Greens, into those of
men brought in from outside. Who these men were, is
a question which cannot now be answered. The allegation is made that they were poor country-people ruined
by the exactions of John the Cappadocian. . . . John

Dismissal
of
ministers
demanded

would probably have smiled if he had heard the allegation; and it is extremely probable that he would have alleged in return, that they were the hired ruffians of wealthy tax-dodgers on whom he had had his eye.[1] . . . The reader can take his choice. . . . At any rate, the force behind the insurrection was no longer the "humane Blue-Greens," anxious for the refugees at the sanctuary of St. Laurence. Its aim was no longer the dismissal of the ministers. What it foreshadowed was a new emperor of the house of Anastasius. The inspiration of the revolt came from the Monophysite party: and its purpose was to prevent the African war. The revolt was political.

VII

The city was searched by the rebels that afternoon for the nephews of Anastasius. Hypatius and Pompeius were in the palace with Justinian, so nothing could be done with them. Probus, the third brother, remained. The deputation which waited upon him found that Probus had foreseen the visit, and had prudently elected to remain no longer. They added his house to the illuminations—a remarkably unpersuasive action—and went away.

The revolt is political

The change in the character of the revolt was reflected in a parallel change in the policy adopted towards it by the government. Towards the Blue-Greens, Justinian had followed a course of extraordinary mildness. No physical force, other than that of the most conventional and most legal kind, had been employed against the cir-

---

[1] For the relations between Justinian and the great landlords, see Vasiliev, *History of the Byzantine Empire* (1928) I. 193. These landlords had armed body-guards, not exclusively for ornament.

cus factions. With a political revolt it was different. A political revolt meant that the emperor and his ministers were fighting for their lives. A rat will put up a desperate battle when cornered, and a man at bay is more dangerous than many rats. . . . More than this, a political revolt is a challenge to a man's spiritual worth. Justinian, in particular, was called upon to consider, and to say, whether he believed that his policy and his purposes were worth fighting for. Were they worthy of being protected by bloodshed and violence? Were his aims good enough to be enforced over the bodies of many men?

Change in Justinian's attitude

He believed that they were.

So believing, he prepared to suppress the revolt by force.

In this respect, Justinian's position was determined by pure accidents which had a kind of providential quality about them. Had he been compelled to rely upon the regular imperial guards, the Domestici and Excubitors, he would have fallen. They were not reliable, and it is doubtful whether they would have obeyed orders. But the mere fact that Belisarius was in Constantinople to confer on the subject of the African war implied that the comitatus of Belisarius was also present. Many of its members were Goths, who had no politics except their master's, and whose moral standards, sound as they were, were often unusually rough. . . . In addition to this, Mundus was in the city with a body of Heruls. These men were not only available to put down the revolt, but were perfectly adapted for doing so. They had none of the associations of family, friendship, language and like-mindedness, which linked the imperial guards with

Military forces available

the populace of Constantinople. As for Monophysitism
—they knew nothing of it, and cared less. If it were to
be war, then these would be the fighting men of Justinian. . . . And Belisarius and Mundus were not commanders of the parade ground and the administrative
office. They were field-service men, who brought to
their work some of the promptitude with weapons, the
habit of shooting to kill, which long service in frontier
wars is apt to breed.

The question was, were they enough?

VIII

On Thursday, Belisarius sallied out with his men to
reconquer Constantinople. Nothing encouraged them to
take a light or friendly view of the insurrection. They
do not seem to have gone far. Outside the Chalkê, in the
Augusteum and the wide street, a wilderness where the
ruins smoked, they found, not the Humane Blue-Greens,
but armed men facing them—more or less amateurs, it
might be, in comparison with the seasoned professionals
of Belisarius, but still armed men.[1]

Thursday Jan. 15th A. D. 532

The clergy of Constantinople, realizing that matters
were rising slowly to a crisis, hurried to intervene. No
great good could have been done by attempting to argue;
but neither side might care to show disrespect to holy
relics. The clergy accordingly, carrying the relics with
them, marched in solemn procession and took up ground

---

[1] See plan facing p. 78. For details Ebersolt, *Grand Palais de Constantinople*
(1910) with map: Mordtmann. *Esquisse topographique de Constantinople;* Holmes,
The Age of Justinian and Theodora (1912) Ch. I. . . . Ebersolt's splendid map is
repeated in Diehl's *Byzantine Portraits* (1927) where it may conveniently be
consulted.

between the parties. Correct as the calculation would have been in normal circumstances, it did not on this occasion work out as hoped. Exactly what happened is uncertain. The Heruls were a pretty rough crew, only slightly sensitive to holiness. Either some of them were struck by missiles, or they misunderstood the intentions of the clergy, for they laid violent hands on the procession and dispersed it, though it is not reported that they harmed the clerics. Fighting became general in the Augusteum and the neighbouring streets. Belisarius seems to have seized the immediate neighbourhood and the head of the Mesê, and to have cut off the access of the mob to the burnt entrance of the palace. He is likely enough to have barricaded and picketed his gains.

The first sally

IX

Whatsoever he did, the fighting, when it was renewed next day (Friday) was no longer in the vicinity of the Augusteum: it had shifted north beyond St. Sophia. The modern world has seen some instances of street-fighting; and this was not unworthy of comparison. The insurgents at last set fire to the city up by the Praetorium, so that the wind blew the flames south, and this second great fire burned along to St. Sophia and the earlier zone of destruction, consuming in its way a hospital full of patients. Saturday saw the struggle renewed further west. Belisarius went down the Mesê, and tried to fight his way up a side-street, so as to get to the other, the western, end of the Brassmarket, from the eastern end of which he had been fended off the day before. The insurgents, ensconced in a building called the Octagon,

Friday and Saturday Jan. 16th–17th A. D. 532

which they had turned into an impromptu fortress, resisted until the soldiers set fire to the place and drove them out. But Belisarius never got to the Brassmarket, for the north wind took up the battle again, and blew the flames back on him. This Saturday fire was the crowning agony. It burned its way down to the Mesê, and then it began to gut the Mesê down to the Forum of Constantine, including the overhead way which spanned the street. . . . When Belisarius came in at nightfall, he had nothing very hopeful to report. He was not making any headway in the task of suppressing the revolution, and he had managed to burn down a good deal of the most expensive part of the city.

By this time the imperial palace, which had never been equipped to stand a siege, was running short of food and water. Justinian gave the word that all non-residents were to leave the palace. He was perhaps by no means sure of the loyalty of all those senators who had chanced to be stranded in his company. At any rate, he sent them off. Those who remained were old perennials like Tribunian and John, who would have to stand or fall with their master. . . . Hypatius and Pompeius protested against being sent away. Their protests only irritated Justinian. He thought that they were protesting too much, and he packed them off with the rest.[1] . . . What was done now would need to be concerted between the die-hards. The small group of men left in the palace, knowing that their days might be numbered and their

Hypatius and Pompeius

[1] It is the custom to assume that Hypatius was innocent. But we must not too readily make this assumption. Justinian was not an unreasonable man; least of all was he subject to panic. The record of Hypatius can be found in Procopius, I. viii. 2, 11–19, I. xi. 24–39. From the last-mentioned reference it is pretty clear that Hypatius had seriously compromised himself upon a former occasion.

doom sealed, prepared to live or die together. They meant to live, if they could. . . . They were none of them in the least doubtful about their own value. When the Lord created them, he had according to their understanding bidden them fight and struggle and survive: and they intended to do so.

So the night of Saturday, the seventeenth of January, 532, passed; and Sunday dawned.

X

They had got their programme prepared—even although events soon began to depart from it. On Sunday morning Justinian himself proceeded to the Hippodrome, and appeared in the imperial box. The Hippodrome was probably occupied already by a fair number of people waiting for something to turn up. It filled at once upon the news that Justinian was present.

The emperor made a last attempt to come to a peaceable understanding with the rebels. Holding up a copy of the Gospels, he swore to make a faithful peace with his enemies, to grant all their demands, and to issue a complete amnesty and indemnity. Some of the audience were impressed: but others continued hostile. There were cries of "Perjurer!" reminders of his oath to Vitalian, and cheers for Hypatius. It was evident that the attempt was a failure. In the meantime, the news had spread that Hypatius and Pompeius were home again. A large crowd marched to the house of Hypatius, cheered him, and pulled him out. His wife, Mary, realizing only too well the meaning of these manifestations, clung to him until she was shoved off; and the procession returned to the

Sunday
Jan. 18th
A. D. 532

Forum of Constantine, which was still unburned. Here they crowned him emperor with a golden chain, as nothing else was handy.

A fairly full meeting of the senate followed. At this meeting the identity of the leaders of the revolt became clear. The discussion assumed thoroughout that the members present possessed ample power to direct and control the operations. It was proposed that an attack should be made on the palace. One voice—that of a senator named Origenes—was against this policy. He counselled a slower approach, and he pointed out that time was on their side. Finally, however, an attack on the palace was agreed upon. Hypatius was carried to the Hippodrome and installed by his devoted adherents in the imperial box. The place was crowded; and probably the noise was deafening.

Hypatius was not of the stuff from which heroes are made. Whatsoever the feelings of the men in the palace, Hypatius had still more despairing sensations. He was the kind of man who feels that his only chance of safety is to betray his side, even when it is the winning side. Up in the royal box the imperial guards were looking on with paternal interest, and more than paternal indifference. While the crowd was cheering, Hypatius got one of the guardsmen, Ephraim, to start off for the palace with the message that the rebels could be caught together in the Hippodrome, if Justinian were quick.

Ephraim had not gone far when he met Thomas, one of the royal physicians. Thomas was doing a private bolt from the palace, but he stopped to speak. He assured Ephraim that it would be wasted time to proceed further. Justinian and the whole court had fled. Ephraim

The Senate
at work

hurried back to the Hippodrome and announced the news. Hypatius began to feel somewhat safer.

XI

But Thomas had left a little too soon. It was true enough that Justinian, returning to the palace, could see no further possible resort. He had played his last card, and he had lost the game. The sea however was still open. A conference was held to discuss the next step. John the Cappadocian advocated flight to Heraclea. With this Belisarius agreed. . . . John was far from being a coward, and Belisarius was sufficiently accustomed to danger to be less alarmed at it than most people. Thomas had left at this point—just a moment too early to realize that the next speaker was to be a person of a hardier heart than John, and a steadier nerve than Belisarius, and was about to transform the situation and the mood of the court. . . . This next speaker was Theodora. . . . Her words were the turning point in the story.

Report that Justinian had fled

XII

Theodora said: "In a crisis like the present we have no time to argue whether a woman's place is the home, and whether she ought to be meek and modest in the presence of the lords of creation. We have got to get a move on quick. My opinion is that this is no time for flight—not even if it is the safest course. Every one who has been born, has to die; but it does not follow that every one who has been made an emperor has to get off his throne. May the day never come when I do! If you want to make

Theodora's
firm stand

yourself safe, emperor, nothing stops you. There is the sea over there, and boats on it and money to pay your way. But if you go, you may presently very much wish you had not. As for me, I stand by the old saying, that the best winding sheet is a purple one."

This seems vastly to have cheered them. After her words there was no further thought of flight. They made ready to see the thing through.

At the very moment, therefore, when the crowd in the Hippodrome was cheering the flight of Justinian, something very different indeed was on foot. Belisarius, followed by steel-clad men, was climbing the spiral stair to the imperial box, and tapping on the door of the guard-room that closed his path; while the eunuch Narses was slipping along to the headquarters of the Blue party, with encouraging money in his satchel and discouraging words in his mouth. He appealed to that sensitive spot in most men's minds—their party loyalty. Did they want, he asked, to see the Greens top dog? They had one of their own men, a true Blue, on the imperial throne. Why should they take trouble to put a Green there instead? . . . The Blues were swayed by such arguments. They began to feel it time to call a halt, and to get their own men

Attempt
to arrest
Hypatius

away from the danger zone. How far they succeeded, we do not know. It is not likely that they had very much time at their disposal for withdrawing the Blues from the Hippodrome.

Belisarius had been unable to make the guardsmen hear. None are so blind as those who will not see; and the guardsmen were not proposing to take any risks. So the door remained unopened. Belisarius returned to the emperor. He was profoundly discouraged. . . . Justinian, however, directed him to try the other side. . . . Accordingly he set out again, and made his way, followed by his men, through the smoking ashes and tottering walls of the Chalkê, round by the Baths of Zeuxippus, and into the opposite gate of the Hippodrome.[1] Pressing in, he found himself in the great covered arcade called the Portico of the Blues. On his left was a little postern door leading up to the imperial box. On his right front was the way into the open arena of the Hippodrome, where tens of thousands of people were cheering Hypatius up in the imperial box above. . . . Belisarius thought quick and hard. If he attacked the little door, for the purpose of reaching and arresting Hypatius, he would soon have the mob on his rear . . . On the other hand, here at last before him was the mob itself, packed tight between the walls of the Hippodrome. It was fixed, ready to be hit: and Belisarius made no mistake, but hit it.

XIII

The entrance of Belisarius into the Hippodrome was sudden, sensational and quite unexpected. It was probably as unexpected to himself as it was to the mob. When Mundus, who had followed him with the Heruls, heard the sound that told of the onslaught of the steel-clad fighting-men upon that mass of humanity, he hurried down to the gate which was known as Dead Man's Gate, burst through it, and made his attack there.

Attack on the Hippodrome

We might sympathize more warmly with the rebels,

[1] That he was able to do this without interruption and without giving the alarm seems to prove that the area round the Chalkê and the Baths of Zeuxippus had, as suggested above (p. 91), been cleared and picketed after the fighting of Thursday. Belisarius was on his own ground.

caught in the Hippodrome, were it not for the memory
of the unfortunate patients in the Hospice of Samson,
whom they themselves had burned to death two days before. They had, indeed, the advantage that the men of
Belisarius and Mundus knew their work and did it well;
thirty thousand persons, at the lowest computation, perished there that day. Most of them, probably, were killed
clean by the cold steel. With them perished what later
ages have named the Nika Sedition, the Revolt of the
Blue-Greens, but which might better be called the
Monophysite Revolt.

XIV

Hypatius, from the imperial box, had seen this lightning change in his fortunes. He made no resistance when
Justus and Boraides, the nephews of Justinian, entered
to arrest him. He and Pompeius were conducted to the
palace to meet the awful frown of Justinian.

Victory of Justinian

They were poor creatures. They never had been much
else. Pompeius wept, and Hypatius argued that he had
meant well. If Justinian condemned them to death it was
perhaps not that he feared them, but that he feared those
whose tools they had been. Their disappearance removed
the figure-heads of any future revolt of the same sort.
He exercised more mercy than his age and country sometimes showed, for he spared their families, and subsequently returned to the latter the remnant of their confiscated property.

No senators were executed. Eighteen of the leaders
were banished and their property confiscated. Some time
later, even these sentences were remitted.

Justinian could afford to be generous, for his victory was complete. He had carried his policy; he had overcome the resistance to it; he had established his own prestige so firmly that it never again was challenged. . . . But the mildness of his punishments were not dictated solely by policy. To the last he had sought to spare those who fought in the revolt; and if he had had his way, there would have been no massacre in the Hippodrome. . . . For long after it, the Hippodrome was closed, and witnessed no more races. For longer still, the Blues and Greens were comparatively mild and polite persons. The change was salutary; but it certainly had not been designed by Justinian.

His clemency

XV

Five weeks and five days Constantinople sat in her ashes, a catastrophic ruin. On the fortieth day the workmen appeared. Gangs began to demolish, to clear and to level. Constantinople arose again. On the site of St. Sophia's grew a new church—that world's wonder, the St. Sophia designed by Anthemius of Tralles.

Anthemius was the man who, when Justinian married Theodora, had built the little domed church of St. Sergius and St. Bacchus to accompany Theodora's house. Now Justinian gave him a mightier work to do. . . . Old, worn, changed by fire, earthquake and the Muslim, the church which still stands at Constantinople is the church which Anthemius built. It arose there, in all its splendour, after the Sunday on which Justinian proposed to fly for his life, and on which Theodora restrained him. It arose there as a witness of his success over the united Blues and Greens.

Something else, besides St. Sophia's, would have been lost to the world had not Theodora held her ground that day. We should never have heard of that other world's wonder, more ponderous than the stone bubble of St. Sophia—the Corpus Juris Civilis, the Code of Justinian, the Roman Law.

Justinian had pursued three ends simultaneously to a common aim. While he restored the rule of civilization he beautified its aspect and he studied its nature. The whole scheme of civilization had fallen into disorder. In proportion as its geographical bounds had become uncertain, so had its very nature become doubtful and questionable. The process of giving it the ancient boundaries implied giving also the ancient definiteness and clarity to its idea, its intellectual principle. The principle of civilization was the body of law through the observance of which men became civilized, and in which their civilization consisted. The wild tribes of uncivilized man, wandering through a world still governed by those laws which are of the forest and the prairie, might entertain all kinds of customs, as struck their fancy or expressed their fears or hopes; but civilized man was such in virtue of having gone past this and sought to live under a law systematic and logical, identical with the reason of mankind. This magnificent pageant of reason, this system of jurisprudence, guiding and channelling the activities of civilized man, had not been arrived at by the arbitrary fiat of legislators, individual or collective. Far from consisting of anything that those who possessed power might dictate, it had been arrived at through a study of the nature of man, the reason of things, and the will of God. Law was not something which men invented, but something which—like the axioms of geometry—they recognized. Its authority lay ultimately not in that men declared it to be true, but in that it *was* true.

This system, like the empire itself, had been in ruins. Almost the first act of Justinian after his accession had been to direct that the law of the civilized world, the Roman law, should be sought for, ascertained and registered. This task he had commissioned the quaestor Tribunian to carry out. Tribunian—with expert assistance—had taken two years or thereabouts to compile the Code, and it had been published by and at the expense of Justinian, in the year 529. This was an outline of what was wanted, rather than the finished product. It was not the Roman Law as we know it, but a preliminary sketch. Justinian sent Tribunian and his colleagues back to their task again. . . . They had been turning and numbering pages, copying, revising and collating, while the Humane Blue-Greens raged through the streets of Constantinople, and the Hospice of Samson, with its unfortunate patients, rose in smoke. . . . If Justinian had bolted, the offices of Tribunian would probably have followed the Hospice of Samson and the church of St. Sophia into the blue heavens. At any rate, Monophysites did not want a Law of Civilization. They were prepared to invent any law they wanted: though perhaps their recent samples had not been of an endearing type . . . Justinian stayed; and Tribunian calmly finished his task.

The work in peril

The larger number of important things have had a dangerous life, and have survived by surprising chances:

even by a kind of miracle. Anthemius' church of St.
Sophia only existed at all because the Humane Blue-
Greens made a bonfire of the old one; and how the build-
ing has remained standing through the centuries is a
marvel to man. The Roman law survived only because
Theodora preferred a purple shroud to a white one.

Its subsequent history can be briefly narrated. In 533,
while Anthemius was still clearing the site of St. Sophia's,
and marking out foundations, Tribunian handed another
pile of manuscript to Justinian. It was the Pandects, or
Digest, and the Institutes. A year after that, while Belisarius was still fighting in Africa, Tribunian produced
the second and revised version of the Code.

The editing and revising of the Roman law was one of
the most tremendous intellectual feats ever accomplished. It was a greater work in some ways than that of
Plato or Aristotle, for it was the distilled essence of a
thousand years of human experience, produced by a man
with a genius for lucidity. The whole history of modern
civilization would have been different, had it not possessed the Civil Law to inspire and guide it. . . . Not all
the things that Justinian intended were accomplished.
When, many years later, he died, he probably entertained that curious illusion of so many able men—a sense
of failure. Yet it has been given to very few men to produce two works so mighty as the Church of St. Sophia
and the Roman Civil Law.

The work
completed

CHAPTER V

THE BEGINNING OF THE RECONQUEST
OF THE WORLD STATE

I

BELISARIUS was going upon no wild-goose chase. The
way had been prepared for him. The emperor's purpose
was so to organize that he might place in Africa, at the
perfect time, a perfect army and a perfect general, who
could be relied upon to do, with perfect promptitude,
the few additional things that would then remain to be
done.

While the perfect general was assembling and drilling
the perfect army, the preliminaries began. Justinian had
an agent in Africa who, during the spring of 533, organized, with the help of a few imperial soldiers, a revolt
in Tripolitana. Geilamir dared not touch it, for his attention was preoccupied by a much more serious event.
The governor of Sardinia repudiated the Vandal government, and sent communications offering to transfer his
allegiance to Justinian. The big merchants at Carthage,
whose interests were bound up with long-distance trade,
were naturally sympathetic with the scheme of a restored empire. Hence, between these uncertainties King
Geilamir was compelled to stake his fortunes on a hazard.
He elected to begin by crushing the Sardinian revolt;
counting, no doubt, upon finishing the task and bringing
back his army and fleet in time to confront the imperial
expeditionary force.

Prelimi-
nary steps

The expectation was by no means an unreasonable
one. Geilamir, however, lost the war before he began it.
The fatal flaw lay not in his intelligence, but in his temperament and character. He was one of those men who
believe that wars are won by heroism and melodrama:
and he did not realize that wars are lost by heroes, and
won by drill-sergeants, diplomatists and financiers. If
any factor in the situation could be called important, it
was the attitude of the power controlling Sicily: but
Geilamir never dreamed of lowering his dignity by assuming towards the Ostrogoths any honeyed diplomatic
smiles, and securing that the Sicilian ports should be
closed to the imperial fleet. . . . It was Justinian who
obtained permission for his fleet to water and revictual
in Sicily: and so important was the success, that as a
consequence the war was half won before the fleet
sailed.

II

With the way before him so prepared, Belisarius
started from Constantinople on the 21st June, 533. Five
hundred transports carried the army, and ninety-two
fighting galleys convoyed them. When, with the flagship
moored off the palace, the patriarch Epiphanius conducted the solemn service of Godspeed to the expedition,
many of those present must have thought of that other
great armada, which Athens in her hey-day sent westward to conquer Syracuse; and they must have thought
that this fleet too, like that, might never return again.
. . . No such expedition westward had ever brought
back laurels. Justinian was following a path on which no

footsteps returned. But for all their thoughts, overt or silent, he steadily pursued his way.

The army was not large, according to the usual standard of armies. It totalled some 16,000 men: [1] but in one respect it differed from any other army which had ever gone upon the same journey. Somewhat over one third of it was cavalry, including not only regular troops, but the comitatus of Belisarius, and two corps of Huns and Heruls, both of them composed of men familiar with the arts of fighting and travelling on the great plains. . . . And this very large body of cavalry was taking its own horses with it. Never before, probably, in human history, had over six thousand trained horses been transported together by sea from Byzantium to Carthage.

The overseas expedition

Before their departure, there was a further ceremony which was destined to have its effect upon the future. Antonina was going with Belisarius. On the eve of departure he solemnly adopted as his godson her protégé Theodosius, an able and handsome youth, who accompanied them as a member of their family circle.

The fleet dropped down to Heraclea. There, after a wait of five days, it took on board the last instalment of cavalry horses—selected Thracian animals especially presented to the expedition by the emperor. For four days it was held up at Abydos by adverse winds: but clearing thence, it made no further stop until it had

The fleet in the Aegean

---

[1] See Bury, *History of the Later Roman Empire*, II. 127.

Regular infantry (Comitatenses and Fœderati)		10,000
Regular cavalry (. . . . . ditto . . . .)		3,500
Comitatus of Belisarius ⎱ special ⎰		1,500
Huns . . . . ⎰ troops ⎱		600
Heruls . . . . ⎰		400
	Total	16,000

doubled the Peloponnesus and reached Methone on the Messenian coast, where it paused to refresh and refit.

It was now fairly launched upon the uncharted sea of adventure.

III

The best modern analogue to the expedition of Belisarius would be a voyage round Cape Horn to the conquest of China. He was leaving safety and support behind him, and was plunging into a world where his life and success, and those of his men, depended solely upon his good sense and power of leadership. He had, himself, no very great enthusiasm over the expedition. Yet his very scepticism about his success was a help towards it. He knew he could take no risks.

While they waited on the wind at Abydos, some of the Huns got drunk and quarrelled, as Huns would do; and two of them murdered a comrade. Belisarius promptly had them court-martialled and hanged. When their chief objected that this was not a punishment consistent with the laws of their people, Belisarius upheld it on the ground of the necessity of maintaining discipline. What is more, he induced them to see his point and to agree with his policy. He had no more trouble with the army on that score. Rough as some of them were, they preferred, in common with the most of mankind, order to anarchy, if only they could obtain the article in a reliable brand.

His next trouble occurred at Methone. When the stores were opened, the biscuit was found to have gone mouldy. By the regulations it ought to have been baked twice in a hot oven to sterilize it and render it crisp. John the Cappadocian, however, intent on economies, had suggested that the biscuit could be baked at the public baths. But the furnaces at the baths were only intended for warming water, not for baking bread; and the stuff which was distributed to the troops at Methone promptly killed some five hundred unfortunate men with dysentery before it was discovered and stopped. Belisarius had the biscuit withdrawn, and replaced at his own expense. He reported the facts to the emperor: but nothing happened to John.

From Methone the fleet touched the island of Zacynthus, and then began the long voyage over the Ionian Sea towards Sicily. This was the most dangerous part of the expedition, and had they not had the prospect of the Sicilian ports before them, the fleet might have had to give up all prospect of reaching Africa. Even as it was they were becalmed, and their passage was dragged out to sixteen days. Water ran short. Antonina seems to have been the only person with sufficient housekeeping instinct to foresee this eventuality; for it turned out that she had laid in a private supply of her own on board the flagship—a fact for which Belisarius and his staff had only too much reason to thank their stars. They reached Sicily with some of the sensations of the Conquistadors landing on the shores of the Indies. Here their first important news awaited them.

Belisarius had expected to be intercepted by a Vandal fleet while making his crossing to Africa; and his views of the probable outcome were not optimistic. To his surprise, however, he heard that the main Vandal fleet was in Sardinia. Procopius discovered a friend at Syra-

Sicily reached

cuse, a merchant who received communications from his agent at Carthage; and from this source he learnt that Geilamir had no information respecting the sailing of the Roman fleet, and had made no special preparation to meet it.

Here was luck! Belisarius was not the kind of man likely to forego the benefit of these providences. Weighing from his Sicilian harbour, he crossed the narrow sea without difficulty. They could go where they liked. The problem was, where ought they to go? All the coast and country was equally strange to the imperial commanders. Some were in favour of sailing direct to Carthage. Belisarius, however, was against this course.

Landing at Caput Vada Sept. 2nd A. D. 533

There was always the chance of the Vandal fleet overtaking them before they got to Carthage. He decided to stick to the programme laid down, and to land in Tripolitana, where the insurrection, daily expecting their advent, welcomed them.

After its great migration the army landed itself, its horses and its supplies, and dug itself in.

IV

Up to the date of its accomplishment this successful landing in Africa was probably the greatest military expedition by a civilized power that had ever been undertaken at sea. It had been more difficult and dangerous than the great raid of the Goths into the Aegean, three centuries earlier, because it was a fully organized expedition, and not a mere scrambling raid; and because it was made in the teeth of a prepared foe. That the Vandal fleet was absent, and had fatally missed its moment, did not in the least alter the fact that it easily could have been present; and had it been waiting to receive the invaders the course of human history might have been altered. . . . But Belisarius had no intention of resting satisfied with the honours. He was after solid military results, and he hastened to strike while advantage remained with him.

One of his first steps was to impose upon his men the strictest orders against looting or violence. The possibility of conquering Africa rested upon the fact that the natives were upon their side. They must remain upon their side. The army promised; and on the whole, kept its promise very well.

They had landed at Caput Vada on September 2nd. Two days later they were at Sullectum, nineteen miles away on the road to Carthage. On the fifth they entered Hadrumetum. On the ninth, travelling along the coast road, with their cavalry advance-guard out in front, and the Huns riding a parallel course inland, on the watch, they reached the delectable place called Grasse. That night, they made contact with enemy scouts. The enemy were evidently not far off. Without troubling to feel for them,[1] Belisarius pressed on rapidly along the road to Carthage. On the thirteenth of September he was approaching the city of Tunis.

The march to Tunis

With the approach to Tunis the conditions of the game changed, and it was necessary for Belisarius to sur-

---

[1] From Procopius III. xvii. (4) it seems that Belisarius must have known Geilamir's position and intentions. He knew Geilamir to be at Hermione. See III. xiv. 10. The exact position of Hermione, however, cannot now be identified. For the detailed geography of the march from Caput Vada to Carthage, see Tissot, *Géographie Comparée de la province romaine d'Afrique* (1884–1888) II. 115, with S. Reinach's Atlas.

vey the ground. Ordering his infantry to dig in at Darbet-es-Sif, he rode forward with his cavalry.

There is a good deal of difference between the kind of war in which one side is definitely aggressive, while the other side is definitely defensive, and that in which both sides are aggressive. The rapidity, and the decisiveness of the events which now befell were due to the sudden clash and contact of two aggressive movements, planned entirely without regard for one another. The high road led through a valley, divided from the sea eastward by a succession of low hills. Westward, beyond a long ridge, lay a dry salt lake. At the further head of the valley was Tunis, filling the gap between converging sea and salt lake. It was a defensible place; but no defenders were there.

Belisarius and his reconnaissance rode on, the Federate cavalry leading the way, the regulars following, and the comitatus closing the rear. When the Federates got to the old posting station called Ad Decimum, they found themselves quite near to Tunis; and here they had their first surprise. Evidently a fight had taken place. All about lay the bodies of Vandals and of Roman cavalry. The local inhabitants explained the mystery.

The arrival at Decimum

The Roman advanced guard, arriving about noon, had run into a party of Vandals who were viewing the ground. In the skirmish that followed, the Vandal commander, after killing twelve Romans with his own hand, had been cut down, and his men had been chased back up the road. It was afterwards found that the pursuit of the Roman cavalry had penetrated some twelve miles or so right up to Carthage, and in the course of it they had dispersed one after another a succession of enemy detachments that were marching upon Tunis.[1] But at the moment this was not known, and the Federates proceeded to ride up the nearest high ground to see what could be seen.

V

What they saw was unexpected. A cloud of dust was rolling up from the south, upon the flank of Belisarius —and presently they could see the glittering ranks of Vandal cavalry in force. A galloper was at once despatched back to Belisarius with the news. There was no time for him to arrive. The long lines of Vandal cavalry coming forward at the trot, rolled up to Decimum and paused there. The Federates, after a brisk skirmish, broke and rode for their lives back to their supports. They dashed into them at such a pace as to sweep the supports away; and the whole crowd went riding back upon Belisarius like a stampeding herd. . . . Had Geilamir been driving his pursuit home after the fugitives, nothing could have stopped them from sweeping Belisarius in turn before their onslaught. . . . By the will of a wonderful Providence the pursuit was nowhere to be seen, and the flight was brought to a halt.

The approach of Geilamir

Geilamir had contrived one of those marvellous bits of paper strategy which depend for their result upon the exact execution to the very minute of great military operations over large areas of ground. The chances were ninety-nine out of a hundred that something would go wrong; and nearly all the ninety-nine had turned up.

---

[1] So effectively "that those who beheld it would have supposed that it was the work of an enemy twenty thousand strong." (Procopius, *History*, III. xviii. 11.)

With the main body of the Vandal force, he had followed the Roman army along the road from Grasse. The moment of their arrival in the defile at Decimum had been calculated to a nicety. At that moment he, following a short cut across the country, would close upon the Roman rear, while his brother Ammatas held them in front, and his nephew Gibamund, crossing the salt lake, descended upon the Roman left. . . . He had arrived at Decimum, only to find that he was in front of Belisarius, instead of behind him. But something worse than this confronted his horrified eyes. The Vandal commander who had been cut down by the Roman advance-guard was Ammatas himself!

The Vandal plan disorganized

It is the custom of historians to rebuke Geilamir for the delay which followed; but from his point of view the occasion was so complete a failure that it was hardly worth while proceeding further. Nearly everything that could go wrong had gone wrong with his admirable paper plans. No sign of Gibamund could be found. As for the Romans—presumably they were still running. Dismounting, Geilamir commanded that the body of Ammatas should be laid out; and he began the rite of mourning for the dead.

VI

The mixed ranks of the Vandal host, at ease while the body of Ammatas was lifted, were struck as if by a whirlwind by the unexpected arrival of Belisarius. Far from being still engaged in flight, the Federates and their supports had been roughly pulled up by their general, sternly reprimanded, and ordered to face the right way.

Belisarius strikes

As soon as he was acquainted with the facts, Belisarius ordered an instant advance upon Decimum. His rapidity caught the Vandals at pause. Their army, in motion, could probably have rolled over the much smaller army of Belisarius. Struck while at stand, and taken by surprise, it broke up in confusion, and began to pour away westward, out of the control of its commanders. Belisarius kept it on the move until nightfall, when he was rejoined by the advance-guard which had so unexpectedly destroyed Ammatas and his force. The Hun flank-guards also came in; and from them the fate of Gibamund was explained.

The Huns, marching parallel with the Roman army, through a district not renowned for natural beauty, had apparently been in a state of profound depression. The sight of strange cavalry—who could only be enemies— crossing the dry salt lake had suddenly cheered and encouraged them. That the Vandals were more than three times their number did not trouble the gentlemen from the steppes. Tightening their girths and unslinging their bows, the Huns proceeded to ride hell-for-leather upon the strangers, killed as many as they could, and chased the rest as long as any were left to chase, hitting them all the way. They returned in the evening light, anxious to meet a few more Vandals. This was the reason for the strange disappearance of Gibamund. *What the Huns did*

Belisarius and his troopers spent the night at Decimum. It was undisturbed by any serious alarm. The Vandal host did not rally, but continued to retreat to Bulla Regia, beyond the Bagradas.

The battle of Decimum is a model example of the complete defeat of a perfect paper scheme by the direct

personal control and prompt decisions of a great tactician. The Vandals had had all the advantages that can be
given by numbers, by individual courage and by knowledge of the ground. But because they acted upon a cut
and dried scheme which involved the exact timing of
three different movements, they were decisively defeated
by those gifts of tactical opportunism which are developed by field service.

VII

The infantry, who had not been engaged at all in the
battle, arrived next morning with Antonina. No obstacle now stood in the way of immediate advance upon
Carthage. That night they camped before the gates of
the great city. The welcome extended to them was
prompt and enthusiastic; [1] all night long the lights of
Carthage were burning through the tropic dark; but
Belisarius was taking no risks. He did not like the idea of
losing his army in the streets of Carthage; and he did
not want his Huns and Heruls to get upon the drink till
they were a little cooler. So they spent the night in meek-
ness and sobriety under the African stars; and on the
fifteenth of September they marched in, horse, foot and
baggage train, with their full battle-equipment. It had
taken them just thirteen days to capture the city of
Hamilcar and Hannibal.

Belisarius
at Carthage

The occupation of Carthage went off without a hitch.
Belisarius had once more strictly cautioned his men as
to their conduct; and they knew him well enough to take
his words seriously. When he arrived at the palace of

[1] Procopius, *History*, III. xx. 1. The picture evoked by Procopius is a striking one.

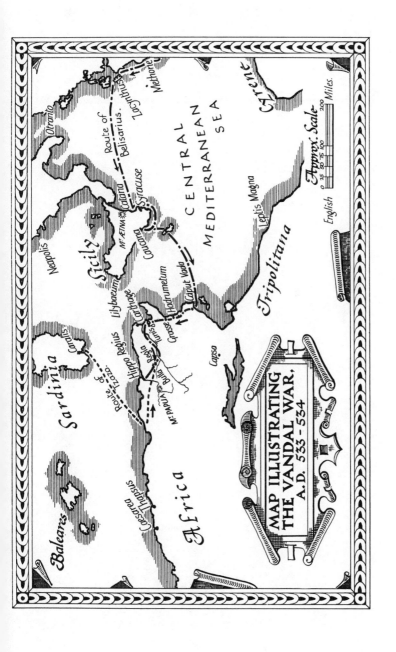

MAP ILLUSTRATING
THE VANDAL WAR,
A.D. 533-534

Geilamir the usual pickets were mounted, and the army
dismissed to quarters.[1] Not a shop needed to be closed,
nor any interruption to be made in the normal daily life
of the city. The fleet, entering the lake of Tunis, once
more formed a secure link with Constantinople.

Belisarius found that many Vandals had taken refuge
in sanctuary. He notified them that they could emerge
without apprehension. One of the first discoveries he
made was that as soon as the Romans landed in Africa the
ex-King Hilderic had, by Geilamir's orders, been slain.
The unfortunate Hilderic had never been much more
than a pawn in the hands of stronger men. His death
meant that no possibility now remained of dividing the
Vandals. Geilamir could claim the loyalty of the entire
Vandal people.

Carthage occupied

When the headquarters mess sat down to lunch, it was
at King Geilamir's high table. Belisarius occupied the
king's chair, and the officers of the royal household
waited at table.

The Romans had entered upon the African expedition
with dark anticipations and gloomy forebodings. Probably none of them could have coined the perfect epigram
that would have expressed their feelings that day.

VIII

The fact that King Geilamir had fled to Bulla implied,
however, that the war was not finished. He had made a

---

[1] When Procopius says that Belisarius "went up to the palace and seated himself
upon Geilamir's throne" he is not implying anything decorative, but only that
Belisarius took the king's office chair (as we should say) where the king could be
seen at regular hours by properly authorized persons. The first interview was, unfortunately, a heated one in which certain sea-faring persons indicated their belief
that they had been robbed by Belisarius' sailors! (Procopius, *History*, III. xx. 21–25.)

rapid and safe retirement out of an unfavourable position, and he now waited, with undamaged forces, for the arrival of his brother Tzazo from Sardinia. Their joint advance down the valley of the Bagradas would be no child's play.

The first step of Belisarius was to survey and repair the defences of Carthage. Although the Vandals had made a practice of dismantling the fortresses throughout Africa,[1] the walls of Carthage had been too considerable for easy destruction, and Geilamir had believed that they were too ruinous now to make their repair possible. Belisarius took a different view, and set to work with vigour upon the task of restoring them to adequate strength.

The omission of the Vandals to complete the dismantling of Carthage was a fatal one. Other cities need not have taken up any one's time or attention had Carthage been adequately dealt with. That Belisarius could hold and defend Carthage made his foothold in Africa sure. Before Geilamir had begun his advance, the native tribes registered their view of the situation by sending in their submission to the power which controlled the great city.

Tzazo had been perfectly successful in Sardinia. He and his army were returning with undiminished confidence in their own power to conquer. He landed without interference from the Romans, and joined Geilamir at Bulla. The meeting of the brothers was emotional, and even sentimental. They wept upon one another's necks,

---

[1] Their aim was to render a war of sieges impossible, and to ensure that all war should be a field war. Very probably the same aim caused the destruction of the Roman cities in Britain. Procopius, *History*, III. v. 8. mentions the policy of Gaiseric in demolishing the walls of the African cities, except Carthage.

while Belisarius was devoting his energies to the more prosaic task of finishing the walls of Carthage.

The aim of the brothers was to draw Belisarius out into the open. A siege of Carthage was not the kind of military operation in which they could expect to shine; but in the field it was hard to see how they could fail of success. Moving down the Bagradas, they established their centre of operations at Tricamaron, some twenty miles west of Carthage. By cutting off the aqueducts and intercepting the food supply they sought to make the position of Belisarius untenable.

Belisarius had no intention of remaining behind the walls of Carthage. He meant those walls to protect his own army from the Vandals, not to protect the Vandals from his own army. By this time he had seen enough of their methods to be quite sure that no troops trained and equipped as they were could hold the field against his own. A whole series of new and unexpected truths was dawning upon his mind. He began to perceive that his horsemen, drilled on the system now customary on the Persian border, could develop a much greater fighting power than any equal number of troops of the ordinary western type. Not only were the armoured bowmen of the east superior as fighters, but the disciplined mobility in which they were trained—a true Roman tradition— rendered it possible to use their collective mass and weight with deliberate purpose and definite plan. And this advantage was placed in the hands of a born tactician, who appreciated to the full the law that an army is not a thing with which to wrestle, but a thing with which to strike.

Return of Tzazo

IX

It was the middle of December before Belisarius moved out.[1] In Africa it was the cool season, when the Goths and the Huns, and the Thracians and Galatians of the imperial army, could take the field without too great a sick list from the heat. The Huns frankly did not like Africa. They were men of the grass-steppe and the greenwood forest; they looked with distaste upon the samples of African desert with which they had been provided. Vandal spies and agents succeeded in starting the belief among them that the government at Constantinople intended to keep them in Africa. The assurances of Belisarius did not suffice to calm their feelings in the face of a prospect so horrid. Even when at last he marched to find Geilamir, the Huns accompanied him in a doubtful frame of mind. They were prepared to smile upon any party which would undertake to send them home.

The camp at Tricamaron had become the rallying point of the whole Vandal people. Here were concentrated into one spot the fighting men, the families and the treasure of the Vandals: and as far as numbers and wealth and the chivalric pomp of war were concerned, the army of Belisarius cut a shabby figure by comparison. The hope of the imperialists lay in their tactics.

The battle of Tricamaron was fought across a brook that flowed past the Roman front. Tzazo's knights, casting aside lance and javelin, prepared for a sword-in-hand

Belisarius advances

---

[1] The geography of the Tricamaron campaign is illustrated in Tissot's study of the Bagradas Valley, Academie des Inscriptions, Memoires Presentes, Series I. Tom. 9. Pt. 2 (1884), with the magnificent maps there given.

onslaught by which they intended to wipe out the Romans.

This assault Belisarius struck before it fell; he played with it, exploited it, and used it to destroy the Vandal army. Leaving his infantry in the rear, out of harm's way, he fought the action with cavalry alone: and chiefly with his own comitatus, under the command of John the Armenian. . . . Three times John's armoured Roman horsemen rode across the brook, wielding spear and sword and bow against the swords of the Vandals. . . . The first time, a small detachment went, and returned in flight followed by a rush of Vandal pursuers. These were met by a second and larger detachment, which drove in the pursuers, recoiled from the Vandal front, and disrupted it by the temptation of a swift retirement. The third time, John advanced his banners, and with loud shouts the Romans charged home; and this time their full force fell upon a Vandal host which had been disordered, entangled and scattered about by successive charges and retreats. Overwhelmed though they were by superior tactical methods, the Vandals fought a desperate and heroic fight. At length Tzazo was slain with the best of his men, and the Vandal host broke and surged back to its camp. . . . Eight hundred Vandal dead were counted, who had fallen to the weapons of the Romans. Only fifty Romans had fallen before the Vandal blade. This proportion of sixteen to one is a grim index to the comparative value of the armoured all-weapon fighter and the Vandal swordsman.

Action and reaction are equal. The Vandals, having fought with unbounded fury, were now seized with a despondence as deep as their courage had been exalted.

Battle of Tricamaron

Flight of Geilamir

The three advances of the Roman armoured cavalry must have been massacres in which the best of the Vandal manhood was shot down indiscriminately with only a faint possibility of reply. Before night the Roman foot, coming into action, assaulted the Vandal camp. Geilamir lost his nerve—a fact which is not altogether incomprehensible if we reflect a little upon the meaning of that sixteen-to-one casualty list. He left secretly, and rode for the Numidian desert. As soon as the Vandals realized his absence, a general dispersal began. They no longer had any organization or any authority to direct them, now that their kings were gone. They made for sanctuary in all the churches of the neighbourhood.

X

Some things no man can do. One of them is to repress human feeling. The Roman army had marched far, lived hard, and beaten superior numbers. . . . The victory was conclusive and final, and the end of the strain had come. It was unfortunate that such a release from the pressure of apprehension and prudence and responsibility should have come at this particular moment. The camp into which the troops burst contained the Vandal women, the Vandal treasure and the Vandal wine. There was no dragging them off. While Geilamir was riding for his life, though no man pursued him, and the Vandal fighting men were crowding the churches of Numidia, Belisarius was passing a sleepless and troubled night. A rally of Vandals, returning sword in hand, could with ease have wiped out their conquerors. . . . But no Vandals came. . . . Only with the dawn could the wakeful

Vandal
camp
sacked

and worried Belisarius convince himself of his luck. He hurried to get hold of the nearest available men. He managed to round up some of the members of his own comitatus, and by degrees the army was got upon parade. In all probability it was a disreputable and discreditable army that morning; but that it existed at all was the wonder.

Much work needed to be done. After sending out scouts to discover the route of Geilamir's flight, Belisarius had to deal with the Vandals in sanctuary, convince them of his good faith, receive their surrender, and place them under proper surveillance. In spite of their heavy losses, they still numbered many thousands.

In dealing with these tasks, Belisarius advanced as far as Hippo Regius, where something of a surprise awaited him. His luck was in. A small party of men, who prudently remained in sanctuary, sent to say that they were commissioned by Boniface, the treasurer of Geilamir, to negotiate terms for the surrender of the royal hoard. They wanted Belisarius to give guarantees that Boniface should be allowed to go free with all his own property. In return Boniface undertook to place Belisarius in possession of the wealth of the Vandal kings.

The treasure ship

The explanation of this remarkable proposal was as remarkable as the proposal itself. Geilamir had foreseen the possibility of defeat, and had packed the bullion in a fast ship which he had moored in the harbour of Hippo Regius. As soon as the battle of Tricamaron had been fought, Boniface, in obedience to his instructions, set sail for Spain. He was blown back into harbour. Realizing the peril of the situation, he offered large rewards to his crew, if they could force the vessel to any port not

under the government of Justinian. Although, by great
efforts they took the ship again out of harbour, it became clear that the case was hopeless. The ship was a
Jonah ship. All their work was cut out, to get back safely
to Hippo Regius. Boniface accepted the situation as an
indication of the will of Heaven, and sent to open negotiations with Belisarius.

Needless to say, Belisarius jumped at the offer. He
doubtless realized that Boniface would take a very handsome percentage as commission; but he was not the man
to worry over trifles of this sort. He gave the pledges required, and Boniface duly carried out the agreement. It
was a stupendous treasure, the real Vandal Hoard, the
savings of a hundred years of piracy and plunder—a
Niblung-gold, a Dragon's-hoard, including amongst its
prizes the Golden Candlesticks and the precious furni-
ture of Solomon's temple at Jerusalem, which Titus had
taken, and which Gaiseric had wrested from the Romans. . . . There may have been greater treasures captured from time to time. The Persian treasure which
Alexander won may have been vaster; but the Vandal
hoard which Belisarius carried back to Carthage, whatsoever its precise rank in the scale, occupies a pretty high
place among the mighty plunders which have excited the
interest of mankind: and perhaps no European again saw
or handled such a mass of wealth until the days, long
afterwards, when the treasures of Atahualpa and Monte-
zuma fell into the hands of Pizarro and Cortes.

The Vandal
hoard

XI

When Belisarius returned to Carthage, it was to notify
Justinian that his commands had been executed. Africa

once more was Roman. The defeat of Geilamir and the death of Tzazo did away with the last traces of effective resistance. One after another, all the provinces of Africa returned to their allegiance to the Roman empire. . . . Wonderful as was the success, and perfectly as Belisarius had carried out the commission entrusted to him, it was not in all ways his own victory. Though he had gone forward when instructed to do so, he had doubted; and although he had taken full advantage of the unexpected powers which he found in his hand, he would never, but for Justinian, have realized their value. It was the emperor who had seen and foreseen and understood and organized victory.

Africa conquered

Some of the reports which came to Justinian from Africa may well have made him uneasy. He had placed very unusual and exceptional powers in the hands of Belisarius. The latter had achieved a victory of a kind which was not unlikely to go to the head of any ordinary man, and he had acquired a treasure such as very few subjects could ever have handled. Certain among his own officers, rightly or wrongly, seem to have got hold of the idea that he never meant to go home again,[1] but would set up as an independent ruler in Africa—and they took the trouble to record their opinion.

Belisarius had some of the temperament which is apt to go with genius. A man who defies the obvious and the commonplace in public, is apt to carry his gifts into private life, where they are less convenient. Justinian accordingly decided that Belisarius had better be out of harm's way. He could not very well send him a blunt

---

[1] Procopius, *History*, IV. viii. 1–2. Apparently the Huns were not the only persons with a horror of being kept permanently in Africa.

order of recall. He did something more skilful—he gave Belisarius the choice between remaining in Africa and returning home.

Questions
respecting
Belisarius

The reports of his secret agents—who had perused some of the letters in question—had already warned Belisarius. But even if he had needed to make up his mind, without doubt Antonina would have supplied the requisite stimulus. He had no desire to be marooned in some far-off corner of the empire, struggling with unwashed Moorish tribesmen, while all the fun of the fair went on busily at Constantinople. . . . He expressed his wish to return home.

Justinian was perfectly satisfied. Not only did the answer amply prove the loyalty and good faith of Belisarius, but it fitted in with the emperor's secret designs and hopes. There was a great future possible for a loyal Belisarius who was willing to employ his military genius in the service of the empire, without fancying that he possessed the talents of a statesman in addition to his own.

XII

Geilamir had retired to the mountains of Numidia, where he sat cold, hungry, bathless, and without a regular income, in the tents of a slightly depressing set of his native subjects. The Vandal king was capable of prodigies of valour, and of resisting tyrants to their teeth; but he was not the man to last out long on a cold water diet and with unwashed shirts.

Pharas and
Geilamir

Pharas, the Herulian chief, who conducted the blockade, entertained not altogether dissimilar sentiments concerning the life of the African wild. Finding that he could not force a path into the mountains, he tried a little diplomacy. The message which he sent in to the king was all the more effective because it dwelt upon feelings common to both.

"I am no high-brow," said Pharas, "any more than you are. All I can do is to state plainly the common sense which I have learned from experience. What on earth can you be doing in that hole? Do you think the sort of independence for which you are holding out is worth having? You are being obliged to live upon someone else, anyhow—and if that is so, why not live upon Justinian? You would be richer as a poor man in Constantinople than as a rich man here. If you think it a disgrace to take pay from Justinian, let me remind you that Belisarius does so, and so do we Heruls, whose blood is as blue as your own. You are offered good terms—an income, a seat in the senate, and the rank of patrician, with the word of Belisarius to guarantee them. I can understand a man holding out as long as he has something to gain by it, but a man who refuses good terms out of mere obstinacy is a fool. Fortunately for you, there is still time to change your mind."

Geilamir admitted the rationality of this advice, but he could not bring himself to accept it. What still rankled in his mind was the unprovoked nature (as he thought it) of the attack made upon him. Quite evidently he, at all events, did not appreciate the conception that the Roman empire was reconquering a sovereignty which had never been extinguished: he still thought of himself as "basileus," an independent sovereign ruler. His notions on this head are an interesting side-light

Hesitation of Geilamir

upon the views of the northern kings concerning their own royal status. . . . Geilamir wound up his reply by asking for a loaf, a sponge, and a lyre.

To the astonished Pharas the Vandal messenger explained this odd request. Geilamir wanted the bread to eat, the sponge to wipe his eyes with, and the lyre on which to celebrate his misfortunes. Pharas obliged; but he was not far wrong in thinking that Geilamir would not stand out very much longer. Every precaution was taken to prevent the king's escape. At last Geilamir gave in.

Belisarius took pains to convince him of the good faith of the Roman offers. A representative waited upon **Surrender** Geilamir, authorized to repeat, in the most solemn way, **of Geilamir** the undertakings given; and the Vandal king formally **March** surrendered. Although, like Pharas, most of the im- **A. D. 534** perialists probably thought him lucky in the prospect of a pension for life and nothing to do for it, Geilamir took a more serious view of himself. At his first meeting with Belisarius, outside Carthage, he broke into loud laughter. It was his way of registering the tragedy that had cast down the house of the Vandals, and the dark destiny that had plunged him into misery. . . . Many of the spectators would have been happy to suffer with him for some of the same rewards.

XIII

In April, Justinian promulgated the new arrangements for the future government of Africa,[1] now once more effectively a part of the Roman empire. The power

---

[1] Cf. Bury, *History of the Later Roman Empire* II. 139.

of the Vandals was abolished; their Arian religion was suppressed. In autumn Belisarius set sail from Carthage, leaving Africa in the able hands of his successor, Solomon.

His arrival home, some fifteen months or so after he had set out, was a truly memorable occasion. Never had any adventure been more abundantly justified by results. To reward the man who had so adequately led it, Justinian went back upon the tradition of five centuries of time, and granted Belisarius the honour of the first Triumph ever seen in Constantinople, and the first celebrated by a private person since the days of Augustus.

It was remarkable enough to justify itself. Although its details were a little unconventional, its substance could compare in splendour with most of its predecessors. The procession began at the house of Belisarius, and wound its way through the chief streets of Constantine to the Hippodrome. Entering the Hippodrome, the procession made the circuit of the race-course, and under the eyes of thousands of spectators halted before the imperial box. . . . The trophies of Vandal arms, the treasures of the Vandal hoard, the seven-branched candlesticks and the golden table [1]—the State-carriage of the Vandal queen—these were perhaps the most valuable —but they were certainly the least dramatic part of the procession. After them King Geilamir, accompanied by his family, his chief men, and the remainder of his noblest tribesmen, followed—a long succession of majes-

Triumph of Belisarius

[1] Procopius tells us that a Jew (unnamed) commented on the ill-luck that had pursued the owners of this particular booty, and expressed the opinion that it would never be at rest anywhere but in Jerusalem. When this was reported to Justinian, he agreed, and sent these wonderful old relics back home. (Procopius, *History* IV. ix. 6–9.)

tic and masculine figures. . . . Geilamir was fully con-
scious of his pathetic dignity, and he pompously mur-
mured, as he moved, the famous and appropriate words:
"Vanity of vanities! All is vanity!" Last of all marched
Belisarius himself, on foot, at the head of his comitatus,
the men who stopped the rout at Decimum and changed
it into victory, and who had formed the centre of the line
at Tricamaron.

Geilamir might repeat, as much as he liked, that All
was Vanity; but he would have found it difficult to deny
that the empire could produce a much larger and more
impressive amount of that kind of vanity than he could.
No Vandal monarchy could have shown the dazzling
glory of Justinian and Theodora, sitting side by side with
diadem and orb and sceptre, and silk of purple and cloth
of gold. Belisarius prostrated himself before the splendour of the Roman empire, the world-state to which all
men must bow. . . . Geilamir at first would not bow.
He wished to take refuge in the levelling doctrine that
all is vanity. But he had now come too far for retreat. He
too must bow. If his conqueror had bowed to the Roman
empire, must not he also? Firm hands quietly pressed him
down. He went unwillingly, as sentimentalists go: he did
not realize that he had already gone at the battle of
Decimum. But down he went; and before the scarlet-
shod foot of Justinian lay the head of the Vandal king.

So perished the Vandal realm. . . . But for eight
hundred years that scene haunted the imagination of the
North. Men who had forgotten Justinian, and who
never knew Geilamir, told the story of the captive king
pressed down before the throne of his conqueror.

The scene in the Hippo-drome

XIV

As far as material fortune went, Geilamir had little to grumble at. He left that scene in the Hippodrome to take up the life of a Galatian country gentleman. His men entered the imperial armies; some took service in the comitatus of Belisarius. The descendants of Hilderic were pensioned at the expense of Justinian and Theodora. . . . There can seldom have been a war which ended more amicably.

Dispersion of the Vandal people

XV

Imperator, triumphator—there needed now but one more classic dignity for Belisarius, and he got it. Justinian nominated him consul for the ensuing year. . . . His entry into office was memorable. Vandal tribesmen bore his curule chair shoulder-high. . . . Gold was scattered amongst the crowd. . . . Justinian knew his man. Belisarius was little like to trouble over a throne, when these headier glories could so much more easily be obtained.

CHAPTER VI

THE HOODWINKING OF KING THEODAHAD

I

BELISARIUS remained in Constantinople, close to Justinian's hand, through the first three months of his year of office. He was none the worse for a rest and a change. But while he was resting, the emperor was working. The task of sweeping the Vandals off the board had been completed only just in time. Before June came, another set of circumstances ripened and was ready for the hand of the reaper.

The Gothic question

We have already noticed the relations between the imperial government and King Theuderic. The death of the king in August, A. D. 526, had meant the minority reign of his grandson Athalaric, and the regency of Athalaric's mother, Amalasuntha. . . . It is hard to refrain from speculating somewhat upon the possible course of events if the boy's father, the Amalung Eutharic, had lived. Almost certainly, the whole subsequent history of Europe would have been different—exactly how different we cannot guess, but assuredly different indeed. But Eutharic had died when his son was four years old, leaving Amalasuntha to struggle with a highly-strung and difficult child, and with Goths whose views of women were definitely of the Prussian type. Amalasuntha was a very clever woman, who carried embodied in herself all the abilities and the energies of the Amalungs. Her son ought to have been as great a man as her father had been. But

Amala-suntha

she could not hold her ground. . . . When, later on, we read of some of the proceedings of the empress Theodora, let us remember that the little Greek had had the example of Amalasuntha vividly before her eyes, and knew by that example how keen, how relentless, how prompt on the nail a woman had to be, to hold her own against men.

Amalasuntha had tried to give her son a civilized education. The Goths, who did not see the necessity, objected that education was an unmanly thing. They were fated, most of them, to feed the kites and crows in punishment for this blasphemy; but Amalasuntha felt it prudent to give way. What the boy really needed was a father. The manly training to which he was subjected soon destroyed him body and soul. He was destined to die at the age of sixteen.

Before this happened, Justinian had already come into direct touch with Amalasuntha. The Gothic queen, never safe from the men who had forced her to surrender charge of her son's education, had written to Justinian asking if he would give her sanctuary in the event of need. Justinian readily consented, and even ordered preparations to be made for her reception in Constantinople. She never went, however, for in the meantime her plans were brought successfully to their consummation. Her three principal opponents all fell to the assassin's knife. She had temporary breathing space.

Attitude of Justinian

II

This took place in the year of the Nika sedition when Belisarius was preparing the armada for Africa. Things being as they were, it was natural enough for Belisarius to find the Sicilian ports at his disposal. The same June that saw the Armada sail, saw the bishop of Ephesus and the bishop of Philippi set out for Italy, in company with Alexander, an agent of Justinian. The object of Alexander's mission was to discuss a secret agreement with Amalasuntha. The queen did not expect Athalaric to last long. When he died, she could no longer retain power, and her enemies were likely enough to take full advantage of that fact. She proposed to save herself by resigning Italy into the hands of Justinian. Armed with this plan, Alexander returned to Constantinople to lay the scheme before Justinian. The two bishops returned with him.

Unknown to Amalasuntha, the bishops carried another secret proposal with them. Its maker was her cousin Theodahad. In the person of Theodahad a new and interesting actor in the drama enters the scene. He was a type of man by no means rare in the history of the northern nations: a preternaturally cunning and **Theodahad** acquisitive man, who seemed to take a deep pleasure in the exercise of malicious ingenuity. If the objections to education put forward by the Goths were founded upon their observation of its effect upon Theodahad, they had a strong case. Theodahad was quite a cultured person, who studied the dialogues of Plato. . . . Apparently he did not study them for philosophical ends, but rather as a training in the art of dialectic: for he showed remarkable ability in wangling landed property out of the hands of other people into his own. Both Theuderic and Amalasuntha had had to repress his energy in this

direction. . . .[1] Theodahad had acquired, by means un-
questionably illegal, a large part of Etruria. . . . His
idea, confided to the bishops, was to sell these to Justinian in return for a pension and a house in Constantinople. The bishops were to lay the idea before the
emperor.

III

These two proposals, reaching Justinian simultaneously, must have been almost embarrassing in the wealth
of opportunity they afforded for political intervention.
Justinian spent the summer in thinking them over. To
judge by later events, he discussed the matter with Theodora: for she was evidently well acquainted with the
details of the two schemes. His envoy, Peter, left Constantinople for Italy in October, 534. We may without
rashness conjecture that the instructions which Justinian gave Peter were paralleled by a second set of instructions, of a very different nature, which Peter received from Theodora.

In any case, as soon as he got to Thessalonica Peter
met the envoys of Amalasuntha. Athalaric had died on
October 2. . . . On October 3, Amalasuntha had done
a very imprudent thing—she had married Theodahad.
Her action was not unreasonable or ill-calculated. The
death of Athalaric left Theodahad the only living male
Amalung. If any one had a right to the kingship of the
Goths, he had. He was the last male descendant of
Irminric. His marriage to Amalasuntha had a real logic

Amalasuntha marries Theodahad

[1] Procopius V, iv. 1–2.

to it; it gave him the throne to which he was entitled; it provided him with a bride fully his equal in birth and descent, the heiress of King Theuderic; and it confirmed Amalasuntha in the power she had nearly lost. . . .[1] But she was herself sane and plain-minded. She did not realize that Theodahad had a kink in his mind. He proceeded to make himself safe by selling her, and then by selling the men to whom he had sold her.

Peter pursued his way, but at Valona he met Liberius and Opilio, delegates from Theodahad, bearing the news that Theodahad had imprisoned Amalasuntha in an island of Lake Bolsena. The new Gothic king had been **Theodahad** pretty quick about his work, and had certainly received **deposes** the support of all Amalasuntha's enemies. Peter stopped **Amala-** his journey and sent an express courier to Constanti- **suntha** nople. As he could clear the roads for a through message, his man arrived long before Liberius and Opilio. Justinian at once sent a letter declaring Amalasuntha to be under his protection. At the same time, or a little later, Peter received a message from Theodora. The empress did not want Amalasuntha in Constantinople. She was taking no risks. The Gothic queen was far too dangerous to allow anywhere in the neighbourhood of Justinian. In cleverness and accomplishment she was no bad match for Theodora; she was also young, and quite presentable; and above all, she was a king's daughter, the heiress of Theuderic, and the representative of a line of sacred kings. . . . It would have been madness—it

---

[1] The family pride of Amalasuntha must not be omitted from the reckoning. Theodahad, as Amalung, was almost the only person of equal birth left for her to marry. This spirit is the old tribal caste spirit—it was not invented by the Hohenzollerns.

would at the best have been hopeless weakness—to allow such a woman foothold in Constantinople.

Like most other men, Peter knew whom to obey. He took Justinian's letter to Italy in his despatch case; and he took Theodora's message in his memory. She is not likely to have written it down.

IV

With all this coming and going, this waiting for instructions and preparation of despatches, it must have been January before Peter arrived in Italy. The imperial commissioner at once delivered Justinian's letter, and let it be known that any injury to Amalasuntha would mean war. Theodahad was now in a quandary from which the most assiduous study of the Socratic method could not extricate him. He was no soldier, and could not risk war. He neither enjoyed it nor wanted it. He could not safely release Amalasuntha. He could not safely kill her. . . . The only thing to do was to keep the situation as it was until he could see his way clearly. It was at this point that Peter's secret instructions from Theodora came into play.

Position of Theodahad

Peter's task was to induce Theodahad to take the responsibility of Amalasuntha's death. To make Theodahad take the responsibility for anything must have been an uncommonly difficult task, and it seems to have taken Peter some three months. With great difficulty, he got Theodahad to see that it was really safer to trust Theodora against Justinian than Justinian against Theodora. The emperor might talk; but as long as the empress was on Theodahad's side, need he fear? Theodora invited him to send all his requests to Constantinople through her.

Theodahad
murders
Amala-
suntha
. . . Persuaded, at last, that this was really the prudent course, Theodahad allowed Amalasuntha to be strangled in her bath.

The murder of the daughter of their famous king, the great Theuderic, profoundly shocked public opinion among the Goths. Peter, after assuring him in his master's name that the deed meant war to the bitter end, left for Constantinople. . . . Theodahad hoped that all was right, as promised. But he had been beaten by a woman whose skill in the calculus of intrigue was greater than his own. Theodora knew that she need not pay her debts, for Justinian was not likely to be long in removing the creditor!

V

Peter arrived with the sensational news at the end of May. He probably reckoned that the excuse for war was so good, and so convenient, that Justinian would not look too closely at the minute details of the case: and if so, he was right. It is uncertain whether Justinian ever heard the true version of Amalasuntha's death. Even if he had done so, his policy would not have been changed. He bent all his energies to the task of punishing the murderer.

This was the situation which came to crisis in the early months of the consulship of Belisarius.

The emperor gave Belisarius his instructions in early June; and at the end of the month, once more imperator, Belisarius sailed for Sicily by the same route as before.

His departure was comparatively unobtrusive; his total forces did not exceed 8,000 men. Justinian did not wish to spend money on military preparations, which might be quite superfluous. For one thing, it was quite possible that Theodahad might resign the crown, and Italy would fall into imperial hands without fighting. On the other hand, if the Goths elected to fight, an invasion of Italy would be a far more formidable task than an invasion of Africa. The Goths were very much more numerous than the Vandals, and their repute as fighting men was of the highest. It might be just as well to be able to back out of a war which proved too big a proposition. Hence for all these reasons the emperor wished Belisarius to begin in a quiet way, without too much unnecessary publicity. . . . Belisarius was quite prepared to exploit these disadvantages. He had spent most of his life in making his difficulties fight for him. To enter southern Italy with a very small army might be the inspired plan. . . . It was the one plan against which no one would have provided.

Justinian acts

The whole set of proceedings was so closely interwoven and interlocked that, far apart as they were in space, they strongly influenced one another. Belisarius landed at Catana, occupied Syracuse, and had practically no trouble in obtaining the surrender of the whole of Sicily. Only at Panormus did he meet with half-hearted resistance from a Gothic garrison. By the end of the year, Sicily was in full possession of Justinian; and Belisarius performed in Syracuse the solemn formality of relinquishing his office as consul. Meanwhile, Mundus had occupied the Gothic province of Dalmatia on the Hadriatic, and had entered Salona. Theodahad made the most

Belisarius occupies Sicily

desperate efforts for peace. He had not wanted war; he did not rely upon war as his instrument, and he was still under the impression that he would obtain a satisfactory settlement if he went the right way about the matter.[1] He induced the pope to go to Constantinople to support the efforts for peace. In the meantime Peter returned to Italy with a scheme of settlement to lay before the Gothic king. The pope's diplomacy produced no effect; and Theodahad must have heard with consternation that he himself was expected to name the terms of settlement.

VI

Since Theodahad had no intention of fighting, the only resource left him was to try to devise terms which Justinian might accept and the Goths would not refuse. He hesitated and reflected. Ultimately he drafted and handed to Peter a document which included the cession of Sicily (but then he had already lost Sicily) and the admission in explicit detail of the emperor's sovranty [2] (which had always been acknowledged in principle).

Problems of Theodahad

Theodahad was not ashamed to make his admission a little more explicit than that of the great Theuderic, and

---

[1] Historians have treated Theodahad somewhat harshly. Once we admit the assertion of Procopius in the Anecdota, that Theodahad murdered Amalasuntha at the instigation of Theodora, his subsequent actions are seen to possess a logic otherwise absent from them. War was deliberately forced upon Theodahad, who believed to the last that faith would be kept with him.

[2] Bury, *History of the Later Roman Empire*, II. 172–173. The form of admission consisted of a number of acts clearly involving the recognition of Justinian's superior status. A crown of gold of 300 lbs. to be sent yearly; 300 soldiers to be furnished; no death penalty on senator or cleric without the emperor's approval; no creation of senators or patricians on his own authority; the emperor's name to stand first on all formal occasions and documents; no statue to the Gothic king without one of the emperor also. . . . These terms are obviously quite nominal— a sort of peppercorn rent.

it is very probable that he would have gone further, had he dared. A man of such education as his own appreciated to the full the significance of the imperial sovranty. He was restrained by the thought of his subjects, who did not share his views. Peter had already started for Constantinople with the document, but at Albano he was overtaken by the couriers of Theodahad, and asked to return.

The core of the conversation which took place between Peter and Theodahad has been reported with fair fullness by the historian.

Th: "Do you really think that the emperor will accept the terms I have drafted?"

Peter: "I daresay he will."

Th: "What will happen if they do not satisfy him?"

Peter: "Then, Highborn, you will have to fight."

Th: "My dear ambassador, is that fair?"

Peter: "What is the matter with it, Excellency? It is fair enough that every man should act up to character."

Th: "What does that mean?"

Peter: "You are a philosopher, and it is very wrong for philosophers to fight. Justinian is a statesman, and it is all quite in order for him to do so."

This was an unanswerable argument. Possibly Theodahad may have seen, moreover, that besides being wrong it is also very foolish of philosophers to fight. In any case, he made his decision. He could not strengthen his terms, lest the Goths refused to ratify them. His only alternative was to throw over the Goths altogether, and to surrender his crown, if Justinian would afford him protection. Then, if the Goths wanted to fight, they could do so to their hearts' content.

Theodahad's decision

A new arrangement was accordingly made. It was agreed that Peter should first deliver to Justinian the letter which Theodahad had already written. If it were rejected (but only if it were rejected) he was to deliver another letter, which Theodahad proceeded to write. In this second letter Theodahad agreed to surrender his royal authority into the hands of Justinian, in consideration of a fixed income for life. He and his wife, the queen Gudeliva, took an oath in Peter's presence to fulfil the terms of this letter. Peter took an oath that he would not deliver the second letter until and unless the first had been rejected.

The suspicions of Theodahad were not far off the mark. Justinian refused to entertain the terms contained in the first letter. It was not worth while; he could obtain more by fighting. So much being certain, Peter delivered the second letter. This was far more to Justinian's mind.

Justinian accepts

A real prospect now existed that he might obtain Italy without fighting. He accepted the terms, and ordered Peter to proceed to Italy to make the necessary arrangements to implement the agreement; while Belisarius was directed to stand by and be ready to occupy Italy.

VII

If Justinian seriously expected this arrangement to be carried out, he was destined to be disappointed. Before Peter could reach Italy again, the Goths had got wind of the project.[1] Peter arrived to find that the Gothic chiefs

[1] The usual story is that the vacillating mind of Theodahad was exalted by the news of the Gothic successes in Dalmatia, and that he now became confident. This cannot be the full truth. Theodahad was certainly not ignorant of the military repute of his fellow Goths. The Gothic fighting men would have laughed at the idea of losing a war. Another story concerns the curious oracle

had taken over the control of affairs. They had evidently told Theodahad that he need not worry about a war. Any fighting that needed to be done, they would do. Peter found a somewhat excited king who now refused to abdicate, or to carry out his oath, and grim men behind him who urged and prompted him. Peter himself, in spite of his status as ambassador, was, together with his colleague, placed under arrest.

It looked at first as if the Gothic chiefs might be right. Not only had Mundus fallen in Dalmatia, so that the imperial army found it necessary to evacuate the province, but Belisarius was not in evidence. He had hastily crossed   Reverse to Africa to deal with a military mutiny which required his personal attention. For a month or more it was possible for the Goths to point with pride to the silence of the imperial government. Where was Justinian? Where were the terrors he had promised? Then in May and June, Constantian, the Constable, entered and reoccupied Dalmatia; and at the end of June Belisarius crossed the Straits of Messina and landed at Rhegium.

The war had begun.

VIII

For some little while the Goths failed to comprehend the events which began to take place under their very eyes. The Gothic commander who defended the Straits went over to the imperial side. As he was the son-in-law

---

about "Africa Capta, Mundus Peribit." The death of Mundus in Dalmatia was a happy solution of the omen. Statesmen are not usually much affected by motives of this kind and the whole anecdote is probably a bit of archaic affectation on the part of Procopius. The preferable course seems to be to assume that the Gothic chiefs discovered the proceedings of Theodahad, and put him under control. Bury, *History of the Later Roman Empire*, II. 174–175. Procopius, V. vii.

of Theodahad, this was hardly encouraging to the Goths. For two hundred and forty miles, from Rhegium to Neapolis, Belisarius and his army marched unopposed along the coastal road, while the fleet sailed parallel with them. He certainly did not hurry. He took more than three months to cover the distance. When, in October, he arrived at Neapolis, there was no sign of any Gothic army, except the garrison.

A deputation of the citizens of Neapolis lost no time in waiting upon Belisarius. They pointed out the unimportance of their city. They urged him to take no notice of them, but to press on to Rome. He reminded them that he had not requested their advice. The Gothic garrison might march out of the city with the honours of war, but the civil population must surrender. He tried to ease the way to surrender by promising the leader of the deputation a heavy recognition in the event of a favourable issue. The citizens retired to consider their decision.

The modern reader, looking on, like some not-yet-embodied spirit, upon that conference, may be seized with an anxious desire to signal to them to agree with their enemy quickly, whilst they are in the way with him. But the reader will not be born for fifteen centuries, and the citizens of Neapolis, unconscious that posterity would ever take any interest in their affairs, proceeded to argue from the data before them. The supporters of the Gothic government persuaded the meeting to ask for conditions which they felt certain Belisarius would refuse. . . . Belisarius, however (a good-natured man) agreed to the conditions. Foiled here, the partisans of the government appealed to the citizen assembly. They con-

Belisarius at Neapolis

tended that Belisarius could not protect them if they surrendered, and could not take the city if they refused. Besides, the Goths, as enemies, might be much more unpleasant than Belisarius was likely to be. The Jewish community, which had no enthusiasm for the prospect of an anti-Semitic imperial rule, supported these arguments. In spite, therefore, of all the concessions which Belisarius was willing to grant, the citizens of Neapolis declined to surrender to the representative of the emperor.

The siege of Neapolis lasted twenty days: a somewhat longer time than Belisarius had expected, or relished. The arguments of the Neapolitans were not altogether untrue. Their city was not very important: and Belisarius found a good deal of difficulty in taking it. He grudged the time. He had already issued orders to resume the march to Rome when the luck turned. He had cut off the city water supply. A soldier, exploring a broken aqueduct, found that the channel into the city could be enlarged to admit a man. A little quiet labour by a working party cleared the way, and unconscious Neapolis was at the mercy of Belisarius.

Before giving the word which he knew meant the unloosing of Huns, Herulians and Isaurians upon Neapolis, he called a further conference. He assured the citizens that it was impossible now that he should not capture their city, and he exhorted them to surrender without bloodshed. Naturally enough, they did not believe him. They thought his assertion another of the famous dodges of Belisarius.

The channel of the aqueduct was accordingly forced at night, the adjoining battlements of Neapolis were seized, and cleared for escalade. Neapolis was sacked;

Siege of Neapolis

The city
stormed

and not until morning could the Huns be called off. By vigorous efforts Belisarius at last restored order. The Gothic garrison was granted quarter, and had no reason to grumble at the treatment it received.

IX

The fall of Neapolis brought matters to a crisis among the Goths. Whether of set purpose or through incapacity, Theodahad had made not the slightest effort of any sort whatever to grapple with the military situation. He may have been a fool, but there are limits to folly. Theodahad merely illustrated the maxim that though a horse may be led to water, it is impossible to make him drink. The Goths had ordered him to fight. This was how he fought.

Before the end of November a meeting of Latin and Campanian Goths was convoked at Regata, in Latium. Their business was of extraordinary gravity. In deposing Theodahad, they ended the long and historic career of the Amalung dynasty. Theodahad was the last of his line. No candidate with any of the old qualifications presented himself. Ultimately they elected a man named Witigis.

The essential weakness of all such methods of procedure was illustrated with remarkable clearness in the election of Witigis. The voluntary choice of a leader is always a compromise. Witigis was not the man for whom most could be said, but the man to whom least was objected. This fact was not immediately visible; but it was destined to influence the rest of the career of the Ostrogothic nation, and to be the little wheel which trans-

Witigis
king of
the Goths

mitted the awful forces of destiny. The fate of Italy was decided when Witigis was elected.

The announcement of his accession was an imposing document. Men are seldom so much in earnest about their principles as when they feel their procedure to be shaky. The document enlarged upon the worthiness of Witigis's title—how he had been elected in the broad and open light of day instead of in the corner of a royal bed-chamber: how the source of his dignity, besides the divine grace, was the free choice of his people. These phrases were meant to veil the fact that Witigis was not descended from any sacred caste, Amalung or other, but was an ordinary person owing his crown exclusively to his sub-jects: and that this fact was a reversion to an older sys-tem, the result of which no one could predict.

If Witigis were to reign, Theodahad must die. The new king, with all his disadvantages, could not main-tain his authority if a sacred king of the old Amalungs were also in Italy. The order was issued to seize Theoda-had, dead or alive. Theodahad, who was in Rome, fled to Ravenna, but was overtaken on the road and slain.[1] He had deep reason to rue the day he ever listened to the en-ticements of Theodora. With him ended the Amalung kings—the first political kings of northern Europe.

Death of Theodahad December A. D. 536

This was December. During the first week of the month Witigis entered Rome and held a conference. His proposal was, that as they were threatened by the Franks on the north and the imperialists on the south, they should

---

[1] Procopius (*History*, V. xi. 9) says that he was slain "like a sacrificial victim." This perhaps only means "very deliberately"; but it may also point to some ritual act committed upon the sacred king.

first dispose of the Franks, and then come southward with the whole of their forces to encounter Belisarius. The reason for this was that the Gothic levy would naturally collect in northern Italy, where most of the Goths lived. There was no obvious reason why they should bring it south and then take it north again, when it was possible to do all the work in one circuit. This view was generally accepted, and the plan ratified by the council.

Other things being equal, common sense is apt to get badly entangled when it attempts to deal with a Quixote of genius; and the present instance was no exception. Witigis reckoned upon regularly placing the larger number of fighting men in the field at the right time and in the right place, and winning his battles in the normal course of events. It was a reasonable expectation, and the Gothic council (which was by no means composed of incompetent amateurs) approved it. So the host of Gothic riders disappeared northwards, to join the levy which was assembling there; and Belisarius and the little Dago army, marching sixteen to the dozen, entered Rome as the Goths left it. We shall see how far reasonable expectations were fulfilled.

Belisarius
enters
Rome
Dec. 9th
A. D. 536

X

The first step of Witigis, after his arrival at Ravenna, was to marry Matasuntha, the daughter of Amalasuntha, and sister of Athalaric. She, the heiress of the Amalungs, might give his reign some semblance of legitimacy: her children would certainly be descendants of Theuderic. . . . Matasuntha showed very little pleasure at the prospect, but she had to submit. Her sympathies and her temperament were akin to those of her mother. She did not enjoy being mated with a man of inferior birth. She did not like the policies and methods which were now in favour among the Goths.

Witigis then took up negotiations with the Frankish kings. These intelligent diplomatists had been induced by Justinian to create a diversion (successfully, as we have seen) in favour of Belisarius, by intervening in the north. Theodahad, a man after their own hearts, had quite understood how to deal with them. By a concession of territory, and a substantial lump sum down, he had even won their promise of help in the war. Witigis now offered to confirm this agreement, and the Frankish kings were willing to conclude it with Theodahad's successor. They managed at the same time to remain on friendly terms with Justinian by sending, not Franks, but non-Frankish subjects, to help in the war. It was almost impossible to pass a bad coin off upon a Frank: and the kings did not regard the agreement as binding until they had got Justinian—as possible next heir—to endorse the transfer of territory. Justinian did so.

The stage cleared

Witigis also wrote to Justinian. He pointed out that since the imprisonment and murder of Amalasuntha were the reasons for the invasion of Italy, these might now be regarded as cancelled by the death of Theodahad and the accession of Witigis. He requested the Catholic bishops of Italy to offer their prayers for peace. He made it quite obvious that, like Theodahad, he desired peace and not war. The reply of Justinian is not preserved. He probably reminded Witigis that the quick and sure way to peace was the simple one of unconditional surrender.

This was far from the thoughts of Witigis. Early in

the year the Gothic levy was summoned, and by February the advance upon Rome had begun. Some twenty thousand men,[1] many of them mailed knights riding armoured horses, rode with the king of the Goths, while the little Dago army was throwing up earthworks and rebuilding masonry in the desperate effort to make Rome defensible.

Witigis moves upon Rome

XI

The approach of the Goths drove in all the outlying detachments which Belisarius had flung northward to watch for the enemy. He held on to Perugia, Spoletium, and Narnia only. His hold on the latter forced Witigis to leave the Flaminian road and to gain Rome through the Sabine country, by the Via Salaria.[2] Belisarius had anticipated this, and had placed a fortified post where the road crossed the Anio. Next day, with his comitatus, he rode towards the bridge, only to find that the garrison had abandoned the post without orders, and that the Goths were over! An exciting skirmish followed. Belisarius was riding a well-trained and experienced horse with a white blaze; and as he rode in the forefront this horse was recognized, and the word was passed among the Goths: "Shoot at the white blaze!" Most of the Goths had no idea what the blaze represented, but they obeyed the catch-word, and Belisarius became the centre of a

---

[1] Following Prof. Bury (*History of the Later Roman Empire,* II. 181, also pp. 183–4. 194–5) who inclines to think that the figure of 150,000 given by Procopius is not the number of the Gothic army, but the total Gothic population in Italy. If so, 30,000 is the largest possible number of Gothic tribesmen available to Witigis. Deducting 10,000 for the Dalmatian campaign, sickness and absentees, 20,000 is a fair guess for the strength of the army which Witigis led against Rome. Even so reduced, it is 4–1 against Belisarius.

[2] For this, see Bury, *op. cit.,* II. 182 f. n. 1. Procopius. *History,* V. xvii.

very fierce struggle. He defended himself with vigour from a general onslaught until his comitatus, placing him in the midst, locked its ranks about him and defied all comers. It was the first clash between the imperialists and the Gothic tribesmen; and the easterners proved their mettle. In the hand-to-hand fighting a thousand Goths fell, and the survivors were driven back upon their supports.

The comitatus lost no time in falling back towards Rome, until the Goths, reinforced, returned to the fight and brought the imperialists again to bay. The comitatus formed up afresh on a hillside, and a second fierce struggle took place in which the Goths again suffered severely. In its next withdrawal the comitatus reached the Salarian Gate. There it met with an unexpected difficulty. The guards, unable to recognize the dust-covered and dishevelled Belisarius, and believing him to have fallen in the fight, hesitated to open the gates, in spite of the exhortations and infuriated threats of their general. Finding himself penned into the gateway and against the wall, Belisarius, as often before and after, saved himself by unflinching bluff. Dusk was falling. In the twilight he turned to bay, marshalled his men, and boldly charged the Gothic pursuit. There was some difficulty in seeing clearly, and the Goths, under the impression that fresh troops were sallying out of the city gate to the rescue of Belisarius, prudently drew off. During the interval Belisarius managed to convince the defenders of his identity, and none too soon was admitted to safety.

During the evening, the Gothic host began to debouch upon Rome. An emissary of the king, named Wacis, arrived outside the Salarian Gate to summon the city to

surrender. His address, however, was not altogether encouraging. He denounced the Romans for abandoning
the Gothic government, and for preferring Dagoes,[1] who
would do them no good—men, said Wacis bitterly, who
had in the past only come to Italy as barn-stormers and
long-shore sneaks. As no one contradicted him, he retired with the honours of war.

Although Belisarius had returned battered and exhausted, and was up half the night arranging for the defence of the city, he seemed very cheerful, and he aroused
adverse criticism among the Romans by expressing an
absolute certainty that he could beat the friends of the
haughty and high-born Wacis. They did not know on
what he based this remarkable optimism, in which perhaps they hardly shared; and he did not at the moment
enlighten them on the subject.[2]

Witigis had not a sufficient number of men adequately
to besiege Rome. He formed seven camps at suitable
points round the city; but even so, his blockade was not
perfect.[3] His first practical step was to cut off the water
supply. The famous aqueducts of Rome, the greatest of
her engineering works, were cut, and water ceased to
flow into the city. There was something epoch-making
in the event. The aqueducts had been the outward and
visible sign of the inward civilization of Rome. They had

[1] Graikoi (Procopius, V. xviii. 40). As used here and in V. xxix. 11. the word
has the peculiar connotation of such modern words as "Bolshie," "Dago" or
"Hun," and Dago seems the nearest equivalent. "Levantine" would once have
conveyed the implication: but the word seems to have dropped out of the
dictionary of abuse.

[2] Procopius, *History*, V. xxvii. 24–29.

[3] If his total forces were 30,000, the seven camps must each have averaged
about 4,000 men each. These numbers, however, represent the full-blooded Gothic
tribesmen and the mercenaries of equal social standing. The servants and
auxiliaries may have much more than doubled these numbers.

fed those baths which made the Romans the cleanest race in history. . . . The popes of succeeding ages were more immediately concerned to wash them with spiritual water, to which the material kind had been a dangerous rival. They preferred a city saved to a city civilized. It is regrettable to think that there has always been some question as to whether later Rome, mediæval Rome, was either civilized or saved.

XII

The cutting of the aqueducts had less effect upon the drinking resources of the city than upon some of its subsidiary activities. The old wells and the river were once more called into service; but the water-mills which were driven by the aqueduct water came to a stop. Belisarius was equal to the emergency. In the full force of the Tiber current he moored boats with the water-wheel slung between them; and by this expedient he provided means of grinding all the corn required. . . . The Goths attempted to float down obstacles to wreck this ingenious scheme. Belisarius at once stretched a boom across the river to intercept them; and the Goths gave up the game. He could usually beat them in a battle of wits.

Before resorting to extreme measures, Witigis communicated with Belisarius. The latter received the envoys publicly, surrounded by his officers and by the Roman senators. Witigis offered generous terms. His spokesman, indeed, took a somewhat patronizing tone, describing the hardship and misery which a prolonged siege would inflict upon the Roman people, who were not suited to bear such trials—figuratively patting the imperial army

Conver-
sations

upon the back, and pointing out its discouraging prospects. If it would accept terms, it might march out with its arms and its baggage.

Belisarius answered in words which appalled and frightened the Romans. He was supremely confident of success: he knew the hand he was playing, and had no doubt of the result. He returned an emphatic refusal to the proposed terms. So far from considering the possibility of retreat, he spoke words of warning to the Goths. He said: "The time will come when you will be happy to hide your heads, and will be unable to do so. Rome is ours by immemorial right. You have no claim to the city. I will never, while I breathe, surrender it."

The envoys retired, unsuccessful; and Witigis began his preparations for the capture of the city by assault.

XIII

On the eighteenth day of the siege, at sunrise, seven columns of Goths advanced against the fortifications of Rome between the Prænestine Gate and the Vatican. Before them rolled the carriages on which the battering rams were swung, and the wheeled towers from which to command the ramparts and protect the breaching parties. Belisarius had a large audience as he stood looking over the battlements of Rome at this terrifying spectacle. The audience had seen all it wanted of the Goths, and its interest now was bent upon Belisarius.

The
Gothic
assault

Belisarius somewhat annoyed a very nervous concourse when he began to smile at the oncoming terror. Their feelings were not alleviated when he passed the word that no action was under any circumstances to be taken until he gave the signal for it. As the rams and towers approached, with creaking of wheels and straining of the ox-teams, the fidgeting on the ramparts increased. Excited Romans began to address audible criticisms at the great commander. Still the Goths were allowed to advance. At last Belisarius took a bow, notched the arrow, drew it to his ear, and transfixed one of the Gothic leaders who were directing operations. Satisfied with his judgment of the distance, he drew a second successful arrow to confirm it, and gave the word— "Shoot at the oxen!"

As he retired to make room for the archers who crowded forward, he explained his provoking smile. He had been amused at the simple faith which imagined that he would let the oxen draw the siege engines into position. . . . And the truth was that the Goths, sword-and-spear men all, found the utmost difficulty in realizing the tactical use of archery. . . . Shot down now by flights of cloth-yard shafts, the oxen were falling and dying in their tracks in front of the siege engines. Not only was the motive power cut off, but a barrier was made in front of the engines which could not be removed under the barrage of the archers. Belisarius had judged the distance well. He had drawn the line exactly at the spot which was furthest from the walls and yet at the same time completely under the command of the bow. The barrier so made was never removed.

Defence of Rome

The Gothic columns nevertheless came up to the assault, though they came up to undamaged fortifications instead of to walls dominated above and breached below. They did not belie the reputation for courage which north European troops in all ages have possessed. Again and again they returned to the onslaught, and were met by the hard-shot shafts of the archers, and the even more terrible missiles of the mechanical artillery, which swept their ranks from the platforms above.[1] Belisarius was everywhere, watching, directing, providing, encouraging. He knew his weak spots, and saw that they were properly attended to. The vastly greater numbers of the Goths meant that one successful entrance, even in some unimportant place, might involve the complete penetration of the defences. . . . But the fierce Huns and Herulians, and the veterans of the Persian wars, fighting behind fortifications, were more than a match for many times their number of Goths. As the light waned, and evening approached, the assault began to slow, and to stop, and dissolve. . . . As the Goths retired, the defenders poured out after them. The cheers for Belisarius were emphasized by the flames which began to arise from the siege towers and battering rams. As it grew dark, the twilight was illuminated by the destruction of the instruments by which the Goths had expected to take Rome.

Repulse of the Gothic assault

XIV

The repulse of the great assault on Rome was a serious military disaster to the Goths—thirty thousand men were said to have fallen upon the Gothic side, though

---

[1] Procopius mentions (V. xxiii. 9–12) a Gothic commander who stood near a tree, directing the operations against the Salarian Gate, and was suddenly pinned to the tree by a bolt from the mechanical artillery, and hung there dead. Elsewhere (V. xxi. 14–19) he describes the tremendous effect of these engine-shot shafts.

in actual fact they cannot have lost anything like this number. But even more serious than the material damage was the moral effect. For the first time the Goths began to suspect that the war would not be a walk over. Their pride would not permit them to look upon the Roman army as anything but riff-raff: but they began distinctly to contemplate the possibility that in Belisarius they had met a wizard and a master-man. From the day of the assault on Rome the legend of Belisarius really began its career.

Belisarius himself realized this fact of his tactical supremacy. It was not one which could be copied. Hard as it would be to train a modern army unskilled in shooting until it equalled an army of old marksmen, it would nevertheless be an easier thing to do than to train archers. The skilled use of the bow involves a much larger number of muscular co-ordinations than the use of the rifle. A bowman must be caught young: and he has all the more advantage if his ancestors were bowmen before him. . . . The Goths could only look blankly upon an art they could never hope to acquire.

Tactical supremacy of Belisarius

XV

Like a wise man, Belisarius was much more interested in his weaknesses than his strengths. In sending his report to Justinian he remarked that so far, from whatsoever reason, he had been successful, but if the success were to continue, the government must take steps to ensure it. Although success or failure are in the hands of God, men are held responsible for their actions. He could only be responsible for the results of the war if he were enabled to fight on terms of fair equality. He needed more men and more supplies.

Belisarius
reports to
Justinian
He went on to press this upon Justinian. Defeat now would mean the loss, not only of Italy, but of the army, and moreover of the prestige of the empire. In addition to this it would involve in ruin all the loyal Romans who had exposed themselves to reprisals. The difficulties in the way of holding Rome were formidable. Not being a port, Rome was hard to reprovision. Too much must not be expected of the Romans, who could not permanently go on maintaining loyal smiles without food to support them.

"As for me," he concluded, "my life is yours, and I shall not be forced out of this place alive. But think how your prestige would suffer if Belisarius were to meet such an end as that."

CHAPTER VII

THE SIEGE OF ROME

I

JUSTINIAN did not need exhortation. He already had re-inforcements on the way under Valerian and Martin. These, despatched in December, had passed the winter in Greece. As soon as the emperor had read the report of Belisarius, he sent an urgent hastener to these troops, and set about the task of raising more.

Meanwhile the repulse of the grand assault turned the siege of Rome into a blockade. It was not at first a very stringent one. Time had to pass before the strangle-hold really closed upon Rome. Belisarius foresaw and anticipated everything. The very day after the assault, when the Goths were too exhausted to act, or even to think, he collected all the women, children, and non-combatant slaves in Rome, and saw them on their road away from the city. Witigis gave no directions to stop them—and in a fierce age, when gentleness and mercy were hardly reckoned virtues at all, this may be booked to his credit. So they disappeared into the distance, going as many trains of refugees have gone before and since. All the remaining able-bodied citizens were put upon the pay-roll of Belisarius, and brought under military discipline: which certainly made for the greatest happiness of the greatest number.

Although Witigis had allowed the non-combatant refugees to make their way out of Rome, he did not extend a like sympathy to the rich and important senators whom he held as hostages. Some of these, warned in time, managed to get away safely; the rest he proceeded to execute. It is probable that both he and Belisarius sincerely deplored their fate; but it is quite certain that neither he nor Belisarius lost any sleep as a consequence. Times were changed for Roman senators since those golden days when Olympus trembled at their nod.

II

Three weeks after the beginning of the siege, the Goths closed the river mouth by occupying Portus, the harbour which had taken the place of Ostia, as the port of Rome. Belisarius had too few men to prevent this, and had to allow the point to be scored against him. Shipping anchored at Antium, further down the coast, whence a side road joined the Appian Way, and gave access to Rome.

Even as late as the sixth week of the siege, when April was well advanced, the blockade was not complete, for Martin and Valerian, arriving with their reinforcements,
rode straight into Rome without serious difficulty—sixteen hundred men, all cavalry, including a corps of Huns. The besieged were considerably strengthened by the arrival of these additions. For some time after they became available the curious spectacle was shown of a fortified town being successfully defended by cavalry. By the expedient of rapid sallies by mounted archers, who struck without coming to close quarters and retreated beneath the shelter of the fortifications, the Goths were kept in a continual state of strain and uncertitude.

Witigis tried to copy this quick-raiding method himself, and was mystified to find that when operated by Gothic sword-and-spear men, it did not work. Even with the facts demonstrated daily before his eyes, he could not credit the tactical superiority of the mounted bowman.

Though the method commended itself to Belisarius as an excellent means of wearing out the besiegers, its very success had an unfortunate effect upon the army. The latter grew so complacent over its own tactical supremacy, that it began to criticize Belisarius, as that artful dodger had been criticized before. He knew, however, the sure and simple method of curing military egotism. Since the army thought him an old slow-coach, too cautious to risk a victory, he submitted to the superior enlightenment of his subordinates, and allowed them to try their hand at more serious warfare.

Belisarius and his army

The blood-letting cure was successful. Faced on the field with overwhelming numbers of Goths, the army was saved from destruction only by the devotion of the infantry reserve, which was destroyed while protecting the retirement of the cavalry to the shelter of the fortifications.[1] Retreat within the gates was carried out with some loss, but without disgrace, and Belisarius for the time being was troubled by no further criticism of his military talents or personal temperament.

III

While adding to the military strength of the defence, the reinforcements were an additional strain upon the

---

[1] Record deserves to be made of Principius, the commander of the reserve, who with forty-two of his men died in protecting the retreat. Procopius, *History*, V. xxix. 39–44.

Blockade
tightened
June A. D.
537

food supply. Since a decisive battle in the open was now
scarcely to be expected, Witigis paid all the more attention to the details of shutting the garrison in. During
June, a treasure convoy bringing money for the payment of the troops and the purchase of stores, ran the
gauntlet from Terracina into Rome; and the blockade
was accordingly made more rigorous on the roads south
of Rome. Finding a spot, between three and four miles
from the city, where two aqueducts twice crossed one another and formed a loop, the Goths turned the loop into
a fortress which effectively blocked the Latin and the
Appian ways. The Romans, in view of the growing short-
age of food, asked Belisarius for a decisive action. He was
not to be moved by their persuasions. Although none
knew better than he how stringent the conditions might
grow, he adhered to his systematic policy. His one chance
was to wear down the Gothic forces by continual attri-
tion, and to destroy their moral by constant small dis-
couragements; and to this one chance he kept.

Since men need a little hope to feed on, Belisarius enlarged upon the subject of the plentiful reinforcements
and the abundant supplies that were shortly going to arrive. As the summer wore, he redoubled his precautions.
He changed the guards of the various gates at regular

Strain
on the
besieged

intervals; he organized strict and regular patrols, both
within and without the walls. Dogs were employed to
relieve the strain on human attention. Belisarius was on
the alert against treachery within as well as craft without. None of this continual watchfulness could be dispensed with. As the defenders went upon rations, and
then upon half rations, the Romans, who suffered the
most, experienced a perceptible fall in their enthusiasm.

Under-feeding implies, for most men, something much more serious than hunger: it implies loss of strength, and greater susceptibility to disease. It is usually accompanied by depression of spirits. Nothing is more wonderful than the transformation which can be effected in the human outlook by missing a few meals. This world is a glorious place; but its glory fades, its hope dies, and not only are its characteristics changed, but that feat which the philosophers assure us is impossible becomes an accomplished fact—the past too is altered, and even the good which once was, becomes so no longer. It is useless to argue with feelings which, to those who experience them, seem to have been begotten before all worlds, and to be greater than time and space. In such an atmosphere traitors are made.

All this Belisarius understood, and as the summer passed without the arrival of any of the reliefs which he had so confidently predicted, he grew seriously uneasy. Unless something was done, instead of wearing out the Goths, the garrison of Rome would itself be worn out. Towards the end of September [1] he despatched the faithful Procopius to ascertain the real situation, and to raise what help he could. . . . Procopius left Rome by night, and managed to run the blockade to Neapolis.

Procopius sent to bring help

IV

It was perhaps after the departure of Procopius that news and advices at last came through to Rome. That,

[1] For the chronology of this autumn, see Bury, *History of the Later Roman Empire*, II. 188, f. n. 1. It is clear however, on planning it out, that Antonina must have left Rome to join Procopius at Naples *after* the episode of Silverius—that is, after November 18th—and this view is taken in the text.

towards the beginning of November, communications arrived for Antonina, is fairly certain; and it is no far-fetched guess that the same post brought letters for Belisarius also.

First of those for Antonina.

The political contest which Justinian was carrying through in the east, while Belisarius was fighting the Goths in Italy, took the form of a religious struggle. For several centuries now, the Roman world had forgotten the possibility and dropped the tradition of political party. The empire had crushed all opposition. The opposition, crushed as politics, revived in the assumed form of religion. Men who could not combine together to oppose a political tendency, were at liberty to combine to advocate a theology. They accordingly did so. They asserted their theology in words and their politics in actions.

Communi-
cations
reach Rome

This was the reason why the rise of Christianity was accompanied by a remarkable series of persecutions of heresies. When Justinian became a theologian, he did so in order to be able to trace and detect, with his own eye, the affiliations of political party within the empire. When he supported the catholic, the universal faith, he was supporting the universal empire, the Roman world-state. The centre of this Catholicism was Rome, the ancient capital of the empire, and still its moral leader. While Belisarius was fighting, Justinian was endeavouring to make clear to the public opinion of Italy the soundness of his own opinions, and the prevalence of those opinions at Constantinople. This propaganda was an essential part of the conquest of Italy.

Theodora entertained her own views. She evidently felt it to be by no means so desirable as Justinian thought

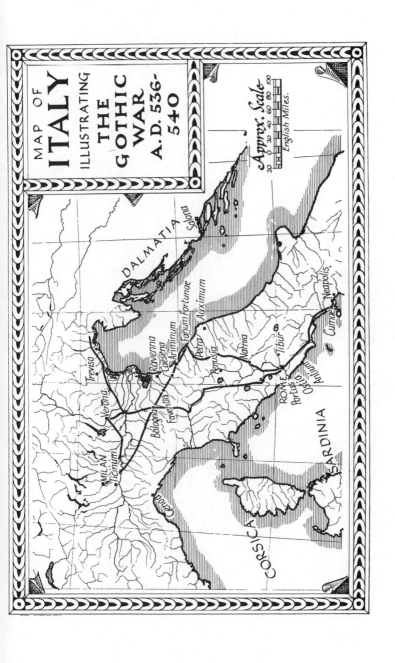

MAP OF
ITALY
ILLUSTRATING
THE
GOTHIC
WAR
A.D. 536-
540

Approx. Scale
20 0 20 40 60 80 100
English Miles.

DALMATIA

Salona

Tarium Fortunae
Auximum
Ravenna
Caesena
Ariminum
Petra
Treviso
Verona
Perusia
Bologna
Faventia
MILAN
Ticinum
Narnia
Tibur
ROME
Portus
Ostia
Antium
Cumae
Neapolis
Carso

CORSICA

SARDINIA

to maintain this ideal of the universal state: and possibly she felt it to be by no means so prudent. To sacrifice the affection and secure possession of the east for the very problematical and largely speculative loyalty of the west was a policy for which she had no passion; and in this she was followed by a number of Byzantine statesmen whose names form a respectable list. It is never wise to kick away the ladder by which one has ascended. The question which largely preoccupied the political thinkers of Constantinople was, By which ladder had they ascended? Was their strength based upon the tradition of the Roman world-state, as Justinian thought, or upon a united bloc of eastern provinces, as Anastasius had evidently believed?

The aim which Theodora set before herself was the bold one of herself getting a grip upon the papacy, the very heart and centre of the catholic world. The intermediary by which she proposed to achieve this aim was the papal representative at Constantinople, the deacon Vigilius.

The proceedings had already gone some way towards success. Theodora and Vigilius had established excellent terms of understanding together. When Pope Agapetus died, the deacon, provided with ample funds by Theodora, and with letters to Belisarius and Antonina, made a dash for Italy. The idea was that in the papal chair he would render Theodora a general support suitable to her aims. The terms of agreement were probably not absolutely definite. As a matter of fact he arrived too late, and his election did not come off. Silverius had already been elected.

Theodora, failing to induce Silverius to give her the

help she wanted, determined that her protégé Vigilius must replace him. To get rid of a pope is not, however, the simplest of tasks. . . . It was upon this subject that Theodora wrote to Antonina in the autumn of this year of the siege of Rome. The letter (as we have seen) in all probability arrived soon after Procopius had left. In order to prevent Belisarius from being inconveniently inquisitive, there were no doubt letters for him also, notifying him of the approaching reinforcements. Engaged with this, he would not trouble over the contents of Antonina's mail.

V

To this day the subsequent mystery has never been adequately elucidated. The one thing certain is that in the middle of November a letter to Witigis was intercepted, in which the Gothic king was notified that the Asinarian Gate would be opened to his men. Now the Asinarian Gate was near the Lateran, where the pope resided. The letter was promptly reported to Belisarius, who instantly arrested the persons on whom suspicion would naturally fall. A number of senators were expelled from the city. The pope himself was requested to call upon Belisarius.

The pope
warned

When he did so, Belisarius pointed out to him that he was on dangerous ground, and had better make terms with his powerful enemies. Silverius declined to swerve from the straight path. He was not arrested nor detained, and on his departure he removed to the Aventine, in order to make it clear that he was not plotting treasonable communication with the enemy. Not very long after-

wards, he received a second summons. He seems to have
recognized that this time the interview would be of
serious import. A crowd of supporters went with him.
These were filtered out by the court etiquette in force
at the headquarters of the imperator. Silverius alone entered the room where Belisarius received.

Antonina was present: and Silverius was confronted
with the evidence of the intercepted letter to Witigis.
He had no means of disproving that he wrote or authorized the letter. It was made quite clear to him that a large
and generous view of his indiscretion would be taken if
the empress were convinced of his loyal devotion. He
would, however, concede nothing.

Exactly what Belisarius really thought of the case is
not so clear as it might be. It was certainly his duty, as
commander of a besieged garrison, to be strict over such
questions as possible treachery; and it is probable that,
on the evidence before him, he had no alternative but to
consider the letter genuine. . . . Most modern judges,
who did not happen to be Antonina's husband, would
consider the letter a highly suspicious document calling
for further careful scrutiny. . . . But Belisarius was
quite aware that more powerful forces were at work, and
that on this question of Silverius his own authority was
secretly superseded by direct imperial command. He was
a prudent man. He took good care to get out of the way.
There was not the slightest reason why he should endanger his own position for the sake of Silverius: and he did
not make the mistake of doing so.

Since Silverius was obstinate, he was placed under arrest, stripped of his pallium, clothed in a monk's habit
and sent to Patara in Lycia.

The pope arrested

Election
of
Vigilius

The rest of the story may be finished here. Five months later, by imperial order, the election of a new pope was begun. Vigilius was elected. . . . But Vigilius was of sterner stuff than Theodahad. He was capable of crime, but not of heterodoxy. He was willing to condone forgery, and to wink at the death of his unfortunate predecessor; but he was not willing to admit that two and two made five, or that the Council of Chalcedon was not in the right. Once in the papal chair, he was pope indeed. . . . But this took place a little later, and does not much affect the subsequent course of the story. Theodahad had been Theodora's tool; but Pope Vigilius made a tool of Theodora.

VI

Either the uneasiness of Belisarius was not perfectly alleviated by the confidence he had in Procopius, or he received advices which notified him that the reinforcements which he expected were now close at hand. At any rate, since he could not go himself, he sent Antonina to follow Procopius, and to bring in the reliefs according to a concerted plan. . . . Antonina was fully equal to the task, and set about it with vigour. Slipping through the Gothic posts, she reached Neapolis in late November. Here she found that the historian had been hard at work helping to make a little history of his own. He had raised a corps of five hundred men, and had loaded a convoy of ships with corn. The reinforcements were still to come. Antonina, however, had not long to wait. Soon after she arrived, eighteen hundred cavalry landed at

Otranto under the command of John, nephew of Vitalian, and began the march to Neapolis by road. A second fleet of transports, doubling the Italian peninsula, disgorged three thousand Isaurians at Neapolis itself.

Antonina sent to bring help

While Antonina, with the Isaurians and the corn ships, went by sea to Ostia, Procopius, his men, John, the cavalry, and a convoy of store wagons, approached Rome by the Appian Way. They were expected. Belisarius made a vigorous sortie upon the Gothic camp near the Flaminian Gate, and the convoy slipped safely into Rome.

War is so often a question of who can hold out longest, that we are hardly surprised to find that at this point the Goths weakened. They were nearly as hungry and quite as uncomfortable as the Romans, and they were (with good reason) far less certain of the ultimate result. When they found out how they had been tricked, their heart was broken. Most of them were men of a type well designed to inflict heavy punishment, but not quite so good at the art of enduring it. Witigis gave up the hope of capturing Rome. Everything he had done had been correct by the text-books. He was correct now in approaching Belisarius for terms of agreement.

The Goths negotiate

Thoroughly in his element, Belisarius took the overtures with the utmost solemnity. Procopius had returned to Rome just in time to record the dialogue which took place between Belisarius and the envoy of Witigis.

We must remember that all this time Antonina and the sea-convoy were down at Ostia, wondering how they were going to get to Rome—a fact of which Belisarius was vividly aware.

VII

The envoy—an Italian—could talk to Belisarius in his own language.[1] He pointed out how unfortunate for all parties this war was. It was time for the leaders to consult the well-being of their followers rather than their own glory. If Belisarius had any objections to the statements he was about to make, he begged him to protest at once.

Belisarius urbanely replied that he had no objection to doing so.

The envoy therefore reminded Belisarius that the Goths had not conquered Italy from the imperial government. Eadwaeccer had repudiated imperial authority and set up a government of his own. The emperor Zeno, desirous of putting down this usurpation, had deputed Theuderic to suppress Eadwaeccer and to restore legitimate government. This was how the Goths came to be in Italy. They had faithfully obeyed the imperial law and custom; they had trenched on no man's lawful rights. Arguments But now, although the imperial government had left Eadwaeccer alone, it was trying to take Italy from the Goths who were its own deputies.

Belisarius observed that this was all very well; but the imperial government had never meant the Goths to take Italy for themselves. Theuderic should have returned the country to its true rulers. He himself, Belisarius, had no authority to give away imperial territory.[2] If the Goths

---

[1] If Belisarius were a Thracian, his native language would be Latin—as was the case with Justinian himself.

[2] Bury (*History of the Later Roman Empire*, II. 190) suggests that both these arguments were wrong. The right of the Goths to Italy rested upon the definite agreement between King Theuderic and the emperor Anastasius—an agreement which neither the envoy nor Belisarius even mentioned.

had any alternative to suggest, he was willing to hear it.

The envoy replied that every one knew quite well that his contention was accurate: but never mind that. The Goths would give up Sicily, which was now important to the imperial government on account of the access it gave to Africa.

"Thank you," said Belisarius. "We shall be pleased in return to present you with Britain, which belonged to us from the earliest years of the empire, and is a good deal larger than Sicily.[1] One good turn deserves another."

If the envoy saw anything funny in this, he did not deign to admit it.

"What if the Goths added Campania?" suggested the envoy.

Belisarius was prudently non-committal.

"Perhaps a yearly sum?" suggested the envoy.

Belisarius could not say.

"Well, if you have no authority, we must go to Constantinople," said the envoy, and he applied for the conclusion of an armistice to allow of this being done.

Belisarius was perfectly willing. Far be it from him to raise objections.

So the envoy returned to Witigis to explain that Belisarius had no authority. Belisarius did not mind in the least. That very night he ordered his horse and rode to Ostia, where the pilgrims were assembled. He instructed the troops to march up to Rome by road; the supplies he directed to come up the river by boat. He was con-

Belisarius declines responsibility

---

[1] The geography of Belisarius was correct. According to Whitaker's Almanack, Great Britain is 88,745 square miles in area and Sicily 10,000—which is probably more than most Englishmen could say off-hand, without reference to books. As Procopius is supposed to have been ludicrously ignorant concerning Britain, it is worth while to note that Belisarius evidently knew its relative size.

fident that the Goths would not interfere. He calculated correctly. Apprehensive of endangering the armistice, they made no hostile movement; and Belisarius, Antonina, the corn-ships, and "all the King's horses and all the King's men," trumphantly entered Rome that night without the loss of a grain or a man.

If not the greatest, it was certainly one of the most amusing of Belisarius' victories!

VIII

Armistice
concluded

After the formal conclusion of the armistice (which was for three months) the positions of the parties were almost reversed. The imperial army in Rome was happy and well fed; the Goths outside were hungry and unhappy. It is no use being a blonde beast if one has not enough to eat. The sea-blockade kept up by the imperial fleet was producing its full effect. As soon as the Goths had consumed the supplies of food available locally, they began to feel the pinch. Witigis withdrew from Portus and from Centumcellae on the sea-coast, as well as from Albano, which were at once occupied by Belisarius. Protests from the Goths had no effect. Belisarius, an expert himself at the game of bluff, merely laughed at their attempts to persuade him that he had no right to occupy positions which they had voluntarily abandoned. As he said, every one knew the reasons why they had left Portus and Centumcellae.

Belisarius indeed trenched as close upon the armistice as he thought the Goths would stand. It is a fine art to draw the line with exact delicacy just short of the degree at which the enemy will endure no more; but Belisarius was good at these things.

The consequences of the defence of Rome became gradually visible. All Italy had watched the struggle, and as soon as the armistice had somewhat slackened the strictness of the siege, messages began to reach Belisarius. There was a deputation from Milan, headed by the archbishop, requesting him to send a force into north-western Italy. The deputation assured him that the revolt of the whole of Liguria would soon follow. Belisarius accepted their assurances; but he had other work in hand at the moment, and the Ligurian campaign had to wait. The conquest of Liguria would open up the land routes to Gaul and Spain. This was too large a business to be contemplated until many other things had first been done.

Results of the defence of Rome

The first step taken by Belisarius was to utilize the presence of John, "the nephew of Vitalian" whose cavalry division had been among the reinforcements which Antonina had brought up from Campania. Both in character and talent, John was the best subordinate commander whom Belisarius had had under him; an energetic and somewhat ascetic man, with perhaps less tactical genius than Belisarius, but with strategical gifts hardly at all inferior. John could be trusted with an independent command. He was now sent north with his own division, strengthened by detachments of the best troops who could be spared from Rome, including men from the comitatus of Belisarius himself. His instructions were to pass the winter on the borders of Picenum, and if the armistice were broken, or when it ran out in the natural course of events, he was to go through the Gothic

John sent to Picenum

lands with fire and sword, making a grand battue of the women and children of the Goths, but being careful to do no injury to Roman subjects. . . . John had no conscientious objection to methods of frightfulness, if ordered. He started for Picenum.

By the despatch of John, it was made certain that any breach of the armistice at Rome would be instantly followed by reprisals in the neighbourhood of Ravenna. This arrangement seems to have been deliberate and calculated, for as we have seen, Belisarius was following a somewhat provocative policy. It might be too much to say that he wanted the armistice to be broken; but he recognized that the Goths had asked for it only in order to serve their own ends—and he therefore had no scruple in making it serve his.

IX

The presence of John, and his availability for responsible employment, set free another person, who now drifts for a moment across the limelight. His chief claim upon our attention lies in the extent to which he indirectly influenced the later development of the tale.

Immediately after the armistice had been declared, a complaint was filed by a person named Praesidius. His case was not very important, but it involved a matter of principle. He was a well-known citizen of Ravenna, who out of zeal for the imperial cause had joined the forces of Belisarius as a volunteer, early in the war. While stopping at a church near Spoletium, the news got about that he was carrying two valuable daggers, decorated with rich jewellers' work. The imperial commander at Spole-

Case of Praesidius

tium, Constantine, sent an officer who relieved Praesidius of these daggers. Praesidius acted with discretion. He did not trouble Belisarius with his private complaint while the siege was preoccupying the great man's attention; but as soon as the truce began, he laid the facts before him.

Belisarius told Constantine to restore the stolen property. Constantine was obdurate. Failing to get his property by decorous appeal, Praesidius tried making a scene—which is often an effective method. He publicly seized the bridle of Belisarius while the latter was out riding, and demanded the return of the property illegally taken from him. In spite of a little judicious bullying and threatening by members of Belisarius' retinue, Praesidius hung on to that bridle until he received an undertaking that he should have redress.

Belisarius, naturally enough, was angry. He called Constantine over the coals at a private conference of higher officers. Constantine flatly refused to return the daggers. Unless Belisarius were to sacrifice discipline altogether among his lieutenant generals, the next step was inevitable. He called in his comites to place Constantine under arrest.

What followed was curious.

"Are you going to kill me?" demanded Constantine.

"Of course not," returned Belisarius. "I am going to force you to return the property of Praesidius."

Constantine, however, for some reason, took alarm; though on the face of things it is not clear why. Drawing his dagger, he lunged at Belisarius, who instantly swung the stalwart form of Bessas between himself and his assailant, while Valerian and Ildiger grappled with Con-

*Incident of
Constantine*

stantine. The comites poured in, disarmed Constantine, and removed him in custody.

This was an ugly episode; but up to this point there was only one side to it. Unless imperial commanders were to become bandits, strong disciplinary action was called for. To make an assault upon the commander-in-chief, with intent to murder him, is in most armies considered a somewhat severe military offence. No one can be surprised to hear that Constantine was executed.

Execution of Constantine

But the execution of Constantine, fully justified as it might seem to be, gave rise to the most surprising and dangerous reactions. Justinian was deeply displeased; and the family and connections of Constantine never forgave Belisarius. Our astonishment at such a point of view is only modified when we ask ourselves why Constantine made his attack upon Belisarius. Why did he ask the remarkable question whether the intention was to murder him? What conceivable reason had he to imagine Belisarius was capable of such an action? Evidently something requires explanation.

Procopius, in his *Anecdota*, does not indeed give the full explanation, but he suggests a reason. The death of Constantine he laid to Antonina's door. Constantine suspected that Antonina intended his death if she could encompass it; and he jumped to a conclusion which in normal circumstances he would never have thought of. He committed a serious military crime out of genuine misunderstanding of the circumstances.

Explanation of the episode

That crime Belisarius perhaps knew to be not quite all that it seemed. Nevertheless, he would be in the abstract justified in executing Constantine. Antonina's influence (whatsoever form it may have taken) persuaded him to take the strict view. By such a vicious circle Constantine was trapped into a crime, condemned and executed; and it is conceivable that Justinian was furious at losing a distinguished officer through such a peculiar logic as this.

Belisarius might have thought twice, had he not had John to take Constantine's place.

The execution of Constantine was the first serious crack in the solidarity and unity of the imperialists. Up to this point, in spite of a good deal of ordinary slander and backbiting, there had been no serious dissensions. But from this point onward there were dissensions of growing gravity. We shall see later on what secret causes Antonina might possess for regarding Constantine as an enemy whose removal was urgent.

X

There was no time, however, to dwell upon the incident at the moment, for soon after it had occurred Belisarius obtained the excuses he needed for renewing the war. The Goths made several daring attempts to get into Rome by stealth. Having sufficient evidence on this head to justify him, Belisarius despatched the necessary orders to John to attack Picenum.

John did not by any means attack a defenceless foe. By this time he had been in the neighbourhood long enough to hint at the possible variety of uses to which his army could be put. A strong Gothic force was watching him. John defeated it in an engagement and slew its leader. Marching northward, he came to Auximum. Here the surprising element in his campaign began. Belisarius had impressed upon him that he was to besiege any

The armistice terminated

fortress he came to, and not to go further unless he took it. John, however, thinking Auximum too serious a difficulty, merely looked it firmly in the face and passed on. Urbinum likewise he left behind him. Ariminum was his aim. The garrison fled to Ravenna, a day's march northward, and without striking a blow John entered Ariminum and proceeded to make himself safe there.

The news that Ariminum, so close to Ravenna, was in the hands of the imperial troops at once terminated the siege of Rome. It had been a long and dreary failure. Now Witigis determined to cut his losses and to retreat upon his impregnable fortress of Ravenna. The armistice had in any case run out without result. By night, the bonfires could be seen in which the Goths burned the **Gothic** stockades of their fortified camps. Their host began to **retreat** cross the Mulvian Bridge and to take the Flaminian Way. When they were half across, Belisarius made a sortie. In the fighting which followed many Goths were slain, many were drowned, and the survivors effected their retreat without the more offensive manifestations of pride. They disappeared northward on the way to Ravenna, leaving Rome, after a struggle of one year and nine days, once more in the hands of the Roman government.

XI

The first step was to rescue John. The advance guard of Belisarius, under Martin and Ildiger, followed along the great Flaminian highway on the heels of the Goths.

Throughout the long wrestle at Rome, Narnia and Spoletium had remained in the hands of imperial garrisons. Hence, instead of Martin and Ildiger finding their way contested, they advanced rapidly, and without serious fighting, until they reached the famous Tunnelled Rock, twenty five miles from the Adriatic Sea. Here their passage was effectively blocked.

The Tunnelled Rock is a spot where the highway, running between a tremendous cliff and a dangerous river, is brought up short by a rock cross-wall. This the emperor Vespasian, centuries before, had tunnelled, in order to make the route possible. The end of the tunnel was closed with a door, and the Romans might have knocked at the door till doomsday for all the effect they could have produced. The only alternative was a long and arduous detour.

Before giving up hope, the generals sent a few men up the cliff to prospect. They found that the Goths who held the tunnel had quarters on the other side, where they lived with their families. Loosening a few rocks, the scouts rolled these down upon the domestic scene. Surrender was prompt. The gates of the tunnel were opened, and the imperial troops had the remarkable experience of capturing an impregnable stronghold which no military force under ordinary circumstances could have captured. Leaving a few men to hold it, they pressed on to Fanum Fortunae.

The Tunnelled Rock captured

At Fanum they turned down to Ancona to obtain a detachment of infantry there; after which they arrived at Ariminum without difficulty.

John had no enthusiasm for being rescued. When they told him that the orders were that the infantry from Ancona should garrison Ariminum, while John, with his valuable cavalry corps, should be withdrawn for more urgent service elsewhere, he simply refused to accept the orders. In his opinion Ariminum was the right place for him. Martin and Ildiger could not stop, for fear of being caught in the coming siege. Witigis invested Ariminum in April. Since the place was too strong to be taken by assault, he blockaded the town. It was not provisioned for a long siege, and soon the garrison was exceedingly hungry. Belisarius did not see why he should disarrange his carefully thought out plans in order to effect the melodramatic rescue of John. Since John apparently liked disobeying orders, he could go on disobeying them till further notice. And in this state the situation remained.

John caught in Ariminum

XII

The insubordination of John was only the first sign of trouble. His disobedience was not personal to himself, but was a hint of the serious schisms which followed the execution of Constantine. As Belisarius advanced with his main body, systematically reducing the strongholds as he went, according to plan, he was surprised to hear the news that a fresh army, nearly as strong as his own,[1] was disembarking in Picenum. Its commander-in-chief was the eunuch Narses, Justinian's Secretary of the Private Treasury.

It has always been the custom to look with a certain amount of surprise and patronage upon Narses. That personage was doubtless accustomed to the same sort of insult when he was alive, so that he is not likely to bother

---

[1] It consisted of 5,000 Roman regulars and 2,000 Heruls. We shall see later that Narses had a marked predilection for the fiercest type of barbarian tribesman, and seemed very successful in handling it.

himself about it now that he is dead. All that need be
observed here is that Narses was one of the big men of **Narses**
his day, a strong character and a powerful intelligence,
deep in the confidence of Justinian. Less of a soldier than
Belisarius, he was far more a man of the world. He had to
a remarkable degree that gift of adequacy to all kinds
of circumstances, and understanding of all kinds of men,
which constitutes the genius of common sense. Although
he could not have invented them, he learnt to use the
methods of Belisarius as skilfully as Belisarius himself.
And he was Justinian's trump card. The advent of
Narses meant that Justinian was angry, and intended to
have his own policy maintained.

Antonina had gone a little too far. Even if Justinian
would not interfere with Theodora, he might feel at liberty to interfere with her instruments. Narses was the
Aulic Councillor who came to watch Belisarius: or possibly it was Antonina he came to watch. He was a very
unusual sort of Aulic Councillor.

A meeting between Narses and Belisarius was at once
arranged. The conference took place at Firmum. The
influence of Narses was immediately felt. In discussing
the progress of the war, and the strategy to be followed,
Belisarius took the view that his plans should not be dis-
arranged for the sake of relieving Ariminum. John had
disobeyed orders, and he could hardly in reason expect
that the whole war should be re-arranged to suit his
caprices. To advance upon Ariminum out of its turn
would be exceedingly dangerous. No risks must be run.

The greater number of officers who were present at
the conference took the same view as Belisarius. Narses,
however, argued strongly against it. He disagreed with

the idea that John should be punished by allowing Ariminum to fall. Serious as the loss of Ariminum would be from a strictly military standpoint, it would be far more serious from the point of view of moral ef-
Narses and Belisarius
fect. Every effort ought to be made to save the city. John could be court-martialled at leisure after he had been saved.

The truth of the matter was that the methods of Belisarius needed such exact obedience from his subordinates, that he was not quite able to act with men who possessed initiative of their own. No argument could dispose of the fact that John's seizure of Ariminum was strategically correct: and this Narses saw.

They were still talking when a despatch, smuggled through the blockade, arrived from John himself. He announced that being unable to hold out longer, he proposed within seven days to surrender.

This settled the matter. Faced with the prospect of losing Ariminum, Belisarius gave way.

XIII

The relief of Ariminum was the most elaborate operation ever planned, up to this point, by Belisarius. First he had to mask the Gothic stronghold of Auximum. Ildiger was then sent with a fleet to enter the harbour of Ariminum, while Martin marched along the sea-coast. Both had definite instructions—if they would adhere to them. Ildiger was not to enter the harbour until notified of the arrival of Martin. The latter, when he arrived, was to light a large and alarming number of camp fires as a signal. . . . Belisarius and Narses, with all the remaining available troops, plunged into the mountains. Their aim was to arrive opposite Ariminum on the north-west simultaneously with the arrival of Martin on the south and Ildiger on the east. This accurate timing was an essential part of the plan.

Steps taken to save John

We have seen the fate of a similar military operation designed by Geilamir a few years earlier.[1] But the conditions for which Belisarius planned were fundamentally different. The destruction of Geilamir's scheme was due to the fact that an aggressive counter-operation threw out the accuracy of the timing. But the operation of Belisarius on the contrary was carried out against an almost passive foe. This passiveness of the Goths was the element which allowed the plan to succeed.

The advance of Belisarius and Narses drove in the Gothic scouts, who alarmed the besiegers of Ariminum. All through an afternoon the Goths watched the north-eastern approaches to the city, ready for action. Night came; and the southern skyline was dotted with a galaxy of fires. The Goths were men who were in the habit of believing the evidence of their senses. That evidence now told them that they were being enveloped by greatly superior forces. They passed an anxious night. Dawn revealed the eastern sea covered by the armada of Ildiger. . . . It was the last straw. The Goths began a retreat that was almost a rout. Had the garrison been capable of a sortie, the whole Gothic army might have been destroyed.

Relief of Ariminum

It was noon before Belisarius reached Ariminum.

[1] See above, Chapter V. Sections iv–vi.

Ildiger had arrived before him. As he met John, Belisarius remarked that he had cause to thank Ildiger. John replied that he had rather more cause to thank Narses.

Still, the relief of Ariminum had been effected.

CHAPTER VIII

THE FALL OF THE GOTHIC MONARCHY

I

THE advance upon Ravenna, the Gothic capital, was the next step; but it was one that required great and complex preparation. Belisarius did not mean to imperil his future operations by leaving intact in his rear the Gothic fortresses which were scattered along the Apennine. John might pass them and seize Ariminum: but although that remarkable military feat had been successful, some one had to do the prosaic horse-work of reducing the fortresses. Many of them were wonderful and impregnable places, which to this day look as if they were accessible to attack only by aeroplane. They might need careful and prolonged blockade.

Reduction of the fortresses

In addition to this, the problem of the north of Italy pressed upon Belisarius. Soon after the termination of the armistice and the retreat of the Goths from Rome, Belisarius had returned to the question of the Milanese deputation which had visited him. He had not sent to Milan: Milan had sent to him. He did no more than fall in with the suggestions made to him. A corps of a thousand men under the command of Mundilas was embarked at Portus and sent to Genoa by sea. From Genoa they advanced northward. With the exception of Ticinum, they occupied all the important fortresses of the northwest of Italy. The promises of the Milanese were fully made good.

Milan was the second greatest city of Italy, and its loss meant the hopeless stultification of the Gothic kingdom. Witigis accordingly despatched Uraias, his nephew, to recapture Milan. Uraias sat down outside the city, which was defended by Mundilas in person with only three hundred men. The rest were scattered in other fortresses. There was, of course, no question of holding Milan with such a garrison. The main work of defence was carried out by the citizens themselves: and they did it well.

This campaign in Liguria, while it helped to disperse the Gothic forces, called into action some other powers which it might have been wiser to leave unaroused.

The Frankish kings were totally unlike the Goths. They were men whose brains and characters had been ground into shape by centuries of contact with the Romans along the Rhine. They were handsome, clever and able men, without one spark of ruth, one trace of honesty or one touch of carelessness. Their words were honeyed, their statements were seldom accurate, and their right hand was a right hand of falsehood.

It was the Frankish smile that now beamed upon the Romans across the Alps. While King Theudebert was writing to Justinian to explain that no Franks were assisting the Goths, ten thousand Burgundians (who were certainly Frankish subjects!) entered Italy to help Uraias with the siege of Milan. The Burgundians did not act altogether like missionaries of a higher culture. They devastated Italy from the Alps to the Apennines, and sacked the city of Genoa. Theudebert expressed his dislike of such behaviour. . . . All the same, although he was careful not to let his left hand know what his right hand was doing, he left no stone unturned to make it sure that the imperial government should be kept as far away as possible from the borders of Gaul. . . . The imperialists, for all their victories, had not yet disposed of the fighting power of the Goths, and they still had to reckon with all the craft of the Franks, which might turn out a problem harder to deal with.

II

Capable as Belisarius might be of dealing with both problems, he was distracted by difficulties of quite another sort. The relief of Ariminum had convinced Narses that Belisarius was not a wholly reliable judge of the military situation. His conviction was so unmistakable that Belisarius cut matters short by calling a general conference of the higher officers, so that the question could be threshed out.

Belisarius and Narses

Belisarius laid before the meeting the real truth of the situation. The relief of Ariminum had not altered or improved the military situation in any way whatsoever. The main forces of the Goths were intact; in Liguria, the imperialists were losing ground, and were in peril; while it was just as necessary as before to capture the fortresses. He therefore tabled his plan, which was to concentrate upon two main objectives—Milan in the north and Auximum in the south.

As he probably expected, Narses at once showed his hand. In opposing this scheme, the treasurer disagreed with the principle of concentrating upon two points only. Narses was prepared to agree to a plan by which he should exercise an independent command against the Aemilian province and Ravenna, while Belisarius at-

tended to Milan and Auximum. This, he thought, secured the indispensable condition of pinning the main
body of the Goths at Ravenna.

Belisarius, however, was not willing to accept any
scheme involving the dispersion of forces and the division of command; and he pointed out the terms of a
memorandum which Justinian had recently circulated
to the higher commanders in Italy. In it the emperor had
observed that in sending his confidential minister Narses
to Italy, he was not giving him a separate command. As
before, Belisarius exercised an absolute command in
chief; and in the interests of the state all subordinate
officers should obey him.

The answer of Narses was a remarkable one. He replied that he did not consider the plan put forward by
Belisarius to be in the interests of the state, and he therefore felt free to disagree with it.

Narses
holds his
ground

What Belisarius thought of this answer is partly betrayed by his conduct. He did not put Narses into irons,
nor expel him from Italy. It is very evident that he
thought the answer inspired from Constantinople; and
he acted as though the interpretation put by Narses upon
the terms of the memorandum were the correct one. At
any rate he avoided a quarrel; and the halting and im-
perfect co-operation between the two commanders continued throughout the year.

III

The policy pursued by the imperial treasurer had some
serious consequences. The first was that, although Beli-

sarius sent as large an army as he could spare to raise the siege of Milan, it was not large enough for the purpose. Martin and Uliaris, its commanders, did not venture to cross the Padus. They contented themselves with watching from a distance. Mundilas sent to urge them to move: but although they promised to do all they could, they did nothing.

After wasting much valuable time, they wrote—not very willingly—to Belisarius to say that with the forces at their disposal the relief of Milan was impossible. This message was not altogether a tactful one to send to Belisarius. The latter was accustomed to perform impossibilities as part of his day's work, and he expected his lieutenants to do the same. They asked for the co-operation of John and Justin, who were working in Aemilia under Narses. . . . John and Justin declined to move at the order of Belisarius. Application to Narses obtained the necessary authority. When this had been secured, John went on the sick list, and operations were suspended.

Siege of Milan

By this time the citizens of Milan were keeping themselves alive by eating dogs and mice. Even so, they held out. The Goths approached Mundilas with suggestions for terms. Mundilas was willing to surrender, on condition that the civilian inhabitants shared in the terms. This the Goths declined. They intended to inflict upon Milan a heavy punishment. Milan was near the Frankish frontier and it is not unreasonable to surmise that Frankish influence stiffened the Gothic attitude. . . . Mundilas stuck to his conditions and refused all terms from which the civilian inhabitants were excluded. . . . His men took a different point of view. They proceeded to surrender the city without regard for any opinions which Mundilas might entertain upon ethical questions.

The Goths carried out their side of the bargain. The imperial garrison was duly received to quarter. Milan itself was taken by storm and sacked. . . . The sack of Milan ranks with such historic atrocities as the sack of Magdeburg. The Burgundians, rather than the Goths, were the men responsible for the worst features of the episode. Procopius believed that the whole male population, numbering some three hundred thousand men, was massacred. The women fell into the hands of the Burgundians, whose perquisite they were. Senators and priests were slain in the churches. Reparatus, the Prætorian Prefect of Italy, the brother of the pope, was hacked to pieces, and his flesh thrown to the dogs. As far as possible the fabric of the city was destroyed. Liguria passed back nominally into Gothic possession, but in reality into that of the Franks. The Frankish king had drawn his frontier line in a very red ink: but there was no doubt of its distinctness.

Milan lost
A. D. 539
(early)

The sack of Milan was a moral shock even to an age not unduly sensitive to proceedings of this sort. To some extent it failed of its full effect by needlessly exceeding the rather wide limits allowed by contemporary public opinion. Belisarius refused to see the general Uliaris, whom he held responsible for allowing Milan to fall. He made no bones about expressing his candid opinion in his report to Justinian. The fall of Milan he attributed to divided military authority. It would never have happened had he possessed in reality the command that he was supposed to enjoy.

IV

Justinian recalled Narses, and confirmed in clear language the absolute and exclusive authority of Belisarius. But the error he had committed was not so easily to be remedied. Narses recalled

The comet—the "Sword Fish"—which began to blaze in the sky during the year 539 was no idle harbinger of trouble. Although the experts—as is not uncommon—differed about its meaning, it was not easy to doubt the reality of the terrors which preceded, accompanied and followed it. The sack of Milan was only the first of many disasters. With the softening of the weather a great Hun army began to pass the Danube: and all that spring and summer it covered the Illyrian provinces, devastating the land. It captured thirty-two fortresses, penetrated Thermopylae, and wrought havoc in all northern Greece; detachments crossed the Straits into Asia, and came back with all the plunder they could carry. When the great army retired, it drove a hundred and twenty thousand captives in its train. . . . So Procopius says. . . . And even if we fancy that he exaggerates, it is well to remember that those who suffered under the invasion probably thought it one of those things which no words could exaggerate.

Old Kobad's son, the young and vigorous Khosru Anosharvan, the new Persian king, was moreover looking with a searching eye upon the western policy of Justinian. He did not like it; and he felt that he was losing ground and wasting time if he stood idly by and watched Justinian recover the ancient power of the Roman empire. That spring he held conferences with his principal henchman upon the Arabian border, the Saracen Al Mundhir. He told Al Mundhir that he wanted a war; and he left the Arab to devise the excuse.

Al Mundhir worked the oracle so perfectly, that for all we can tell his excuse may have been genuine. He drifted with great naturalness into an embittered dispute with his neighbour, the pro-Roman Harith. They argued over the real ownership of certain bits of third-rate pasturage. The intervention of Justinian was then invoked, and the emperor sent two arbitrators to decide the conflicting claims.

This was what Khosru wanted. He now appeared before the curtain in person, with a grievous and abominably plausible tale of the insults and injuries to which he had been subjected by the emperor and the arbitrators. He had a letter which Justinian was alleged to have writ-

Policy of
Persia

ten to Al Mundhir, seeking by the offer of filthy lucre to corrupt the saintly innocence of that pure white soul. He also had a letter which the emperor was alleged to have written to the Huns, inciting them to invade the Persian empire. With vast indignation, Khosru was proposing to denounce the treaty he had concluded with the Romans.

Just as he had worked himself up to this point, a new factor began to influence the situation.

We know that Witigis had invoked the help of the Franks. Whether he had anything to do with the Hunnish invasion is another matter; but we do know that at this critical moment he attempted to open negotiations with Khosru. No Goth would have been of any service; so he induced two north Italians, a bishop and a priest, to undertake the task. In Thrace they picked up an interpreter; and as the two countries were at peace they had no particular difficulty in entering Persia.

V

According to Procopius, these obscure and humble ambassadors made a speech before the King of Kings which impressed him. They told him that Justinian was aiming at the creation of a world-state. If the emperor could crush the Goths, the power so placed at his disposal would enable him in turn to crush Persia. They exhorted Khosru not to neglect the happy moment, but to act before it was too late.

These views so agreed with the opinions of Khosru himself that it became now only a matter of finding the most advantageous method of reopening war. The situation in Armenia proved to be the direct cause required; and it was due so completely to the deliberate policy of Justinian that the war arose, by a logical chain of events, from this policy, and not by any unsatisfactory jumble of accident.[1] Needless severity, imprudent rivalry—attempts to save time, money and men by forcing new methods upon the Armenians instead of waiting upon the effects of persuasion and conciliation—these things ended in general disaffection and an Armenian deputation to Khosru. The King of Kings was delighted at the turn of events. His council was like most other councils. It did not readily respond to arguments based upon profound political principles. Very probably it regarded with indifference the improbable contingency of Justinian

Goths and Persians

---

[1] For the details, see Procopius, *History*, II. iii. passim; and Bury, *History of the Later Roman Empire*, II. 92–93.

creating a world-state. But the Armenian question was different. Commercial considerations made Armenia a topic of lively interest. A long discussion ended in Khosru obtaining what he wanted. As it was then autumn the war was authorized for the following spring.

The imperial government was neither quite able, nor altogether willing, to believe that the Persians meant war. During the winter, Justinian wrote a personal letter to Khosru. After remarking that most men of intelligence did their best to avoid war, which was easier begun than ended, he disclaimed any evil or hostile purpose in his communications to Al Mundhir, or to the Huns. He drew Khosru's attention to the mischievous activities of Mundhir, and finally asked him not to strain trifles into reasons for war, considering how much suffering war may cause. Khosru did not answer this letter. He might possibly have suggested that Justinian should begin the application of these admirable sentiments nearer home— say in Italy. It was perhaps simpler to make no answer.

As a matter of fact, Justinian had actually begun to reconsider the Italian war. As early as June he had information that communications were passing between Witigis and Khosru, and he made ready to hedge. The King of Kings was a very serious enemy. In resources, numbers, prestige, and capacity for maintaining a long and exhausting struggle, the Persians were infinitely more dangerous than the Goths. . . . Throughout this year, therefore, Justinian was pondering over his problems. With Milan fallen, Illyricum over-run, and Persia threatening war, he had to debate very carefully with himself concerning the right steps to take. Above all, the financial

Justinian's
difficulties

problem had to be faced. Could he, with all this war in progress, raise a revenue commensurate with its needs?

Belisarius, however, showed real strength. He may have been, in his private character, as temperamental as the historians represent; but he certainly did not display himself in that light during the autumn after the recall of Narses. He went on steadily, quietly and inexorably with the task of capturing the fortresses. . . . Theudebert himself appeared in Italy during this time. The Frankish king made not the slightest apology to any one for grabbing everything upon which he could lay his hands. It was only too obvious that his sole object was to prevent the existence of any strong political power at the gates of Gaul. Witigis had lost Liguria quite as much as Justinian had. The total result was, therefore, that with the gradual reduction of the fortresses Witigis, at Ravenna, at last found himself face to face upon somewhat narrow ground with Belisarius and the imperial army. As the autumn wore, the work and patience of Belisarius had their full reward. He could advance with perfect safety upon the Gothic capital.

Franks in Italy

VI

King Witigis must have been the least romantic of men, for everything he touched turned into prose. The siege of Ravenna and the last stand of Witigis were as unexciting as a drive in a four-wheeled cab. The war was conducted for the most part by urbane gentlemen equipped with notes and instructions, while the army, save for a few unimportant operations, yawned in

Negotiations

cantonments. Towards the end of the year Belisarius heard that Frankish envoys were on the way to Ravenna. He was correctly informed.

The Franks (who were apparently unaware that they had ever been on anything but the most affectionate terms with the Goths) came with a proposal for an alliance between the Goths and the Franks against the empire. The idea was that after turning the imperial army out of Italy, the allies could divide Italy into spheres of influence—exactly what proportion was to exist between the Frankish and the Gothic sections they left in some obscurity.

Belisarius hastened to intervene. His own representatives lost no time in putting before Witigis the far, far better prospects of an agreement with the imperial government. They touched without enthusiasm upon the subject of the honesty and truthfulness of Franks. Their remarks upon this head were favourably received by Witigis and his council, who agreed that it was preferable to reach an understanding with the emperor. Negotiations were therefore formally opened.

Early in the New Year plenipotentiaries arrived with full instructions from Justinian. The emperor—a little nervous at the threatening situation in the east—was willing to agree to very generous terms. He would agree to the retention by Witigis of Italy north of the Padus;[1] he asked an indemnity of half the Gothic royal hoard—

[1] At this time, Italy north of the Padus was for the most part occupied by the Franks. It is not certain that Justinian realized this; but in any case his offer was not intended in a cynical spirit, for Witigis, armed with a legal title, and able to concentrate his attention upon the project, was in a much better position than the Franks to establish effective authority through the territory. The chief objection of the Franks was to having the empire as a neighbour. They might have come to an agreement with the Goths.

the bullion reserve by which the northern kingship governed.

The terms surprised every one. The Goths of course accepted. Justinian was probably offering them far more than they could hope to obtain by fighting. No one realized this better than Belisarius. The latter was struck with consternation when he perused conditions which sacrificed so many of the gains he had laboured so hard to make. To him they must have seemed almost an affront —as if all the skill and patience he had displayed were valued no higher than this!

It is possible that Belisarius would have taken a different view of the case if he could have talked the matter over personally with the emperor. He was a soldier; and perhaps there were many points which Justinian could have demonstrated, that did not occur to Belisarius. At any rate, when the plenipotentiaries requested him to countersign the treaty as imperator and grand commander in Italy, he refused to do so.

Belisarius against the terms

The imperial army, far from being a service in which rigid despotism stamped out individuality, was full of strong personalities who seldom hesitated to express themselves with embarrassing candour. Many of them were very candid on this occasion. Belisarius therefore called a conference.

He told his officers that no one was better aware than he of the large element of luck in war, and the way in which the whole tide of war could be turned by a defence in the last ditch. It might be wise to make terms with one's antagonist while one was in the way with him. But one thing he must insist upon. No one must afterwards turn round and blame Belisarius for consenting to such easy terms. He wished them to say whether they approved the terms in the treaty, or thought it practicable to enforce more suitable ones.

Faced by a request to comment upon the terms of the treaty, none of the officers ventured to criticize Justinian's draft. They unanimously approved.

Belisarius then asked them to put their opinions into writing. They did so. He was pleased to have these declarations; for he felt very sure that there would afterwards be adverse criticism of the treaty, with its extraordinary gap between the terms drafted, and those it was possible, by military action, to enforce. He wished to be absolved from responsibility on this score.

The treaty suspended

Witigis and his advisers, however, had by now taken alarm. They felt sure that though they could not discover it themselves, some snag must exist somewhere in the treaty. It was too good to be quite genuine. They now refused to accept the treaty unless it were endorsed and guaranteed by Belisarius. . . . It is interesting to notice the estimate they had formed of the honesty and honourable dealing of the great Thracian.

As a consequence of all these proceedings the treaty, absurdly favourable as it was to the Goths, was suspended. It had over-reached itself by the very generosity of its terms to a defeated foe.

VII

The Goths, who of their own accord had chosen Witigis to be their king, had been amazingly loyal to him. Perhaps they had had little alternative. They had chosen a man on whom they could all agree; it was their fault, not his, if he were a commonplace man. But the break-down of the negotiations over the treaty was too much. They really could not stand any more. Even so they did not directly condemn Witigis. Something far more remarkable took place. They began to contemplate the possibility of offering a crown to Belisarius.

Just as their Arianism had prevented them from associating cordially with Catholic Italians, so their Amalung dynasty had prevented them in the past from nominating an emperor. The Amalungs were now gone; none was left except Matasuntha, a woman. No barrier any longer **Belisarius** existed to prevent the Goths from creating a Roman **offered a** **crown** emperor, an absolute sovereign, owing allegiance to no overlord. They never put forward the Amalungs as emperors. A Roman emperor must be a Roman. Only a Roman citizen could hold the unqualified sovereign rule by the grace of God which constituted the monarch of the world-state. Belisarius was a Roman citizen. He had conquered Italy at the head of a pack of mongrel curs, largely Levantines, Armenians and broken Goths. What could he not do at the head of the blue-blooded tribesmen of the Goths? An alliance of Belisarius and the Goths might be the stroke of genius which would recreate the empire with not only a new emperor, but also just that one thing which for centuries it had lacked, a gentile aristocracy.

The scheme was possible. More, it has even to this day something of the air of a genuine inspiration. The man who started the idea—whosoever he may have been—was no fool. He had hit upon a plan which might alter the course of history.

When the proposal was laid before Belisarius himself,

he needed to make, very quickly, a decision of extraordinary importance, such as comes very rarely to men.

We do not know his intimate thoughts; but it is not altogether difficult to guess some of the factors which swayed his mind. It is hardly likely that he shared the view which the Gothic tribesmen took of themselves. He was a man of pretty wide experience, who had met a great variety of fellow men in all kinds of unusual circumstances; and although this experience may have convinced him that Goths were splendid war-beasts, it probably had not persuaded him that they were especially fit to rule an empire. Moreover, the whole life of Belisarius, both before and after this episode, hints that he was acutely aware of his own limitations. A soldier he knew himself to be, and he never fiddled or fretted over his claims to military eminence; but he never thought himself cut out for a monarch, and never showed any desire to shoulder the work of one. If he thought, for one dazzling instant, of himself as an emperor ruling by support of the Goths, it was only to pity himself profoundly. . . . No. It might look very fine in the abstract; but it was not practical politics.

His
attitude

Belisarius showed, throughout his life, that he sincerely preferred a world in which Belisarius reaped the military laurels, and Justinian did the horse-work of government. He had no wish to stick his own neck into the collar.

VIII

Emphatic as his views might be on this head, he was sufficiently diplomatic to smile cordially upon the Gothic intermediaries. So satisfied were they with their welcome,

that the news began to spread inside Ravenna. Even
Witigis heard of it. The king had done his duty to the
best of his power, and he was now sick of his job. He sent
to Belisarius urging him to fall in with the scheme. The
advice, if not unselfish, was at least disinterested.

Belisarius promptly summoned a fresh conference of
officers and asked for the attendance of the imperial
plenipotentiaries. The question he put before them was,
what view they would take if he could, without violence,
recover the whole of Italy, capture Witigis, and seize the
whole of his hoard. . . . The meeting thought it a highly
desirable aim, and agreed that he ought to achieve it if
he really perceived a way. Having got this put on record
for future use, Belisarius found the path clear for his
next step.

Famine was nibbling at Ravenna. Blockaded by sea and
land, the Goths found it impossible to keep the city adequately supplied. This threat of famine had been one of
the agencies which impelled Witigis to negotiate. Beli- First steps
sarius now dispersed his principal lieutenants in all directions on military duties. By this expedient he also got
rid of a number of witnesses whose presence might have
been awkward.

As soon as he was free, he sent in to Ravenna to accept
the proposals made to him. Under cover of renewed
negotiations concerning the treaty a whole set of fresh
negotiations were started concerning a very different
subject indeed. Conditions and stipulations were arranged. Belisarius pledged himself to hold harmless all
persons and all property among the Goths. His formal
oath as monarch, by which he would step into possession
of the fealty and homage of the Goths, he postponed un-

til he should be in Ravenna. The reservation was natural
enough, as it was not quite clear how the solemnities of
taking these crucial oaths could be performed by deputy.
The Goths had no doubt that he would take these oaths.
The formal entry into Ravenna was arranged.

It was in May that the Roman fleet entered Classis, the
port of Ravenna, laden with food for the starving city.
The gates were opened—and not the whole imperial
army, but Belisarius and his comitatus only, a small body
of conquerors, marched through streets crowded with a
much larger number of the conquered. . . . There
seems to have been some difference of opinion among the
Goths themselves. According to the historian, the Gothic
women were enraged beyond measure at the sight of the
undersized little army which had overcome the lords of
Italy, and they spat in the faces of their husbands and
sons; but we are not told of the precise extent of such
a remarkable manifestation of opinion, and in any case,
Belisarius and his men would no doubt freely have admitted their own inferiority in a beauty contest. They
were entering Ravenna as soldiers, not as hairdressers.

Once inside Ravenna, the work of Belisarius was swift
and deadly. Witigis was arrested, together with a certain
number of the chief men of the Goths. The royal treasury
was seized. The rest of the Goths were dismissed to their
homes. . . . When at last they realized the fact that
Belisarius had not taken, and never would take, the oaths
of a king and emperor, it was too late to object. Their
combination had been destroyed.

The capture of Ravenna was an extraordinary episode
in human history. Not its least extraordinary feature
was the perfect humanity and good temper which dis-

Belisarius
enters
Ravenna

The mask
removed

tinguished it. To walk into the stronghold of men like the Goths, and to act as Belisarius acted, is a feat not given to many men who have lived in this world.

IX

A month later, with Witigis, the hostages and the treasure, Belisarius sailed from Ravenna. His journey home was rapid: but when he arrived at Constantinople it was to meet a cold and not very friendly Justinian, and news of a startling nature, hardly less terrible than the sack of Milan. This news was the tidings of the fall of Antioch.

The loyalty of Belisarius was beyond question, and Justinian never very seriously questioned it; but the actions of Belisarius in Italy concerning the settlement of the Gothic war had been almost as upsetting to Justinian as flat rebellion would have been. He had shown, at the lightest reckoning, indiscretion; and some might even call it by a harder name. The emperor, with his finger upon the pulse of empire, had thought out and arranged a coherent and intelligible policy, and had embodied it in the treaty of peace. This treaty, which Belisarius did not understand, and was incapable of estimating in its true value, would have created, for some years to come, a Gothic buffer-state in northern Italy, parting the empire from the Franks and Germans. Belisarius, having signed this treaty, could rapidly and promptly have left Italy and returned to take charge of the threatening Persian war. . . . He had done none of these things. Instead, he had destroyed the whole scheme of the Gothic buffer-state, and had left the imperial forces

Belisarius and Justinian

in Italy struggling with an expensive and troublesome guerilla war, which might at any moment expand into something even more serious. He had wasted four or five months, and allowed Khosru to march unchecked into Syria, and to inflict upon the empire one of the most appalling disasters it had ever suffered. . . . If, after these things, Belisarius expected a warm and affecting greeting, he was a sanguine man.

X

The Persian campaign had followed the lines Khosru had projected. Marching up the Euphrates, the Persian army had advanced into Syria. Khosru, a man of power and intelligence, was a highly successful organizer, and there was no man in the imperial army capable of dealing with him. What the Roman side was like without Belisarius grew only too obvious as day after day went by and Khosru did as he chose.

The Persian front

Justinian had made arrangements which, if carried out, would have avoided all the troubles that followed. He had settled that Belisarius should have the Syrian command from the sea to the Euphrates, while the sector from the Euphrates eastward should fall to Bouzes. Although some saw an "Irishman's rise" in the appointment of Belisarius to a comparatively narrow sector instead of his former general command in chief, it is very evident that Justinian's intention was not to restrict the authority of his best commander, but to set him free from worrying and irrelevant details, so that he could concentrate his attention exclusively upon the really dangerous front of the war. . . . As Belisarius was still wasting his time in Italy trying to improve upon the emperor's plans, Bouzes in the meantime temporarily took the whole eastern command.

Making his headquarters at Hierapolis, Bouzes determined to avoid a war of sieges, and to rely more upon a mobile field force for harassing the Persian advance, and for preventing Khosru from settling to the work of capturing fortified places. These were admirable maxims. Putting them into operation, he disappeared with his mobile field force, and nobody knew whither he had gone. As far as Syria was concerned, Bouzes might as well have been in Italy with Belisarius.

As soon as Justinian heard of the Persian advance, he realized the need for urgent measures. He at once despatched his nephew Germanus to Antioch, with three hundred men hastily got together and the promise of an army to follow. Germanus arrived at Antioch, surveyed the city, and pointed out that if it were to be held against Antioch military action, a certain number of alterations were necessary in the defences. The city architects at once declared that it was impracticable to carry out the alterations in the time at their disposal. With the fortifications in this unsatisfactory state, and no army arriving, Germanus took a pessimistic view of the prospects. Antioch accordingly determined to buy itself off.

Negotiations being set on foot through Megas, bishop of Beroea, the King of Kings lent a favourable ear. An indemnity of ten centenaria of gold was fixed as the price of Antioch. Khosru undertook, indeed, to leave Roman territory in consideration of this sum. On the return of

Megas to Antioch, the bishop found that imperial envoys to Persia had arrived, in the persons of John the son of Rufinus, and Julian, the emperor's confidential secretary. Julian forbade the payment of any indemnity. The bishop therefore was unable to obtain the ratification of the terms he had arranged with Khosru.

The view of the situation taken by good judges may be gauged by the fact that the bishop of Antioch lost no time in fleeing to Cilicia, whither Germanus was not long in following him. Many of the citizens of Antioch fled with all their portable wealth, and more would have done so had not six thousand troops arrived—an army nearly as large as that with which Belisarius had begun the conquest of Italy. Khosru, when he appeared, was by no means unreasonable. He still offered to accept an indemnity of ten centenaria, and some people thought it obvious that he would have taken even a smaller sum. Antioch would have found little difficulty in raising such a ransom.

But here, finally, the ultimate difference intervened. The people of Antioch were accustomed to that particular brand of popular humour which is nowadays considered the product of democratic institutions, and is familiar to us on the music hall stage and in the political cartoon. . . . Roman emperors accepted it with philosophy, as part of the scheme of things. . . . Khosru, an oriental brought up to a totally different system of manners, did not accept with philosophy the ribald remarks addressed to him by the populace. He was horrified and deeply insulted: and he determined to take Antioch by assault.

Antioch
in danger

XI

Even now, Antioch might have escaped: but her doom pursued her. There was an absence of proper organization in the defence. Belisarius should have been there, and he was not there. The collapse of some temporary structures employed as part of the fortifications led to a panic. The soldiers left their post, and abandoned the city, marching out through one of the gates which the Persians had not invested. When the Persians made escalade to the undefended walls, they at first could hardly credit the evidence of their senses. . . . Even now, Antioch might have escaped . . . But the amateur defenders of the city, no longer controlled or advised by responsible professional soldiers, vainly imagined that they ought to defend their hearths and homes. . . . A massacre followed. The Persians slew every living thing they could catch before they were called off. Practically the whole of the city within the walls was plundered and burnt out with fire. The remnant of the citizens of Antioch was rounded up for transport into Asia.

The sack of Antioch was a shock to the whole Roman empire. The modern world, though it has seen one or two things which have made it cry out with horror, has not seen the sack of Glasgow or Chicago: and Antioch, in the sixth century, corresponded in relative magnitude to such cities as these. The prestige of Justinian was shaken to its foundation. Even those who would not have granted that the fault was his, unconsciously saw him as of smaller stature and meaner power.

Faults of omission and negligence are not easy to pun-

Antioch falls

ish, for it is not always possible to bring home clearly
to the guilty parties their responsibility for the consequences of what they have not done. But it is evident
that though Justinian could hardly punish the conqueror
of Italy for the fall of Antioch, he was deeply displeased,
disappointed, and offended. This time, Belisarius was not
granted a triumph. He had brought back another of
those kings of his—but he was not allowed to lead him
in procession. He had brought back another royal hoard
—but he was not permitted to exhibit it.

Witigis was well treated. With the rank of patrician,
and an estate in Asia, he lived for two years after he lost
the kingship of the Goths. Most of the Goths who accompanied him passed into the imperial army. They had
singularly little to grumble at.

Yet Witigis may have heard with astonishment and
admiration the lordly doings of Khosru. After wiping
out Antioch, where he had been insulted, the King of
Kings indulged in a little sea-bathing at Seleucia, a holi-
day resort not often available to monarchs of Persia. He
visited the famous gardens and fountains of Daphne: an
excursion well worth while, as Procopius observes.

At Apamea, he decided to patronize the local races;
and being informed that Justinian was a Blue, Khosru
decided to become a Green—the first Persian monarch
who had ever ornamented that party. Unfortunately a
Blue driver headed the field. Khosru, unprepared for
these western manners, ordered him to be put back. . . .
The King of Kings and the Green faction then won the
race amid loud and prolonged cheering; and it may be
presumed that they were proud of it.

He returned home by easy marches, weighed down

with the plunder of Syria, and driving before him the surviving inhabitants of Antioch. Wonderful as had been the doings of Belisarius in Africa and Italy, it seemed as if a Persian army could do pretty much as it liked with the Roman empire.

CHAPTER IX

THE DESTRUCTION OF THE INSTRUMENT:
(1) THE WORK OF ANTONINA

I

SINCE Antioch had fallen and the King of Kings, with his train of miserable captives, had vanished leisurely down the Euphrates, there was no especial reason for hurrying Belisarius to the front. He had worked hard, with no holidays, for some five years. It was time for a rest. It was time, also, for him to stand still a little while in the light so that his friends and his foes could look at him.

The worst of Belisarius was that he was not an individual. He was a combination, a syndicate. No one could be quite sure whether they were dealing with the senior or the junior partner in the combination—that is to say, with Antonina or with Belisarius. The great soldier, of course, had his enemies who would gladly have seen him in trouble. To destroy Belisarius might have been a comparatively easy job. But any one who tried it found themselves facing, not the good-humoured tolerant man, but the fierce and resolute woman, whose heart was flint and her brow brass—and her intelligence uncommonly quick. Her morals may have been open to suspicion—at any rate, her enemies said so—but her brains were not.

Antonina had evidently been realizing for some time

past the need of re-insurance. She elected to bank for safety upon an alliance with the empress.

Antonina's policy

There was wisdom in this, because they had a real common ground in their fear of John the Cappadocian. For both Theodora and Antonina John was the real foe, the dangerous foe. He was dangerous, not only because of his ability and his ambition, but because he possessed the emperor's ear. Justinian listened to few men more than to him.

The return of Belisarius had not been marked by any public demonstrations of affection on the part of John. The historian assures us, indeed, that John showed a distinctly unfriendly spirit.[1] Only a habitual optimist could have expected him to be enthusiastic about a man who, against all reason, had proved John's predictions untrue. Even fools are hurt when their feeble prophecies are falsified. Much more was John incensed and alienated when his perfectly true, his clearly rational, his square and solid based commonsense was blown to the winds by this ridiculous Quixote with his elderly wife and her train of young men. . . . Belisarius ought to have left his bones to bleach on African desert sands, as John had very reasonably said he would. . . . John was not among the cheering crowd when Belisarius marched up the Mesê with a captive king in his train. He was probably in his office, swearing at his amanuensis. . . . John, we may guess, was one of the men who underlined and emphasized the faults of Belisarius when the latter returned with another captive king whom he had no business to have.

Hostility of John

Belisarius harboured no ill-feeling. With Antonina it was different.

[1] Procopius, *History*, I. xxv. 11–12.

II

We have already seen that there is some ground for
thinking that John was the man who set going those
stories of Theodora which can still bring a blush to the
cheek of elderly scholars of blameless life. The historian
Procopius, when he was old and angry, recorded these
stories though he had not himself witnessed them, and so
repeated them only upon hearsay. . . . He repeated
some other stories, which, remarkably enough, he had in
a similar way not actually witnessed, but had heard.[1] It
is no very wild guess to suspect that these other stories
also received some colour from the art of John the Cappadocian. How far they were true we cannot tell. Probably, without being in all ways true, they were not altogether untrue. They were stories of Antonina and her
conduct in Italy.

John certainly provoked the full attention and most
resolute enmity of Antonina. He was just the sort of man
who would spread himself with enjoyment over the task
of repeating with artistic touches the scandalous story
of Antonina and her godson Theodosius. He would enjoy it all the more since it set the hero Belisarius in a
ridiculous light. . . . That something of the kind did
happen, we may infer from the fact that, on their arrival
in Constantinople, Theodosius decisively separated himself from the party. The reason given is that he felt his
position to be too prominently before the public. He
could not stand the general comments. He joined a monas-
tic order and took the tonsure at Ephesus. . . . We are

Attack on Antonina

[1] See Bury, *History of the Later Roman Empire,* II. 192 f. n. 1.

not told who did the talking; but the inference from the whole set of circumstances is that the scandal-monger was John.

The feelings of both Antonina and Theodosius are comprehensible if the scandals were those reported by Procopius. They began as far back as the voyage to Africa, when Theodosius, newly baptized and adopted, accompanied them on the flagship. We get a vivid picture, told us, as it were, behind the hand of the historian, of the stout Antonina, violently and not too discreetly obsessed by a youth young enough to be her grandson; and the absurd Belisarius expertly succeeding with his eagle eye in detecting nearly everything that happened except, oddly enough, *that* . . . Antonina (it was alleged) carried her young man about with her whithersoever she went. At Carthage Belisarius, a little less tactful than usual, found on one occasion that he had walked in where angels might have feared to tread. In successfully failing to see anything wrong, he achieved one of the most peculiar triumphs of his career . . . So the historian says.[1] If John did not get the full value out of all this, he was a fool.

Antonina and Theodosius

III

But this was merely preliminary. The subsequent developments of the story had far greater popular appeal. When Belisarius sailed for Sicily, he took Antonina with him, and Antonina took Theodosius. . . . It is rather difficult to see why, in the alleged circumstances,

[1] Procopius, *Anecdota*, A', γ'–δ'.

Antonina should have troubled to go travelling about Italy with an army, at a good deal of personal discomfort, when she could have stayed at home with Theodosius; but scandal, like all forms of romantic poetry, has conventions which we must not disturb by the undue intrusion of daylight and actuality.

Belisarius was still at Syracuse, after his conquest of Sicily, when a woman named Macedonia had an interview with him. After she had made Belisarius swear the most binding oaths that he would never betray her, Macedonia told him the whole story of Antonina and her passion for Theodosius. As Belisarius had presumably seen a good deal of it, we may wonder why he needed any information. . . . She also produced two boys as witnesses; though since Belisarius had declined to believe his own eyes, it is not clear what reason she had for thinking that he would believe any one else's.

Case of Macedonia

Belisarius (the reader will remember that this is scandal) believed the testimony of the two boys, though he had disbelieved his own: and he flew into a great fury, although he had known everything all along. He sent some of his men to kill Theodosius. The latter, warned in time, fled to Ephesus. Feeling it wiser to be on good terms with Antonina than obedient to Belisarius, the would-be assassins revealed everything to her.

It can hardly have been really necessary to do this; for apparently every one was in the secret. Constantine, as a friend and colleague, sympathized with Belisarius in his failure to "bump off" Theodosius. The memorable words he uttered were: "I would have put the old lady on the spot, rather than the boy." . . . When Antonina heard this, she laid it to heart for future action.

IV

The scandal-monger, whether Procopius or John, had at this point to account for the awkward fact that Antonina and Belisarius continued to dwell together in a perfectly amiable and happy relationship. His solution was ingenious. It was due, he thinks, possibly to enchantment, or conceivably Antonina petted him back into good humour. The reader is at liberty to say, from all that he has heard of Belisarius, which of these alternatives is the more probable, or the least improbable. In any event, Antonina persuaded him of her innocence. Belisarius became furious again—though in daylight he was an unusually cool customer, who hardly ever lost his head or his temper—and he undertook to deliver up Macedonia and the boys to the vengeance of Antonina. . . . And what did Antonina do? We shall find it hard to credit! The wicked old woman actually chopped them up, put the pieces into sacks, and threw the sacks into the sea. She was assisted in this deed by one Eugenius, who helped in another well known atrocity—the arrest of Pope Silverius. From this latter circumstance we can see that Eugenius was fully capable of any crime; and apparently we are to deduce that Antonina herself did some of the chopping up.

Soon afterwards, Antonina had her revenge also upon Constantine. These foregoing facts, the historian tells us, are the true reason why Belisarius executed Constantine.

Theodosius, though reconciled with Belisarius, declined to return to Italy while Antonina's son Photius was with her. Photius was jealous of him. The reason given for the jealousy of Photius is that although he was the son of

Antonina, he was entirely neglected; while Theodosius, during his governorships of Carthage and Ravenna, amassed a fortune of one hundred centenaria.[1] Not until Photius had been driven from Italy by threats against his life did Theodosius return: and then, free from Photius and secure against Belisarius, the wicked couple enjoyed their abominable intrigue to the full.

V

This story, ridiculous and impossible as it is when examined, had probably a core of truth. It is probably true that Antonina and Belisarius were a devoted couple, with great confidence in one another. It is probably true that determined efforts were made to sow dissension between them, which signally failed. It is likely enough that Antonina made a tame pet of Theodosius, and that the great soldier usually failed to notice the existence of that somewhat insignificant person. . . . The reason for the attempts to create discord between Antonina and Belisarius is that she stood on guard over him while he fought. While she was there, it was impossible for his enemies to get rid of him. Belisarius owed his career to the steady watchfulness of Antonina.

John—if it were John—overshot his mark. We know, at any rate, that Macedonia the dancer was a political agent, who had worked for Justinian in times past. That she took part in an attempt to sow dissension between Belisarius and his wife is only what we might expect. It

---

[1] While remotely possible, this seems so unlikely as to be incredible. For how long did Theodosius enjoy these posts? It does seem true, however, that Theodosius was employed in responsible positions. Procopius, *History*, VI. xxviii. 8.

is not impossible that Antonina strongly suspected Constantine of similar complicity. This is the simplest and most natural method of accounting for the extraordinary circumstances connected with his death. If he had been an agent of John, it is easy to understand that the latter would leave no stone unturned to represent the execution in an invidious light at Constantinople. Hitherto, Antonina had been compelled to stand up passively while these attacks were levelled at her. Her return with Belisarius forced a crisis. John was making desperate efforts to damage them. It was very necessary therefore to destroy John.

Antonina seems to have set about the task with careful circumspection. She gave no hint of her programme. As long as Belisarius remained in Constantinople, she remained with him. Not until, in the spring of 541, he left for the Persian front, and was safe in the wilds of Asia, did she act. On this occasion she did not accompany him. She remained behind.

The counter-attack

It was necessary to have a reason for remaining. The unwilling Theodosius was again roped in, while Antonina proceeded to play, with great realism, the comedy of How she lied to her husband.

Theodosius had probably been sincere when he expressed his resolute intention of remaining a monk. . . . Antonina had conducted herself in a somewhat striking manner over the retreat of Theodosius. She had openly bewailed his loss, and had passed the word to the bewildered Belisarius, who obediently bewailed it also. To the amusement of the general public, he succeeded on obtaining pressure from high quarters upon Theodosius. The public was delighted when, as Belisarius disappeared southward to fight the Persians, Theodosius, vowing that he never would consent, consented to return to Constantinople. Antonina's alibi was perfectly satisfactory. No one doubted the nature of her reason for remaining behind. . . . Above all, it was probably the only reason that would have convinced John.

VI

Antonina had not been an actress for nothing. Her line of attack was upon the weaknesses of John, and even upon his most human and amiable weaknesses. He had a daughter, Euphemia; and, John being what he was, it was almost a foregone conclusion that though she had the intelligence of her father, he would guard her from experience with the utmost care, and make certain that she should be a sweet and innocent child. . . . John adored his sweet ideal of female charm. . . . And it was there that Antonina prepared to strike.

Point of attack

John might, of course, have defended himself, had he realized whence the blow would come; but that was particularly the thing which Antonina masked. It seems never to have occurred to him to prevent any acquaintance between Antonina and his daughter. Euphemia fell almost at once before the experienced siren. In a few days, Antonina had all the snowdrop secrets of that maiden heart.

There was no necessity for Antonina to speak anything but the truth. She knew the repute of John. She knew his ambition; she realized that one of his causes of dislike for Belisarius was the possibility that the latter might be a dangerous rival in the struggle for empire if Justinian died. John was sure that he was destined to **Euphemia** wear the mantle of Augustus—and Euphemia knew it too.

When they were alone, one day, Antonina expressed the disappointment she and Belisarius had felt at the treatment they had recently received. It seemed so hard that, after Belisarius had done so much, and had brought two kings captive to Constantinople, Justinian should be cold and unappreciative.

Such sentiments as these gratified the tender Euphemia. John's daughter, knowing how her father feared the empress, felt very happy to think that Belisarius and Antonina should be alienated from that terrible foe. She pointed out, with much good sense, that the fault really lay with Belisarius and Antonina themselves, seeing that, when they had the power to alter things, they neglected to use it.

Then Antonina baited the trap.

A revolution, she told Euphemia, could not be carried out by soldiers alone. It needed the co-operation of the civil administration if it were to be successful. Now, if John were willing, there might be some hope of success. . . . Euphemia promised to tell him so.

VII

John was very far from being a foolish or an unsophisticated man. He undoubtedly looked hard at that message, and turned it round in his mind; but turn it as he might, he saw nothing against it. Here was a possible

The trap

way to the fulfilment of his ambitions! He at once said that he was willing to meet Antonina and talk the matter over: and he bade Euphemia arrange the meeting.

As far as we can see, the whole common sense of the matter was upon John's side. He had no real reason to fear Antonina; because for one thing Antonina had never shown any active hostility. She had defended herself and her husband; but she had not been aggressive. John, being a bold and confident man, did not fear those things which he had no reason to fear. Moreover, all that Antonina said was acknowledged truth. Finally, she could not betray John without betraying herself.

Antonina added one more refinement of subtlety to her part. She impressed upon Euphemia that it was not altogether safe for her and John to meet; curiosity and suspicion might be aroused, and their proposed arrangements might be made impossible. She was, however, leaving almost at once to join Belisarius, and she suggested

The secret meeting

that John should meet her near the park called Rufinianae, not far outside the city. It was a private estate of Belisarius, and there would be no difficulty.

To this John agreed, and the day was fixed.

When Theodora heard this story, she was delighted, and warmly approved of the plan. Her encouragement and assistance helped Antonina to carry the plan through its second and most dangerous phase. The interview with John might not be child's play. Theodora at once engaged the interest of Narses, the secretary of the private treasury, and Marcellus, the commander of the imperial guard. They agreed to go down to Rufinianae with an adequate force, and to investigate whether John were really guilty of planning a *coup d'état*. If he were, they would of course have no compunction about cutting him down. All this seems to have been arranged without consulting the emperor, whose friendship with John was well known, and who would be biased in his favour. The party of investigation had already started before the first whisper reached the ears of Justinian. He at once sent another personal friend of John's to him with the warning not, on any account, to meet Antonina secretly. . . . The advice was certainly generous. Had John taken it, he would have saved himself much trouble. But he is probably not the only man who has had a dislike of altering a programme, once it is fixed. He decided to go.

About midnight, close by the wall of the park, he met Antonina. He did not guess that behind the wall were Narses, Marcellus, and a party of guardsmen.

VIII

The meeting went off as arranged. . . . John, always impetuous, had already said in a loud and decisive voice quite enough to endanger his head, when Narses and **John's escape** Marcellus broke cover. Their attempt to take him, dead or alive, was unsuccessful. John was one of the very few civilians in the empire who were authorized to possess a comitatus; and some of his henchmen were waiting close at hand. In the clash which ensued Marcellus, not John, was cut down; John mounted, and galloped for Constantinople.

John the Cappadocian is a leading instance of the imprudence of losing one's nerve. Had he lived on water, he might have died great and respected. But the wine and the women that gilded John's dreams now wrought their revenge. When he arrived in the city he ought to have gone straight to Justinian and confessed everything —or nearly everything. The historian thought that the emperor would almost certainly have forgiven him his indiscretion and protected him from its results. But this was just what John could not make up his mind about. He was fool enough to take sanctuary. Before he had recovered himself, Theodora was with Justinian, and John's chance was over. He had lost it, not through his crime, but through his blunder.

John's false step

The fall of John was now complete. From the moment at which he entered sanctuary he never again filled the office of Praetorian prefect, nor possessed any public rank. He left, some time after, for Cyzicus, where in order to protect himself he entered the church, and took priest's orders. He was very unwilling, however, to confirm his ordination by actually celebrating the holy rites. He still hoped against hope that some day he might throw off his churchman's gown and return to his prefecture. But the day never came.

We need not too deeply pity John. The rules of the game, as played at Constantinople, did not forbid "kicking or hacking." He would have done the same to Antonina if she had not got her blow in first. . . . Justinian, in accepting the result, was kind to his old friend, and took care that the ex-minister should retain all his property, and should be adequately provided for.

Exit John.

IX

But when Antonina, full of satisfaction at a great work successfully accomplished, reached Belisarius in Syria, a horrid and alarming surprise awaited her.

Belisarius, in all good faith, had proceeded to his Syrian command, and taken up the duties. It was not a particularly thrilling time. The King of Kings was in the east fighting the Huns. The Roman army was in an unsatisfactory state, and called for the attention of the drill sergeant and the quartermaster rather than for grand strategy. The local commanders seemed to be gifted with a somewhat worrying combination of ignorance and inexperience. In accordance with his orders from the emperor, Belisarius arranged for a little raiding into Persian territory.

Surprise for Antonina

With Belisarius, Photius his step-son, the son of Antonina, was serving. Photius was emphatically not popular with his mother's friends, and they lost no opportunity of letting him know it. If he had taken part against her during the Italian campaign, we have no difficulty in perceiving a satisfactory explanation of their conduct. Photius, however, explained it differently. It was due, he thought, to Antonina writing constantly to set people against him. His method of conducting reprisals was liable to strengthen the prejudices of Antonina's friends, and to lend colour to their suspicions. Photius appeared before Belisarius with a man fresh from Constantinople, who had a scandalous tale to tell.

The work of Photius

Antonina had presumably not taken her husband into her confidence—or not sufficiently so—respecting the little comedy she had staged to explain her action in staying behind. This may have been a mistake. Belisarius was horrified when he heard the tale told from the point of view of the general public. He, Belisarius, had gone with idiotic and fatuous complacency beaming away to Syria, while the wicked Antonina . . . It was too much! He implored Photius to help him. They ought not, he said, to put up with this abominable treatment. Photius agreed. The latter reminded him, however, of the unfortunate fate of Macedonia. The two therefore swore most sacred and unbreakable oaths of eternal fidelity. They undertook to stand by each other through thick and thin. They swore so hard, that the suspicion is suggested that neither was quite satisfied about the other.

The military events proved dull and uninspiring, and far from adequate to divert the mind of Belisarius from other matters. Finding Nisibis too strong to be attacked, he gave his army a little experience in the siege of Sisauranon. While so engaged, he sent Harith with his Saracens, and a few Roman troops, to make a cavalry raid into Assyria. Harith went; but never came back again. This was worrying. The Goths and Vandals, moreover, did not stand the Mesopotamian heat very well. The subordinate commanders were nervous about Al Mundhir, who might swoop down upon them at any minute. When Belisarius, unable to take Sisauranon by force, at last talked it into surrender, the general opinion was still in favour of going home. In the middle of this, Antonina arrived. She was considerably surprised to find herself put under arrest by a stern and outraged husband, and committed to custody. What she said is not upon record—but few readers will have much difficulty in imagining it.

Belisarius in diffi- culties

On their reaching Roman territory, the truth at any rate about Harith emerged. That Arabian blackguard, not wanting to share his plunder with the rest of the army, had persuaded his Roman colleagues to go back by another road. Belisarius never caught him, and the army which had been besieging Sisauranon was poorer by its share of prize-money.[1]

X

Belisarius, with Antonina a very angry prisoner, was not clear as to his next step. The statements of Procopius hint that some suggestion was made to him that he should do away with her; but if so, the reception he gave to it did not encourage further explorations along the same lines. His perplexity was founded upon the substantial fact that he was very fond of Antonina. People who did not like Antonina found this so hard to credit that they exchanged fresh murmurs about the use of enchantment on her part. But who amongst us can really understand the inexplicable charm other people have for some one else?

What should he do with her?

If the problem were at deadlock here, it progressed actively elsewhere. While Belisarius was pondering over the problem of what to do with Antonina, Photius had set out for Ephesus, taking with him Antonina's steward Calligonus. By tickling up Calligonus judiciously with the whip at intervals, Photius induced him to make "confessions" which unfortunately have not been preserved

[1] Procopius thought that if Belisarius had gone forward he might have taken Ctesiphon, and recovered the prisoners taken at Antioch. Belisarius very evidently did not think so. (*Anecdota*, B′, ϛ′.)

for our benefit. . . . Calligonus, however, was probably quite sufficiently a man of the world to know that it did not much matter what he said, as long as it was false. If Photius wasted his time in extracting confessions from Calligonus, it cannot have been very long before he discovered that they were "dud."

Antonina's friends had not been idle. A fast express to Ephesus warned Theodosius in time. He hastily took sanctuary in the church of St. John the Apostle. He ought here to have been safe. The bishop of Ephesus was induced, however—Procopius says bribed—to surrender the fugitive. While these things were going on, another express had reached Constantinople, and had called upon the help of a mightier providence—the empress Theodora.

Theodora invoked

With the empress, Antonina's credit stood high; she had only to call, and the powers of Theodora were let loose to her aid. Before he had reached any definite conclusion on any subject, Belisarius received a summons to report himself at Constantinople with his wife. A similar call reached Photius. These commands were forms of polite arrest. Any disregard of them would have been followed by very substantial arrest indeed. But before the full effect could be exercised upon Photius, he had had Theodosius smuggled away from Ephesus. Calligonus however went with him to Constantinople.

With Belisarius and Photius a large number of their friends and associates were also arrested—not always in the polite form extended to the principals.

Belisarius was directed to apologize to his wife for his behaviour. If he did so with stiffness, it was no doubt because Antonina had expressed opinions about him which had somewhat hurt his feelings.

The next thing was to find Theodosius and Calligonus. Failure in this task was not accepted by Theodora as final. She meant to have the information she had asked for—and she proceeded to get it. The lash was used to exercise persuasion upon the subordinates of Photius. . . . Some of them, the historian whispers to us, disappeared and left no trace; some were sent into exile. . . . Photius himself was a tough customer. Though subjected to the more select treatment of being beaten with rods, he refused to divulge anything.[1]

Theodora to the rescue

Fortunately perhaps for Photius, before it became necessary to resort to stronger measures the empress's investigators had found Theodosius far away in Cilicia, where some of Photius's soldiers had been holding him prisoner. Beneath the magic of Theodora's imperious will and complete organization, Theodosius was wafted rapidly back to Constantinople, fed, washed, dressed, combed, and put upon his feet in a beautiful apartment. The empress sent for Antonina. . . . The historian, for once in a way, lets us follow Antonina right into the presence of the wonderful little Greek woman, and we catch some scent and suggestion of her silk-clad presence, her long-lashed eyes, and soft voice.

She said: "Dearest lady, I received a pearl yesterday, so beautiful that its like was never seen. If you would like to look at it, I will gladly show it to you."

Antonina and Theodora

---

[1] Procopius says that he did not betray Belisarius (*Anecdota*, Γ', δ'). It is not quite easy to understand, however, what there was to betray. Possibly the oaths they had sworn to one another would have seemed aggravation of their offence, as implying conspiracy.

Antonina was charmed.

Theodora stepped to a side room, and from it haled forth the clean, polished and blushing Theodosius.

XI

Antonina was obliged to finish, before the critical eyes of another and an even better actress, her comedy of How she had lied to her husband. The historian tells us that she did it well. Her clasped hands, her faint cries of gratitude, her tender exclamations of saviour, bene-factress and mistress, passed as adequate with Theodora. . . . It was a most pleasing episode. . . . And yet it was the empress, not Antonina, who undertook the care of Theodosius. Theodora took him over as a pet, and kept him some time. Her little dicky-bird,[1] however, did not last long. He died of dysentery—possibly origi-nated in some insanitary Cilician crag-castle where he had been imprisoned.

For Photius, there was none of these pleasant things. He remained in prison for three years; and although the prison was probably far from luxurious, we may be fairly sure that Theodora did not pay for his keep without some intelligible reason for the policy. Whatsoever her sus-picions may have been, she never obtained any direct confirmation of them from Photius.

Three times he escaped. The first time he took sanc-tuary at the altar of the Church of the Theotokos. He was taken away from it by force. The second time, he

Photius in custody

---

[1] Theodora playfully said that she would appoint him commander-in-chief of all the Roman armies (Procopius, *Anecdota*, Γ', ς')—a dig at Belisarius which some modern historians have taken quite seriously!

tried the font at Sancta Sophia. Theodora's minions, to the shocked consternation of clergy and people, did not worry about this either, as long as they got their man. They carried him off, and no one dared intervene. The third time involved some peculiar transactions. The prophet Zacharias, appearing to him in a dream, promised him assistance in escaping. What form the assistance took is not mentioned, but Photius found the information and help so reliable that he got clean away, and managed to reach Jerusalem. There he took the tonsure and became a monk. He remained unmolested in this status for many years, until both Theodora and Justinian were dead. . . . The glimpse we get of him in those later years shows that he was by no means a perfectly pleasant person.[1]

The story of the three escapes of Photius from prison is an indication that he was not without powerful friends, whose money and influence could penetrate even the defences of Theodora. His faith to them was not unrewarded. If we knew their names, we might be singularly enlightened respecting the inwardness of some of these efforts to destroy Antonina and Belisarius.

Procopius remarks that Belisarius never made any effort to carry out his oaths of faithfulness to Photius— **Belisarius and Photius** so apparently he was not among these powerful friends. The historian thought that it was this ignoring of his solemn oath which was the cause why Belisarius had bad luck for the rest of his life.[2] But we shall presently see

---

[1] Bury, *History of the Later Roman Empire*, II. 61, f. n. 2, quoting John of Ephesus, *Hist. Eccl.* Part 3, Book i. 31, 32.

[2] How little ground there was for this assertion can be seen by the success of Belisarius as narrated in the next section, following Procopius, *History*, II. xx. xxi.

that there was another explanation of that ill luck, much
more satisfying to the modern mind. And in order
to be quite clear on that subject, it is well to note that
Belisarius is not likely to have been particularly fond
of Theodora after the events of this year. He may have
been wrong in his actions and misled in his views; but
only by degrees did he gradually return to his normal
state of feeling.

XII

He was helped, next spring, by the stirring news that
he was at last seriously needed in Syria. Khosru had
planned another great campaign, aimed, this time, at
Jerusalem.[1] A vast army came up the western bank of the
Euphrates. To oppose this in the field was impossible to
the local troops. They could only take refuge in the
strongholds and watch. . . .

The
Persian
campaign
A. D. 542

The story of Antioch, however, was not destined to be
repeated. How much difference a single man can sometimes make we see in the actions of Belisarius. He rode
express from Constantinople, and arrived in Syria without an army, and with only the equipment he stood up
in, but keen to get to business. One of the earliest events
that chanced after his arrival was a letter from Hierapolis,
where Justus (the emperor's nephew) Bouzes and other
officers had joined forces. They invited him to join them;
and they reported that Khosru was rapidly advancing,
and that his objective was unknown.

Belisarius felt that this letter displayed too much in-

---

[1] A Persian conquest of Egypt (which former ages had shown to be quite practicable) would give Persia control of the Red Sea trade route to Ethiopia and India.

terest in the objectives of Khosru, and too little in his own. He established his headquarters at Europus on the Euphrates, and ordered all available troops to rendezvous there. To Hierapolis he wrote, saying that if Khosru were not intending to attack Roman subjects the plan of stopping in Hierapolis was sound, for safety first is a prudent rule; but if he were proposing to attack a choice and undefended province of Justinian, it would be their duty to fall fighting, rather than to save their own skins. He concluded his letter by summoning them promptly to Europus. Leaving Justus with a garrison, they came.

The King of Kings, on hearing that the famous conqueror of the Goths and Vandals was in front of him, was impressed. He felt the necessity of knowing something of this dangerous enemy, whom he had not before encountered; and he sent one of his confidential secretaries, Abandanes, to report upon what kind of man Belisarius was. An excuse was easily found for asking an interview.

Bluff as a science

Belisarius perfectly understood the object with which the request was made. The handsome little pageant which he staged for the benefit of his visitor might have been advertised as The Perfect Commander and His Ideal Army. Abandanes was deeply impressed. His report to Khosru gave a highly favourable description of Belisarius and his men, and carefully pointed out the disadvantages of the Persian position. Suppose, said Abandanes, that the King of Kings were victorious—it would only be over a servant of Justinian; whereas if he were defeated, how damaging it would be to his dignity! The Romans, moreover, had their fortresses in which to take refuge in the event of defeat; but if the Persians were beaten upon this ground, not even a messenger would get back to

Persia. . . . These arguments were most effective in persuading Khosru. He decided upon retreat.

The difficulty was to choose the route. After consideration, he resolved to cross the river and march eastward. Belisarius recognized that with his much smaller forces it was totally impossible to prevent Khosru from doing anything he liked. To have frightened off a great army was, however, quite enough for credit. He therefore raised no serious objection when the Persians began to bridge the river and to cross. He took up, indeed, a benevolent attitude, as if it had been purely by his grace and generosity that the Persians were allowed to cross the river.

The
Persian
with-
drawal

Khosru, as soon as he was over, sent to Belisarius calling attention to the friendliness of his own actions, and notifying him that he expected peace envoys from Justinian. Belisarius then crossed, and sent a message warmly acknowledging his action, and promising that the envoys would soon come. He requested Khosru to treat as friendly country, the territory through which he was about to march. Khosru promised, if he might have hostages. John, the son of Basilius of Edessa, was sent, much (as the historian informs us) against his will. The whole transaction was thought a much greater glory to Belisarius than his conquest of Geilamir or Witigis; for with almost every possible disadvantage against him he had induced a much superior army to retire without fighting.

The King of Kings had captured and razed Callinicum before the hostage arrived; but from the moment of John's arrival, the attitude of Khosru was strictly correct. He retired, without further military action, over his own borders.

XIII

But besides the reason known to the Greek historian, there was another reason which may have induced Khosru to retreat without fighting. That summer, the plague broke out at Pelusium, and he is likely enough to have received the news while on campaign.

Pelusium is in Egypt; and it is possible that the outbreak was originally due to transmission by the ships engaged in the Indian trade. The pestilence spread. Westward and southward, it reached Alexandria, and then it reached Nubia and Ethiopia. But its worst effects were seen when it spread eastward into Palestine, and from Palestine into Syria. It was experienced in Constantinople. That winter, it hung more or less suspended. The retreat of Khosru had been nothing but prudence. He had left Syria just in time.

Earthquake, war and the comet Sword Fish had fought against Justinian. A much more terrible enemy was now threatening. As the spring returned the plague spread with increasing rapidity and deadliness. By the middle of spring it was in Constantinople. It swept through Asia Minor, Armenia and Mesopotamia. For all the caution of Khosru, it entered Persian territory. Westward, it reached Africa, penetrated Italy, and passed the Alps into Gaul. Men might flee from earthquake and war, and at a pinch might shut their eyes to the grisly threats of the comet Sword Fish; but they could not flee from the pestilence, which with seven-leagued boots and hideous unreason pursued them and felt for them, like some blind Cyclops, which slew without knowing why it slew.

Plague (Summer A. D. 542)

The Plague spreads A. D. 543

CHAPTER X

THE DESTRUCTION OF THE INSTRUMENT:
(II) THE WORK OF THEODORA

I

THE first approach of the terror in Constantinople was heralded by spectres and apparitions—not those homely and domestic ghosts from which the householder can hide under the blankets, but strangers out of the void, as novel and as terrifying as the wild Hun of the steppes. Those who experienced the encounter reported that the strangers struck them; and where they had been struck, the deadly sign of the plague—the bubonic swelling— followed . . . Some of these died raving of prodigies and strange things, curdling to the blood of those who nursed them. Some fell into heavy sleep, and slept their lives away. If nursed and fed they ate without waking; and if not, they would die of starvation in their sleep. . . . Generally speaking, the Christian is armed against supernatural terrors. But those who, on meeting these spectral visitors, defended themselves with the Holy Name, found that the weapon would not act. Though they fled to sanctuary, they found no refuge. . . . And prosaic physicians, who examined professionally into the terror, explained the reason. The spectres were not there. They were delusions of people already sick. . . . It was not in the streets of Constantinople, but in the minds of men, that they walked and struck. Even in sleep they

The portents

The plague demons

appeared to the doomed persons, warning them with iron touch.

If any imagined that because they had received no warning, they would go free, they were undeceived. The larger number of the patients were struck down without preliminary warning, with a light fever which seemed too trifling a thing for a man to die of. But a day or two later the bubonic swelling appeared: and they were in the grip of the plague.[1]

II

The cases at first were not numerous, and the statistics of mortality in Constantinople hardly rose above the normal figures. Then they grew: and they grew greater; and at last they rose in a steady peak to the terrifying and overwhelming numbers which are among the most soul-shattering effects of great pestilences. The plague lasted, in all, as a serious visitation, about four months. For three of these it raged with epidemic violence. For some unknown period—perhaps a fortnight or three weeks, but hardly more—it was at its height,[2] a silent, invisible, in-

The
mortality
begins

[1] The great historic pestilences have been reported with differences of detail which make it probable that they did not exactly repeat themselves. Most of them do seem, however, to have belonged to one type or family; they were not contagious or infectious diseases as commonly understood, but were rat-diseases spread by the bite of fleas which had absorbed blood from the black rat. The plague in Europe was stayed rather through the activities of the brown rat, which killed out the black, than by sanitation, which did not make its mark till much later. See Bell, *The Great Plague in London*, p. 247 et seq.

[2] The mortality reached 5,000, 10,000 or even more per day. (Procopius, II. xxiii. 1.) John of Ephesus gives 12,000 or 16,000 per day. As 5,000 a day for three months would mean 450,000 deaths, we must no doubt grade these figures. The higher numbers must refer to a few days at the peak of the crisis. The government seems to have made a real effort to gather reasonably accurate figures, though Procopius suggests that it was not always possible to do so. J. B. Bury, (*History of the Later Roman Empire*, II. 65) thinks that the total mortality at Constantinople might be round about 300,000.

tangible thing slaying its hundreds of thousands with an irresistible force which filled Constantinople with corpses and with fear. . . . No battle—not even those in which high explosive and poison gas have been used without stint—ever spread such irresistible and such terrible death. But it had one grim likeness to battle—no one could tell who would be taken and who would be left.

Constantinople came as well out of the test as most cities which have suffered a like ordeal. In western Europe, centuries later, the Black Death drove people to despair and to feverish enjoyment of the moment: but the same terror crowded the churches and converted the sinners of Constantinople—at least for the time being, which is as much as can be expected. In a time in which chaos reigned supreme, and all the ordinary life of the city was entirely suspended, exhausted families still clung to delirious patients, and fed those who lay lost in sleep. Grim men, whose names nobody chronicled, wheeled the ambulances down to the waterside, stacked high with dead; dug the great common graves, and stamped the earth firmly down on those who lay there. People of wealth and distinction died abandoned, unwashed and **The terror** hungry, because their household had been wiped out, and no one was left. Slaves roamed about in unexpected and unwelcomed freedom, because the steward who handed out the daily rations, and the master who paid for them, were dead. The trade of the city was completely dislocated. How to obtain the common necessities of life became a serious question, and not for the poor alone. Many houses were closed; sometimes because every one within was dead; sometimes because frightened people had locked themselves away, and would not open. . . . Their precautions were useless. The plague penetrated locked doors and closed windows and caught them; while on the other hand it was soon found by those concerned that the physician might work in the midst of the pestilence without fear, and the men who dug the graves and buried the dead had no cause for alarm. It was quite certain that the plague was not catching. It did not pass from person to person.

One of the most disturbing and demoralizing aspects of the plague was its apparent irrationality. The medical science of the day—which was very far from despicable —was baffled. No method of treatment could be relied upon; most prophecies proved false. The disease could not be classified under any known head. Attempts to understand its cause and its nature were fruitless. One thing only seemed clear. If the bubonic swelling sappurated, the patient might live. But this event could not be compelled or controlled. Nothing could be controlled. All that could be done was to hang on to faith and sanity till the thing should be past—if it were destined to pass. For all that any one could tell, the whole human race might be perishing. In a year's time, the sea might be lapping and the wind wailing round the coasts of a manless world.

III

One advantage attached to Constantinople. The city was not left to chance help. As soon as the emergency began to become visible, Justinian appointed one of his private secretaries to deal with it, and provided financial help and military aid. The imperial guardsmen, under the

Organization

direction of Theodorus, formed a sanitary corps which began to tackle the work for which private effort was inadequate. Those households which could, were left to nurse their own sick and bury their own dead. But as the mortality began to climb the steep to its height, all private effort became more and more futile. The cemeteries were filled to overflowing. In vain they were extended. At last all people could do was to dump bodies by the quayside and leave them.

The guardsmen—probably with assistance from unemployed persons glad to earn a little money and food —proceeded to collect the dead out of the thousand streets of Constantinople, and out of the silent houses where doors had to be burst in, to find perhaps only corpses inside, or pale and frightened people who thought these new-comers the Plague-Demons. At the quayside the bodies were counted and checked, stacked in barges and transported over the Golden Horn to Galata. Here the huge communal graves were dug. As the mortality reached its summit, even this was not enough. The dead arrived quicker than the trenches could be dug. They were dropped into the great towers of the fortifications of Galata, and left there. When the wind was in the east, the city knew it.

How long the mortality stayed at this nightmare pitch, we do not know. How soon it began to drop; how fast it fell on its downward grade, no pen recorded. It was probably towards the end that Justinian himself fell sick. He lay for some time between life and death.[1]

Justinian falls sick

[1] Theodora evidently never took the plague. If the surmise is accurate, that the disease was flea-borne, that elaborate toilette of hers was probably more effective than armour plate as a defence. It was noticed at a subsequent visitation that

The plague had been raging throughout the east. For the time being it had put an effective stop to the war. The Persian army was affected, and Khosru retreated into Assyria, which up to this point had been comparatively free from the sickness. There was even some talk of peace, which Justinian did not encourage. The news of his own illness therefore found the Roman army quiet in quarters in Syria, with plenty of time upon its hands. The commanders had nothing to do; and as the fatal habit of human beings is, they talked.

Instinctively, their thoughts drifted to the really interesting problem. Suppose Justinian died? What then about Theodora? The partnership had been too close and too effective for one of the two to die, and the other to fade meekly into the background. There was the problem of Theodora's money. She controlled very large resources, which Justinian had deliberately placed in her hands for her own protection. While she held these, it would be no simple matter to displace her from her position. They gave her an independence which would make very difficult the position of any emperor who succeeded Justinian. And yet the traditions of the empire certainly did not contemplate the rule of a woman. If Justinian died, a man ought to succeed him. All the same, it was very improbable that Theodora, with her energy, her power and her skill, would give way. It was quite likely that she could secure the ratification of her own title at Constantinople, or alternatively nominate any one she chose.

The problem of Theodora

women suffered less than men. (Bury, *History of the Later Roman Empire,* II. 66. f. n. 4. quoting Agathias v. 10.) The bitter assertion of Procopius, that the worst people came off best, probably reflects the same fact.

Most of the military commanders held old-fashioned views about women. They lived too near Asia.

Who really spoke the incriminating words is uncertain: but some one said: "I shall refuse to acknowledge any one imposed upon us by Constantinople."

IV

For Theodora, waiting day by day and hour by hour for news of Justinian's condition, the matter was one of life and death. She is not likely to have worried much about the theory of woman's true place in the world. Steel will bite and hemlock kill both women and men alike: and craft and courage and force can be employed in self-defence equally well by both. We need not doubt that, waiting for the news which should decide the future, she meant to use to the utmost every weapon there was in defence of her man and herself: of them both, if it might be—of herself, if necessary.

Justinian
recovers

Justinian lived. Possibly his abstemious life worked for him; but whatsoever the cause, the bubonic swelling sappurated, the deadly poison was drained out of his system, and he began to recover.

When the news reached Syria, the military commanders had uncomfortable recollections of words which might be repeated, with unpleasant consequences. Some of them hastened to be first in the field, and reported the episode. Theodora was still in charge. She called them all to Constantinople. When they arrived there, Bouzes vanished. What had become of him, no one knew, and no one dared to enquire. Against Belisarius nothing was ever proved, but he was dismissed from his command, his

licence to employ a comitatus was revoked, and he was
placed under courteous arrest. This meant that he was
not entitled to receive the visits of his friends. The command in Syria was handed over to Martin.

The natural inference from these severe measures is
that Belisarius (who was not pleased with the conduct of
Theodora) had spoken the incriminating words, and
that Bouzes had approved them. Justinian and Theodora
owed Belisarius a little too much, and they knew him to
be too loyal a man, for sharper measures; but he himself
was the last person to grasp that fact, from which it is a
fair deduction that his conscience was not as clear as it
should have been.

It was two years and four months later before a dazed
and blinking figure sought again the places and the people that had once known Bouzes. He had spent that time
in solitary confinement in a dark cell in Theodora's palace of Hormisdas, never knowing day from night, and
never hearing the voice of his gaoler. . . . What recantation he had made, what guarantees he had given, and
what agreement he had come to with Theodora, has not
been recorded: but he was released from the bastille, and
restored to his employments. He had had his lesson, and
although it was a sharp one, there have been men who
had more to complain of than he.

The fate of Bouzes was of interest to Bouzes: but perhaps it never mattered much to any one else. With Belisarius it was different. The revocation of his licence to
maintain a comitatus threw upon the market those
fighting men who had been the real conquerors of
Africa and of Italy. Such an occasion was historic.
There was a scramble to engage them. Lots were cast in

Bouzes
arrested

order to ensure fairness in distribution. Finally they were dispersed among various military commanders and, so Procopius says, "some of the palace eunuchs"— by which last he perhaps means Narses. . . . Not only so, but the private treasury of Belisarius was seized, and he no longer had the power of maintaining men, even if he had retained the authority to do so.

Disgrace of Belisarius

Few episodes in the history of Constantinople impressed the imagination of the man in the street as did the fall of Belisarius. Its visible effect would have been far greater, had it not followed immediately after such a cataclysm as the great pestilence. No one was in a mood to spare much attention or pity for any one save himself. Yet what happened to Belisarius went echoing along the ages, even if in strange and legendary forms, until it found a home in modern English poetry.

Men stared in incredulity and wonder at the sight of a Belisarius no longer rich, no longer great or courted by others, but a solitary, somewhat gloomy man, wrapped in his own thoughts, starting at shadows, and looking for the assassin's knife at every corner.

V

Was it just? Was it right? Wait a moment! It was not brought about only for the obvious reasons. The causes were much more complex. Belisarius had started the process when he wrecked the scheme of the Italian treaty —the effects of which were growing very visible now. He had hastened it when he put his trust in Photius rather than in his wife. It was his own fault if he bore a grudge against Theodora for compelling him to make his

Case against Belisarius

peace with Antonina. The peace had been a hollow one. He had now carried his grudge to the point of a threat of civil war. . . . When the blow fell, and broke him, he had only himself to blame.

Theodora was not at all a likely person to palter or fumble over such a threat as he had been guilty of. She threw her thunderbolt with a promptitude that any one who knew her might have expected. Pray, what had Belisarius himself expected? . . . There was a strain of weakness in him. He pitied himself too much, with the self-conscious pity of the tragedian. . . . Theodora had no pity of that kind. She had been brought up on the comic stage.

There was subtlety in the way in which Theodora, starting upon the case at this extreme end, began to work back steadily to the beginning. Belisarius might have spared himself the trouble of looking for assassins at every corner. He was not going to be treated quite so seriously as that. He was dealing with a comedienne. She let him worry and fret to his heart's content, until he had worried himself into black despair. He realized, at last, the awful truth. He had lost everything! He had been the second man in the empire; and wealth, power, fame, admiration—all were gone.

His
downfall

He attended at court as usual. There was a great difference between the old Belisarius, with his splendid retainers, and the present one, with his half dozen cheap servants. The stage was set for him, although he did not know it. He did not see anything funny, poor fellow! in the fact that emperor and empress gave him the cold shoulder, and that he was openly laughed at by their minions and toadies. He went home one evening, nothing achieved, nothing forwarded, looking cautiously back at every corner for danger, though none came. When he reached his house, he walked into the hall and sat down upon his couch, an utterly disheartened man.[1] He felt at the end of all things.

Antonina was walking to and fro. Apparently they were barely upon speaking terms: and Procopius tells us quite definitely that she was not a party to the events which followed. Theodora was the sole author of the thrilling little sketch of The Forgiving Wife.

Immediately after sunset a palace officer named Quadratus appeared unexpectedly at the door. He had passed across the courtyard without being noticed—probably His despair because there was no longer any adequate watch at the gate. Quadratus announced that he was the bearer of a message from the empress.

This was the last straw. Satisfied that his death warrant had come, the wretched Belisarius drew up his hands and feet, and laid himself upon the bed in a suitable position.

Quadratus, however, remained at the door holding his letter, and presently Belisarius interrupted his dramatic pose for the prosaic task of receiving and reading it. It was not at all what he expected.

According to Procopius, it ran: "You are not unaware, Excellency, of all your offences against me; but my debt to your wife is such that for her sake I have made up my mind to pardon you; and I give her your life as a present from me. Do not, for the future, worry

---

[1] Procopius here (*Anecdota*, Δ′, ε′–ζ′) a little overshoots his mark. He supplies particulars concerning the disgraceful and unmanly emotions of Belisarius which the latter is certainly not likely to have supplied. But if Belisarius did not, who did?

THE EAST ROMAN FRONTIER A.D. 530

CASPIAN SEA

PERSIA

Persepolis

PERSIAN GULF

R. Araxes

R. Tigris

R. Euphrates

Ctesiphon

Theodosiopolis

LAZICA

Amida

Daras

Nisibis

Samosata

Edessa

Callinicum

Circesium

Hiera-polis

Chalcis

Palmyra

DESERT

Antioch

Jerusalem

BLACK SEA

Constantinople

Nicomedia

Ancyra

ROMAN EMPIRE

CYPRUS

Alexandria

EGYPT

ILLYRIA

CRETE

MEDITERRANEAN

AFRICA

Approx. Scale

0 100 200 300

English Miles

about your life or fortune; your conduct will show whether you are a worthy husband."

Belisarius belonged to an age and to a country somewhat more demonstrative than our own. In the reaction of the moment his excitement and joy were such that he fell prostrate with emotion at Antonina's feet, embraced them and kissed them, declaring that she was his saviour to whom he owed all, and devoting himself thenceforward to being no longer merely a husband, but her faithful slave.

Belisarius pardoned

It is a pity that we do not know what Antonina said in reply.

VI

Belisarius had now acquired the right attitude of mind respecting Theodora, and had acknowledged her good will in reconciling him with Antonina. All that remained was for him to finish unravelling his sins by similarly putting himself right in respect of the Italian situation. This, unfortunately, was not quite so easy.

The rehabilitation of Belisarius included certain modifications. His wealth was not restored to him intact. One third was deducted. Sixty centenars of gold—a treasure of six thousand pounds weight bullion—were returned. Even this was a much larger sum than it seemed altogether safe for a subject to possess. He was therefore linked to the imperial family by the betrothal of his only daughter and heiress, Joannina, to Anastasius, the grandson of Theodora.

Whether Theodora perfectly comprehended all the problems involved we have no means of discovering.

We know that she was not overwhelmed with enthusiasm over plans for reconquering the world-state. Her own point of view (as we have seen) was all in favour of cultivating the loyalty of a definite, circumscribed eastern realm. She therefore was not much concerned with some of the consequences which might conceivably flow from her treatment of Belisarius. The breaking up of his comitatus was a historical event of great importance. This comitatus, and nothing else, had been the military power which forced a drawn war with Kobad, had suppressed the Nika sedition, overthrown Geilamir, worn down Witigis, and overawed Khosru. It, chosen with care, trained through many years of constant association, connected with its leader by quick sympathy and close familiarity, was the core of the imperial army. A woman might think that the same men, dispersed and scattered in a dozen other military corps with different leaders, would still pull the same weight. It was a disastrous error. Their power had been in their association, their cumulation. All the deeds they had done were due to their corporate strength, not to the simple addition of one man to another man. It is probable that even Antonina very imperfectly grasped these ideas. The explanations and expostulations of Belisarius would not have their full effect upon hearers who did not understand the values with which he was dealing. . . . And it was not safe for him to say too much. He was lucky to have got off as lightly as he did.

Problems involved

We must not forget the other side of the case. Theodora might have replied that no subject ought to possess a power greater than was possessed by his sovereign, and that if Belisarius claimed the right to do so, then he was

Case for Theodora

logically committed to the responsibility of sovranty.
Belisarius had actually employed the power so placed
in his hands to modify, without authority, and with disastrous results, the commands of his sovereign. He had
threatened to employ it against any future sovereign
who did not meet with his approval. . . . If these actions were not questionable, what actions ever could be?
If Belisarius did not mean any harm, he was all the more
dangerous. Theodora could make out a very respectable
case for claiming that it was much more important to
safeguard the authority of the emperor, and to maintain the inward strength of the governing power, than
to conquer Italy. For one was essential, while the other
was merely incidental.

Whether, in this matter, Theodora were in the right
or Belisarius, in any case Theodora was the person who
had the deciding word. She decided; and we shall see
what came of her decision.

VII

Even though the occasion and the manner had their
awkwardness, the reconciliation between Belisarius and
Antonina seems to have been sincere and permanent.
Their relations were never again disturbed. The two re-
sumed their old footing. But the re-establishment of
complete confidence between them had one or two
singular results. It must have been at this time that
Procopius ceased to be an ally of Belisarius.[1] When, some

Belisarius
reconciled
with
Antonina

---

[1] The suggestion is Dr. Hodgkin's (*Italy and Her Invaders*, IV. 452–453.) It
is by no means certain; but it is very probable, and the assumption helps to
clear up the difficulties of the narrative.

years later, the historian began to write the scandalous
chapters of the *Anecdota*, he betrayed the reason. He had
been, and he remained to the end, among the enemies of
Antonina and Theodora. He was a partisan of Photius,
and he may have been one of the men who had influenced
Belisarius against his wife. Photius had gone. Now Procopius also went. . . . He departed, in his mind bitterly
charging the great soldier with the desertion of Photius,
and raging against Antonina.[1]

Belisarius lost no time in putting in his claim to a new
command. Antonina would not hear of the Persian
border, where so much of an unpleasant nature had happened to them. Ultimately, it was decided that Belisarius should go to Italy—the most appropriate place
for him, from Theodora's point of view. But it was not
as imperator that he was to go. The rank he received
was that of Constable—*Comes Stabuli*: which was a
rank of the second class.

The plague itself had been a revolution: and it is quite
conceivable that in the midst of the changes which had
transformed a world, Belisarius felt less acutely the
changes in his own fortunes. Justinian, mending steadily
during the summer months, was never quite the man he
had been. The first sharp edge had been taken off his
mind. . . . The results of a great pestilence are almost
inconceivable to those who have never seen one. The
hundreds of thousands of deaths, which had swept away
families, friends and acquaintances, had destroyed the
familiar social landmarks. They replaced with strange

**Results of
the plague**

---

[1] Antonina, he savagely remarks, was at least sixty! It is a form of argument
giving great scope for retort. If old age be a crime, we are all would-be
criminals.

faces the old accustomed persons: and in many instances
there were no replacements, but crumbling houses and
empty corners; fields half-cultivated, or falling back
into waste; shipping lines that no longer sailed, shops
that remained permanently closed, hammers that were
for ever still. . . . Even the physical features of the
earth seem changed when the people who inhabit them
become different. The natural recuperative power of
humanity soon sets to work to refill the world: but it
takes time. Many a year passed before the world recovered from the blast of death which had swept over it.
When it recovered, it was a new world.

The entire administration of the empire was affected
by the economic difficulties created by the plague. Every
branch of activity needed to be surveyed and revised;
but of none can this have been so true as of the financial.
The system of taxation was soon in confusion, and it
was scarcely restored in Justinian's time. Wealth had
shifted, vanished, and emerged as features of a land-
scape sometimes do after earthquake. To get all this
back into familiar order was work for many years. As
one result, Justinian's government was now a poor government, hard put to it to get in its revenues, and face
to face with passionate outcry from taxpayers.

The empire impover-ished

Justinian was therefore very unwilling to spend
money. For the rest of his reign prudence indicated the
utmost economy; and even though he cut expenditure
below the level of prudence, it remained difficult to obtain sufficient revenue for the imperial services.

Special arrangements thus needed to be made for the
Italian command of Belisarius. He was still a very rich
man. The understanding finally reached was that he

should make his command self-supporting. There was no particular reason to doubt that he could do it. The previous wars in Africa and Italy had certainly paid for themselves. . . . But it was an innovation that, instead of being under the financial control of the government, an imperial commander should have an independent treasury, not controlled or surveyed by the government, but supplied and expended by himself alone. . . . Justinian's ambition of restoring the empire to its old boundaries was already a dream when it had to be carried out by methods of such a kind. Political unity, and unified

Belisarius returns to Italy

political control, are always based upon the control of finance; and an independent treasury for the Italian command almost inevitably involved an independent Italian kingdom.

In some quarters—so Procopius says—it was confidently expected that Belisarius would in fact raise the banner of independence as soon as he was well away from Constantinople. Procopius may be referring only to his own expectation. If so, he was disappointed. Belisarius did not consider the events which had just passed an adequate reason for revolt. Procopius attributes his attitude to the unaccountable influence of Antonina over her husband.

VIII

But Belisarius, whatsoever his faults may have been, was wiser than some of his critics. He knew his own limitations. He knew himself to be just a military expert —a specialist whose ability as a soldier did not in the least imply any ability as a statesman. He would not

have lasted six months as a would-be sovran, whether
at Byzantium or elsewhere. He was not really interested
in the sort of work a sovereign has to do—the sort of
work at which Justinian was ready and willing to work **The new**
sixteen hours a day. If Belisarius required any advice on **Justinian**
this head, he needed only to watch the development of
affairs in Constantinople. He was not the type of man
who enjoyed facing the difficulties which Justinian now
had to face.

The emperor had been struck down in the zenith of
his days, and the fullness of his career. He emerged from
that valley of the shadow of death to find that the world
had suffered a sea-change. Everything was now wrong.
While twice two still, in theory, made four, he could
only rely in practice upon receiving three and a half.
And while in principle it was just as far from Jericho
to Jerusalem as it was from Jerusalem to Jericho, in
practice there was a frictional drag that falsified the
count. A spiritual challenge lay before him. His hopes,
his ideals, his aims might now be—and perhaps were—
impossible. But they were not cancelled. . . . As in the
case of Balaam, the Lord said to him, Go!—but was angry
because he went.

Justinian himself, a little blunted, a little less capable
than of old, was quite prepared to press on inexorably
along the old path. The peasant blood in him was an
unbending, a stubborn element, which did not know
how to retreat. But it grew ever clearer that he would
press on almost alone. The band of faithful who surrounded him was dwindling. . . . Procopius wrote it **Legend of**
all down in his history. The subjects of Justinian saw, **the Demon**
with awe and a touch of terror, the growing sternness of **Emperor**

Cæsar, as he realized that he confronted the impossible;
the growing resolution in his heart, as all human resolution became vain. Startled sentinels, drowsing at their
posts in the dark, at the dead of night, heard the meas-
ured footfall of a man, and saw Cæsar pass by. The
story was told that he had been seen pacing the cor-
ridors of the palace without a head. . . . He had always
been a restless man, unable to keep still. Now his rest-
lessness became terrifying. The legend grew—the legend
of the Demon Emperor,[1] who, like Philip Vanderdecken,
had set himself to carry out his purposes in the teeth of
the will of God.

Procopius reflected the ideas of a large proportion
of the Roman governing classes when he embroidered
and decorated this theme. As they realized the cost, they
shrank from a policy which proposed to reach its end
in spite of war, plague, famine, earthquake, and the
probable ruin of nations. . . . In many respects they
were wrong, and Justinian was right; they were foolish
and incapable, and he was a wise and strong man. But
they were right in one matter—he was now beginning
to set himself against the common sense of things, and
against the stream of history. . . . No one can doubt

Meaning of
the legend
the terror and hatred that inspired the men for whom
Procopius spoke. They were shocked at his determination, frightened at the sternness with which he set his

---

[1] Procopius, *Anecdota*, IB′, δ′–ι′. The historian tells more than one story of
Justinian being seen without a head. On one occasion it was observed (not by
Procopius, of course!) to fade out like the Cheshire cat. The legend is worth
study, for it is one of the rare cases in which we can identify the origin of such
a legend, not among ignorant and illiterate people, but at the hands of a highly
educated writer.

heart. A man so hard, who would work all night, and was scarcely ever seen to rest—such a man could hardly be human. So the legend grew.

Belisarius was far indeed from any such temper. He had no ambition to sit in such seats, or to confront such problems. He preferred the simpler life of a soldier.

The events connected with the recall, the disgrace, the rehabilitation of Belisarius, and the arrangements for his new command, took some nine months. During May, in the year after the plague, Belisarius set out for Dalmatia, this time taking Antonina with him. In Thrace he began the collection of a new comitatus. It was not a large one, for when he reached Salona and met Vitalius, the Illyrian commander, their united forces amounted only to 4,000 men [1]—hardly a full sized army. After assisting in the work of organizing the relief of Otranto, he set out for Pola in Istria. Thence he reached Ravenna.

Belisarius was no worse a soldier than ever he had been. The curious weakness which now marked his conduct of war was due to no failing of his own, but to the unmistakable fact that his wonderful instrument of victory had been taken away from him. A promising campaign in the province of Aemilia, south of the Padus, came to a lamentable end by the desertion of the Illyrian troops, who were unpaid, and who heard that the Huns were raiding in Illyria. The whole of Aemilia had therefore to be abandoned. Bologna was lost; and Auximum, so hard-won a few years earlier, followed. A whole year's work by the conqueror of Geilamir and Witigis

Situation in Italy

---

[1] At the end of the Italian war in 540, the comitatus of Belisarius was 7,000 strong. (Procopius, *History*, VII. i. 20.)

amounted to the relief of Otranto, and the refortifica-
tion of Pesaro; and that was all he had to show for his
pains.

In the meantime, the attention and the resources of
Justinian had been engaged elsewhere—on that very
Persian frontier the command of which Antonina had
refused.

IX

For the moment the eyes of all the empire were on
Khosru. The Goths could wait; the question of the reconquest of Italy could wait; the question which Khosru
raised was whether the empire could maintain itself at
all. His assault was of a type before which the Goths
paled into insignificance. It began by an attack upon the
city of Edessa, which for the time being became a representative position. If Edessa went, the whole Romano-
Persian frontier would cave in. If it held out, Khosru
would come no further. All the men, money and brains
that Justinian could gather he poured into Edessa.

Mesopo-
tamia

Edessa had a legendary history which made the city
especially significant. According to old Bishop Eusebius,[1]
the archives of Edessa in his day, during the reigns of
Diocletian and Constantine, still contained a letter written by Abgarus, king of Edessa, to Jesus Christ, inviting
him to Edessa. "I have here a little city and an honest,
which will suffice us both," wrote Abgarus: and the inhabitants of the "little city" preserved the tradition
with pride. . . . They were still prouder of the letter

---

[1] Eusebius, *H.E.* II. 13. Edessa also possessed a miraculous handkerchief, sent
by Jesus to Abgarus, bearing an imprint of the sacred countenance.

from Jesus which answered Abgarus, explaining why he could not come to Edessa, but promising after his assumption to send a disciple. This disciple was Thaddaeus, the brother of St. Thomas.

If the tradition had stopped at this point it would have been quite sufficiently impressive; but it went on to maintain that Jesus had said, in his letter, that *no Persians would ever be able to take Edessa.*[1] It was this assertion which especially provoked the Fire-Worshipping Persians, and encouraged the Edessaeans. A trial of strength over Edessa was not only a military, but a religious struggle.

Even so, the Edessaeans numbered a strong party not devoured with eagerness for a war. They would have agreed to pay Khosru any practicable indemnity. Khosru began, therefore, by demanding an indemnity so large that the city could not pay it: and when he was refused, he invested Edessa.

Siege of Edessa

Khosru had no intention of wasting time and money over a blockade. On the eighth day of the siege his preparations for attack became visible. Squared trunks of trees were laid out in a great rectangle; then a mound was built of earth within the trunks, and a fresh layer of great baulks laid on this; after which a layer of rough stones followed, and the whole unit was repeated. As the mound rose, it was extended and pushed forward. Its object was to command the defences of Edessa, and to give access to the battlements. That it would succeed in these aims was as certain as anything human could be.

The building of the mound was delayed by the sallies

---

[1] Evagrius (*H.E.* IV. 26.) denies the genuineness of this legend and correctly points out that the alleged passage is not in the letter as given by Eusebius.

of the garrison. The Huns did especially deadly work, one of them, named Argek, killing twenty-seven of the working party single-handed. But Khosru ordered up troops to meet these sallies; and it became quite obvious that the building of the mound could not be stopped by such means. The citizens tried the expedient of negotiation; but although their deputation was headed by an old tutor of Khosru, who had enjoyed high favour in the Persian court, it could not obtain possible terms. Khosru meant to have Edessa. Another deputation was simply shown out without seeing the King of Kings. . . . Brains were set to work, and some genius suggested heightening the wall. As the besiegers could easily keep pace with this, no object was achieved, and the plan was abandoned. Things looked very unpromising for Edessa.

Danger of the city

Frustrated in all these expedients, the idea of mining the mound was taken up. Edessa is not altogether the place where we might have expected to find men capable of such a type of work; but the skilled direction was obtained, the shafts sunk, and the tunnels driven under the mound. As the excavators reached the danger line, the sound of their digging was detected by the Persians, who immediately sank a shaft to intercept them. The Romans at once refilled the end of their tunnel, and paused to think out another plan.

X

The unknown engineer who conducted the attack upon the mound was evidently an expert acquainted with all the knowledge of his day. He now designed a chamber at the end of the tunnel, just under the edge of the mound, and packed it with highly inflammable material treated with bitumen, sulphur, and oil of cedar.[1] Reserves of fuel were prepared in readiness.

As soon as the mound was completed, the commander of the garrison renewed the offer of negotiation. This form of turning the other cheek being rejected by the Persians, the Romans set fire to their mine. The mound was evidently loosely packed, and would conduct a draught through its midst. As soon as smoke began to rise, the garrison of Edessa began to shoot burning arrows, and to fling fire-pots upon the mound. The Persians had a busy time in extinguishing the fires so caused, and it never occurred to them that there was more smoke about than would be caused by the missiles from the wall. Khosru, however, seems to have thought that not everything was sufficiently accounted for; and an inspection in person enabled him to identify the trouble. The mound was on fire within. Before the eyes of the grinning Christians who crowded the walls of Edessa, the whole resources of the Fire-Worshippers were called up to deal with the awkward behaviour of their divinity.

The countermine

Under the direction of Khosru, water was poured in upon the fire. When it touched the treated fuel the results were sensational. A vast column of smoke began to arise, so great that it was visible to the people of Carrhae thirty miles away. The water spread the flames, which by degrees gained complete mastery. Little by

Effects of the countermine

[1] "Bitumen" includes naphtha and petroleum. Oil of cedar is a solvent of the type of turpentine. The sulphur, under heat, would give off sulphurous acid fumes. Exactly how the three were combined may be a question; but certainly they could create a very fierce fire, unquenchable by water, a dense smoke, and fumes that would produce most of the effects of poison gas.

little the timbering of the mound was burnt out, and the mound itself became a mere heap of hot and smoking rubble.

This set-back was a turning point in the siege of Edessa. Khosru rested his men for six days. He did not judge it expedient to repeat the work which had been wasted on the mound. At the end of this time he organized an assault with escalade. It was made at dawn, when the garrison would be at its sleepiest. The attack was beaten off: and a smaller assault later in the day upon the great gate was no more successful. As it was impossible to penetrate the defences by direct assault, and the mound had probably by now cooled after the fire, he ordered the surface of the mound to be levelled and prepared. From this he attempted a fresh assault which was pressed home with the utmost determination. It was beaten off only by the most desperate efforts of the defenders. Non-combatants—even children—were pressed into the service. The free use of boiling oil at last forced the Persians to give up. The King of Kings was told that his commands could not be carried out. He refused to receive such a report. Ordered back to the assault, the Persians made one last attempt. . . . They were repulsed. Very reluctantly Khosru accepted a verdict against which there was no chance of appeal. He saw that Edessa could not be taken.

Failure of the Persians

The Edessaeans were too prudent, and lived too near Persia, to make themselves unpleasant over their success. They were ready to salve the feelings of the King of Kings by a handsome contribution to the cost of the war. In paying five centenaria, they doubtless reflected that they would have lost a great deal more if the Persians had got into Edessa. . . .

But the triumphant defence of Edessa, compared with the disastrous loss of Antioch four years earlier, seemed to hint that the methods and assistance of Belisarius were not indispensable, and that the defence of the Persian frontier might be more prosperous if he were prudently omitted altogether from the reckoning.

XI

The defence of Edessa switched the Persian war away into Colchis. Khosru made no further attempt to force a way through the heavily fortified frontiers of Syria and Mesopotamia. The sack of Antioch remained his only great success. The powerful city-fortresses, if held with anything resembling skill and determination, were an impregnable barrier. We hear no more for a long time of serious hostilities in Mesopotamia: and before they were renewed again, Justinian had long been dead, and a new world had come into being.

Results of the defence

But Justinian's policy shows that he was far from thinking that the change of fighting ground involved any diminution in the importance of the war. A permanent acquisition of Colchis by the Persians would assuredly mean the placing of a Persian fleet on the Black Sea, the extension of Persian influence northwards, and Persian command of the trade routes eastward. One of the most earnest wishes of Justinian was to circumvent the Persian monopoly of the eastern trade routes. For this purpose the possession of Colchis was absolutely indispensable, for it gave access to the only route which was not under Persian domination. Colchis represented one of the main positions in the Persian campaign to envelop the empire and cut her off from free access to the east.

The year after the siege of Edessa, Justinian made an armistice for five years with Khosru. He undertook to pay as consideration four centenaria a year—a peppercorn price which was no doubt intended chiefly to mollify the dignity of the King of Kings. Khosru had so **Partial** little hope or expectation of obtaining more by continu- **armistice** ing the war, that he agreed to a provisional peace upon **with** **Persia** the Mesopotamian border. He refused, however, to include Colchis in the arrangement; so that as regards the latter, the war continued in a desultory sort of way.

Justinian's object was to give the resources of the empire an opportunity to recover themselves from the troubles of the plague year. He wished to accumulate reserves for more serious operations in the east; and he wished to be free for a few years to see the question of Italy brought to its due conclusion.

CHAPTER XI

TOTILA, AND THE SECOND STRUGGLE WITH THE GOTHS

I

THE Italy on which Belisarius rather helplessly gazed was the direct result of his own work. The troubles he suffered, and the difficulties he met, were due to his own action in wrecking the treaty with Witigis, and to all the consequences which immediately ensued.

Wars are like wounds—unless they heal quite clean, complications are liable to follow. There were certain ragged edges that troubled Italy. One was the question *Condition* of the Gothic kingship. Had Witigis remained at *of Italy* Ravenna, all might have been much easier. As it was, the Goths could settle neither to a king they wanted, nor to a king the Romans approved; in fact, they could settle to no king at all.

Optimism might have allowed men to believe beforehand in the possibility of conquering Italy from the Goths, but only ignorance could ever have led them to suppose that the Goths would sit down meekly and permanently under conquest. This irritation over the question of the kingship kept the Goths awake and ready for trouble: and the rapid succession of candidates ensured the probability that before long Destiny, the dealer, would deal a genuine king.

Even before Belisarius had sailed from Ravenna with *The Gothic* Witigis, the Gothic lords, realizing that he never meant *kingship* to accept the kingship himself, had approached one of the few men who still held out in the north. Uraias, who held Pavia, was a nephew of Witigis. Possibly he felt that the experiment of electing a king from outside the limits of the sacred castes had been ominously unsuccessful.[1] At any rate, he refused, recommending them to try Ildibad, who held Verona. Now Ildibad, a nephew of the Visigothic King Theudis, might, in virtue of that relationship, claim to possess fortunate blood in his veins. Ildibad accepted, on the prudent condition that Belisarius should quite definitely express his rejection of the Gothic kingship. Belisarius, duly approached, had given the deputation the necessary positive assurance: and Ildibad was confirmed as king of the Goths.

Ildibad lasted for less than a year. He was not a rich man, and his wife came to him with a sob-story of the pride and wealth of the wife of Uraias. Ildibad caused Uraias to be slain. Then one of Ildibad's own men, a Gepid, murdered his lord. (May 5th.) The Rugians then elected a candidate of their own, Eraric, who was generally regarded as no king of the Goths; but, since the Goths had no immediate candidate, Eraric was allowed to remain. He was, however, a somewhat slimy customer. The terms which Justinian had offered Witigis amounted, in effect, to a Padus boundary. Eraric persuaded the Goths to endorse an offer to accept these terms. By this means, without raising suspicion, he succeeded in getting an embassy sent to Constantinople. But certain members of the embassy had been charged,

---

[1] He observed that it was commonly believed that men of the same descent shared the same fortune—(Procopius, *History*, VI. xxx. 12.)—a noteworthy maxim which perfectly explains some features of early kingship.

in addition, with secret communications to the emperor. Eraric offered his Gothic kingdom for sale.

Whether or not the full purport of this secret proposal became known among the Gothic lords, they were not disposed to be content with him. After a little thought and discussion, a new candidate was hit upon. This man was Totila, or Baduila, a nephew of Ildibad and therefore probably connected with the family of Theudis.[1] He held the fortress of Treviso,[2] which his uncle had given him. . . . And now, after Destiny had dealt the cards steadily, one after another, without success, she dealt a king. . . . He was about twenty-five years old, or thereabouts: a young man in the prime of his energy. Time would try whether he possessed the royal fortune.

Totila approached

II

Totila was not in the least a fool, and he was not particularly an idealist. He had come to the conclusion that the Goths were the losing side, and that it was no use wasting time in their company. His negotiations with the imperial commander for the surrender of Treviso were interrupted by proposals from the Goths which entirely changed his views. A Gothic nation with Totila for its king was something worth fighting for. For that, he was ready to fight.

He had, unfortunately, already arranged to surrender Treviso; and like a prudent man, he did not care to

[1] Procopius (VII. xvi. 24.) represents Pelagius as addressing him as "gennaie," i.e., "highborn."

[2] Treviso was the extreme eastern fortress of Ildibad's dominions, beyond Verona, towards Aquileia. It marked how much territory Ildibad had won back from the imperialists.

Accession
of Totila,
September
or October
A. D. 541

break his word without reason. In accepting the Gothic proposals he stipulated that Eraric should be put out of the way before a given date. That date was the date of the surrender of Treviso. The Goths carried out the contract; Totila was declared king of the Goths; and, as the king of the Goths had been no party to the surrender of Treviso, the town remained Gothic.

If a city that is set on a hill cannot be hid, still less is it possible to ignore the advent of a certain type of man. By the accession of Totila the whole relation between the empire and the Goths was altered; the spiritual atmosphere was changed as if the sun had risen after a troublesome night. The Goths, with Eraric or Witigis for a king, may have been poor creatures; under Totila they became suddenly once more the Goths of Theuderic and Irminric. Long before Totila had accomplished any great action Justinian detected him as one lion might scent another. He recognized the smell of a king.

The anger of Justinian was directed against the men who were chiefly responsible—his commanders in Italy. The empire had an emperor adequate to command upon a great scale; how was it that it could not supply adequate subordinates capable of intelligent action upon a

Anger of
Justinian

comparatively small one? . . . His anger was justified: but the workman was quarrelling with his tools—which is always a dangerous thing to do. If they were not capable of doing what he wanted, why did he ask them to do it? If they could not work together, what was the reason? But this question was precisely the one which Justinian could not ask himself. The answer might have been too difficult to face.

The whole situation in Italy had gone wrong from

the start. Belisarius had begun it; and it is conceivable
that but for his action in wrecking the treaty with
Witigis, it would never have become as wrong as it did.
The financial administration which, at Justinian's direction, Alexander the Logothete proceeded to set up in
reconquered Italy, might have had different effects had
Italy been pacified on the basis of an accepted and agreed
treaty. As it was, the war was still lingering on; there
was no indisputable acceptation of, or agreement on,
any basis of pacification. Alexander did not look cordially upon the demands of the army for financial assistance. Any opportunity of docking it he embraced
with promptitude. His consequent unpopularity with
the military was surpassed only by his unpopularity
with the Italian official classes, who received from him
notice to submit complete accounts of all monies received and expended during the Gothic occupation of
Italy. This was quite in order, since in theory they were
responsible to the emperor for all actions performed
during the reign of his Gothic viceroys. But what the
Italian ex-ministers thought of Alexander, and what
they trusted would happen to him, are matters best left
in a decent obscurity. Worst of all, Alexander proceeded
to scrutinize, with a keen and intelligent eye, all the
account books placed before him. It was very unpleasant
for everybody.

New civil government

The Italians were helpless; but the military were
better able to create unpleasantness in return, and they
seem to have done so. When they felt themselves neglected by the financial authorities, they did a little informal tax-collecting on their own account. As none
of it was audited by Alexander, the procedure was prob-

ably very summary, and the arithmetic of an optimistic kind.

Few of these things did much to heighten the enthusiasm of the Italians for imperial rule.

III

The difficulties and friction which arose in the imperial governing machine in Italy might in time have been overcome. There is even a certain suggestion about the course of events that Justinian had had his whole scheme mapped out beforehand; and after the default of Belisarius he was unable to modify it, but had to **Conference of Ravenna** apply the scheme, although the circumstances had changed. But the accession of Totila altered everything. Awkwardnesses became crimes: inconveniences became treasons. The emperor's stern criticisms led the military governors to hold a conference at Ravenna. As a result, it was decided to take really vigorous steps. An army of 12,000 men was provided, and Verona was to be its objective.

With such an army, Belisarius might have conquered half Europe. A committee of military governors—men who were capable enough as separate individuals—could not even conquer Verona with it. Negotiations had been conducted for the opening of a gate by a party within. This went off according to programme. A detachment was then sent forward to enter and occupy the town. This too was accomplished. The Goths, panic stricken, promptly left the town as the occupying detachment entered it. When morning dawned the Goths, after spending an uncomfortable night on a hillside, noticed that the rest of the programme was hanging fire. The army, instead of advancing to complete and confirm the occupation of Verona, was arguing in committee about the disposal of the prize-money. The Goths stole back. The occupying detachment, feeling that the emergency was pressing, retreated by the short and quick method of jumping off the wall—not always with happy results. The army, adjourning its committee meeting, retired without having taken Verona.

It was not yet at the end of its troubles. Before it could reach the safe seclusion of Ravenna, it was overtaken by less than half its number of Goths under the personal command of Totila. At the battle of Faventia it was smashed and dispersed by the Gothic riders, and all its standards were captured.

Battle of
Faventia
Spring
A. D. 542

From this moment Totila never looked back. He won another considerable battle at Mucellium in Etruria: he captured the fortified tunnel of Petra Pertusa, besides other fortresses. But he did not rest content with these successes. It became clear to him—as it had been clear to Gaiseric, and was clear to all the best brains among the northern tribesmen—that for men armed and trained as the Goths were, a war of sieges was a losing war. His aim must be to employ to the full the mobility of his riders as a striking force. Totila's perception of this fundamental principle divides him as if by an unbridgeable gulf from such a leader as Witigis, whose conception of war was of the boot-and-bludgeon type. It brought once more into the struggle—this time on the Gothic side—the decisive factor of human intelligence.

While, therefore, Belisarius, on the Persian border, was shepherding Khosru back home over the Euphrates,

Totila was marching south upon the comparatively open country and unprepared towns of southern Italy, undoing all the work that Belisarius had done, by much the same method of mingled promptitude and politeness which Belisarius had employed. He was soon in practical possession of all Italy south of the Vulturnus; and the significance of this lay in the fact that he levied and collected taxation. Not only was the country lost again to the empire, but it equipped and maintained the revived Gothic kingdom.

His south Italian campaign culminated in his appearance in Campania. The alarmed inhabitants were surprised to find that the Gothic king was genial and humane to inoffensive persons. Instead of eating them alive, he treated well and dismissed with courtesy the families of Roman senators who still dwelt in the Campanian villas. Last and most important of all his actions was the siege of Neapolis.

Totila in southern Italy

IV

This second siege of Neapolis [1] lasted some nine months. Totila was still wise. The investment was a blockade rather than a siege. As it progressed, it grew into something symbolic. It ceased to be merely a struggle over an actual town in southern Italy, and became the type of a war in heaven. If Justinian could hold Neapolis, the future of the world remained with the Roman empire. If Totila could take Neapolis, the future of the world might be obscure and difficult to predict— but it would not lie with the Roman empire. Whatso-

Siege of Neapolis

[1] For the first, see Ch. VI, viii above.

ever else might happen, the empire would make, keep, or break itself over the contest.

Justinian could not bring Belisarius to Italy on the spur of the moment. To do so would have been opening the gates of the eastern frontier to the armies of Khosru. Belisarius, as we have seen, was busy in taking care that the King of Kings should be fended off from Jerusalem and the road to Egypt. This simultaneous attack on the empire, by the Persians and the Goths, was a large part of the secret why Justinian could not exert greater power in Italy. The policy which he did follow, however, was strong and individual. He put a civilian in supreme command as Praetorian prefect of Italy, with a military lieutenant, an officer named Demetrius, trained in the school of Belisarius. Troops were sent—Thracians, Armenians and Huns.

Demetrius is a promising name for a soldier. The new commander arrived ahead of his troops in Sicily, made himself acquainted with the latest information, and proceeded with great promptitude to act upon it. Neapolis was starving. Demetrius took steps to relieve the city.

As his fleet sailed, we approach the critical moment, the great divide in human history. Up to this moment, the Roman empire—the empire of Augustus and Constantine—was still in the running for victory. No one could deny the possibility that the Gothic war might be followed by a Frankish war, and then by a British war, and the complete restoration of the old frontier. That no such thing happened was due partly to the insufficient forces at the disposal of Demetrius. He was a bold man, and the bluff he put up was impressive. Even the Goths, hearing of the approaching fleet, and assuming as a

Attempt
to relieve
Neapolis

matter of course that it was manned by the normal number of fighting men, were impressed. Had Demetrius pushed straight to Neapolis, he might have forced a Gothic retreat, relieved Neapolis, and changed the course of history by means of his fleet of unarmed grain ships.

But—and it is a moral instance for the instruction of youth—at the critical moment the heart of Demetrius misgave him. He took refuge in prudence, and steered for Rome, to pick up some fighting men. The garrison of Rome totally refused to associate itself with such a wild goose chase, and Demetrius sailed back to Neapolis. But by this time the real truth had become known. Totila had organized an impromptu fleet, with which he proceeded to fall upon the relieving fleet. Demetrius, with a few of his men, escaped in boats. The grain ships fell into the hands of Totila.

Repulse of
Demetrius

The divide was now passed: from this decisive moment onwards, all the rivers of human life began to flow another way. It had become certain that the Roman empire would not dominate the future of Europe: for it had become certain that the empire would not quite succeed in dominating Italy.

V

Such things as this are visible only on a long retrospect. They were unsuspected by the men who fought over Neapolis. If we could foresee the future, there would be no future. . . . They went on fighting as if nothing had happened.

Demetrius, arriving back in Sicily, found that his

army had at last arrived, together with the Praetorian prefect. Urgent messages from Neapolis begged the prefect to make another attempt to relieve the starving city. With the approval of his superior, Demetrius organized a fresh attempt. Midwinter was at hand, but the need was too urgent for these considerations to weigh in the scale.

The second effort to relieve Neapolis nearly succeeded. The fleet, this time with its fighting men as well as its food supplies, reached Neapolis in safety. Before it could take any steps to achieve its purpose, a Mediterranean winter squall arose, blew the ships on shore, and wrecked the entire fleet. Demetrius himself this time was among the prisoners.

Second attempt fails

If Neapolis were now isolated, with hardly any prospect of help, it was due to no fault of Justinian. If, by degrees, the garrison and inhabitants saw the inevitability of surrender, it was due to no fault of theirs. They starved on as long as they could. Totila—a robust man—talked sound sense and rough good nature. He offered excellent terms to which no one could object. The garrison should march out with the honours of war. Neapolis went on starving, and wondering if it were worth while. At last the commander undertook to surrender if no relief arrived within thirty days.

"Thirty days!" said Totila. "Say three months—and meanwhile I will just sit and wait."

Neapolis did not wait three months, nor even thirty days. It threw in its hand and surrendered. This was some time in March or April, probably about the time when the plague mortality was climbing to its height in Constantinople.

VI

There was something very typical about Totila. Having given his word, and the city having accepted it and
opened the gates of Neapolis, he seemed to the bewildered Neapolitans almost extravagant in his kindness. He did not need any legal documents with seals and preambles to tie him to his undertakings. He fed the city like a father, rationing the starving inhabitants strictly for a day or two, and gradually increasing the ration up to normal. When the garrison, having tried to get to Rome by sea, were held at Neapolis by the wind, Totila gave them horses and saw them all sent off by road. . . . His conduct produced just the effect on which he probably calculated. The little birds ate out of his hand.

The Gothic king now began to turn his attention north towards Rome. The imperial commanders in Italy signed an unanimous protest to Justinian that their resources were insufficient to hold the country against Totila. Justinian, hovering somewhere between life and death, was probably in no condition to take any active measures. So the position stood.

Totila entrusted to members of the Neapolitan garrison a letter which was addressed to the Roman senate. In it he argued his case. He contended that it was to the advantage of Italy that the Gothic rule should be restored, because it had been a better rule than the imperial. . . . The commander at Rome could not prevent this letter from reaching senators, but he could and did prevent them from making any response. Totila had to guess at the effect produced upon the Roman opinion. As the year wore, he prepared to move north.

His arrival before Rome was heralded by the sudden appearance of large posters in the city, in which he rehearsed the solemn undertaking to do no injury to the Romans. After detaching a force to finish the war in southern Italy by the seizure of Otranto, the Goths packed their wagons and set out for Rome.

Totila moves upon Rome Spring A. D. 544

The second siege of Rome thus began in circumstances very different from the first, seven years earlier. Both sides were weaker; and that very fact seemed to put off a clear decision. Totila began the same kind of blockade that had been so effective against Neapolis. Bessas, the imperial commander, adopted a purely defensive policy which, although it made the task of the garrison easier, imposed a much greater strain on the civil inhabitants. This passive quality in the siege of Rome was offset by great Gothic activity in central Italy. Totila's mobile columns took one fortress after another. When he seized Tibur, the head of the great Valerian highway that gave access to southern Picenum, he gave an example of the frightfulness that he could employ when the little birds did not eat out of his hand. . . . Perhaps this, taken with his amiability on other occasions, was not without its effect. Most people are influenced by a broad and consistent logic. They were quite capable of perceiving that Totila spared the humble and warred down the proud: and they acted accordingly.

Such was the situation into which Belisarius stepped when he came back to Italy. He reprovisioned Otranto, as we have seen, and won a few small successes. For the rest, he could only see the new Gothic power of Totila sweeping slowly and steadily north; he could find no means of checking it, still less of crushing it; at the end

Arrival of Belisarius (May 544 to May 545)

of the year he could only sit down and write to Justinian, and describe the situation as it was. The commanders in Italy had already informed the emperor of their opinion. The emperor had sent Belisarius, and now Belisarius in turn despatched his report.

VII

Before he came to Italy, and had seen with his own eyes the state of affairs, Belisarius had offered to make the war pay its own expenses. The first truth he now grasped was that such a policy was impossible.[1] Totila had established a start which could not be overtaken. The Gothic king now held all southern and most of central Italy—the richest parts of the peninsula. Like another eminent man of more modern date, Totila was not himself an agricultural labourer. He was not interested in possessing and cultivating the land of Italy. He was perfectly willing to allow its legal owners to continue owning it and cultivating it. All he wanted was that they should pay their taxes according to the legal assessments. The landlords, for the most part, did not worry very much whether they paid their taxes to a Thracian at Constantinople or to a Goth at Ravenna. The advantages and objections were about equal. Totila, therefore, and not Belisarius, was the man who was making the war pay its expenses. Belisarius could not build up a new comitatus from the resources available to him in Italy. . . . And probably there were certain limits

Financing the War

---

[1] For his own statement of the case see Procopius, *History*, VII. xii. 3–10, his letter to Justinian, which contains the whole facts, and shows signs of being a genuine composition of Belisarius.

of prudence that he did not intend to pass. He did not mean, for instance, to keep a comitatus out of his own capital, until that capital ran dry. He meant to stop the process long before that point was reached.

Even if he had had the money from local resources, the local resources would not furnish him with the type of man he wanted for the new comitatus. The best men of the imperial army in Italy were now in the pay of Totila; and the remainder were not a subject for enthusiasm. . . . In brief, if the war were to be fought, it needed a bigger backing than Belisarius was prepared to give it. It needed the backing of the imperial treasury itself.

Such was the report that Belisarius sent. It reached Justinian during the spring of the year after the siege of Edessa; and the peace which Justinian made with Khosru must have been based largely upon the necessity of providing, out of resources which had suddenly shrunk, for the Italian war.

Government aid necessary

Difficult as matters might be for Belisarius, they were no less difficult for Justinian, who was precluded, out of regard for his imperial prestige, from explaining some awkward facts. It was, however, obviously necessary, now that Khosru was brought to standstill, to attend in turn to Totila; for the Gothic king was a dangerous man. Totila showed more real military talent than the great Theuderic had displayed, and, in addition, certain keen perceptions concerning the mentality of the people he dealt with. His combination of geniality and terrorism was a deadly one. If Totila completed the conquest of Italy, he would be in a position to extend his power further still at the expense of Justinian. An understanding between the Goth and the Persian, such as even the ponderous Witigis had succeeded in effecting, might crack the empire like a nut. . . . And even if we, wise after the event, can see that Justinian had less to fear than perhaps he thought, he, without our advantages, had to take the possibilities as well as the probabilities into account.

VIII

Belisarius
waits

Belisarius employed as his courier John, "the nephew of Vitalian," that same John who had once seized Ariminum, and had been saved only by the action of Narses. John had some of the dazzling ability and the erratic temperament of the south-east European. While John travelled to Constantinople, Belisarius retired to Dyrrachium to compose a hastener.

John had promised to return promptly; but promises are not always easy to fulfil. It is probable, too, that the requests of Belisarius could not be met quite so easily or quickly as he wished. Not only did the money need some consideration, but the question of the men was not free from complications. Belisarius did not get his old comitatus back—at any rate, he did not get all of it or the most part of it. The commanders who had engaged its old members are not likely to have been willing to part with them. New troops had to be found, men suitable for the climate of Italy. . . . During the period through which all these arrangements dragged on, John did something which was a little surprising. He got married.

No one has ever quite clearly established the precise

motives which inspired John; but the motives which lead any man to get married are usually complex, and in the case of such a man as John, we may guess that they were more complex than usual. John's action, more-over, had one very peculiar feature—it involved him in sharp conflict with Theodora.

Marriage of John

The bride was a daughter of Germanus, the nephew of the emperor. John's marriage did not exactly bring him into the succession to the imperial throne, for a good many male heirs stood between him and it; but it did bring him into the imperial family circle. Germanus was a very important person indeed. Without belonging to the small, select tribe of men of genius, he was one of those individuals who not infrequently do very well in the world—a capable, competent man, with man-ners that made him liked and admired, and a relation-ship to Justinian that gave him a great influence, which, as far as we can see, he used tolerably well. He headed a discreet and blameless party of opposition to Theodora. Not for him were the rough ways, the Rabelaisian stories and the open enmity of John the Cappadocian. All that he did, he did with decorum. Theodora did not get many chances against Germanus. Her policy was to make things warm for his agents and followers. Among these, the new son-in-law proudly inserted himself.

Belisarius had had reason, long before this, to object strongly to the proceedings of John. His feelings now must have been still more incensed. But John was a per-son not altogether easy to object to; he seems to have been the kind of man who is always full of zealous and convincing arguments in support of whatsoever he has done. He did not in the least avoid Belisarius, but met

John's Return

him, rather late in the year, at Dyrrachium with the reinforcements he had obtained.

History has not vouchsafed to give us details of the conversation (probably heated) between John and Belisarius. If John contended that Theodora was opposed to help being given to Belisarius from the treasury, and if he maintained that only by the influence of Germanus could it be successfully achieved—then Belisarius, knowing what he knew, would have had some difficulty in refuting him. The fact remained that John, as before, had emerged from the episode with kudos, and Belisarius had not. . . . It probably did not delight Belisarius to hear that Narses had been sent to raise a force of Heruls, with the object of co-operating in the Italian campaign. His memories of co-operation with Narses were not such as to make him wish for a repetition of the experience.

So, whatsoever the true reason may have been, Belisarius did not get his comitatus again; and although he did get reinforcements and help from the treasury, they came late, and were not all that he might have wished.

Belisarius disappointed

IX

The delay meant that Totila had finished the conquest of middle Italy, and cut Belisarius off from the possibility of marching to the relief of Rome. Before Belisarius could get his new army effectively into the field, Totila had moreover extended his power northwards by the capture of Placentia, where the great Aemilian-Lepidian highway crossed the Padus on its road to Milan and the north-west. The defenders of Placentia, like those of Neapolis, waited and waited, and starved and starved. It is even said that they resorted to cannibalism. All was useless; their endurance was wasted; no help came. But Belisarius was determined that Rome should be saved. Since he could not march to Rome across Italy, he would sail thither by sea.

John did not want this plan. What he proposed to do was to land at Brundusium and march upon Rome by the old route followed by Sulla, which was weakly defended, and was much less difficult. This plan Belisarius was not likely to accept. As John was obdurate, they finally agreed to divide their forces, and each to carry out his own plan. Belisarius could consent, because there was much to be said for this combined land and sea attack.

The real reason, however, for John's attitude was that he had begun to feel unsafe, not so much with Belisarius **Difficulties** as with Antonina. Belisarius, even if he felt strongly over the way in which he had been treated, would not do more than talk. But the episodes of Pope Silverius, of Constantine, and of John the Cappadocian, conveyed an unpleasant suggestion that Antonina might, at the instigation of Theodora, do more than talk. She might —and there were reasons why she would. The help of Theodora might become necessary, if Belisarius were to get the full amount of money and reinforcements that he needed. John probably did not suppose that Antonina, without a struggle, would allow her famous husband to sink into the position of a second-rate soldier. Belisarius had undertaken the Italian war—at her instigation— under a misapprehension of the circumstances. It would

be Antonina's task to obtain the powerful help necessary. And Theodora, like another Herodias, might ask
for the head of another John.

John's campaign in southern Italy was successful. He
reached and captured Canusium; but he took good care
never to go anywhere near Antonina. As far, therefore,
as Belisarius was concerned, John might as well not have
existed at all. The operations of Belisarius against Totila
constituted the fighting that really counted in the making of history.

X

Belisarius sent on an advance guard to encourage the
Romans until he could himself arrive. The commander
at Rome, however, was defending the city with a force
of only 3,000 men; he was therefore fixedly determined
to run no risks, and he refused to take any step in co-
operation. Perhaps he knew his man; for Totila, keenly
on the watch, seized the first chance of cutting up the
new arrivals. Hence the moral encouragement to the
Romans was not what it might have been. An attempt
of the pope to run corn-ships from Sicily through the
blockade very nearly succeeded. They were captured at
the very mouth of the harbour at Portus. A bishop who
was on board was brought before Totila and examined.
The king believed him to be prevaricating, and ordered
his hands to be cut off as a warning to others. . . .
Whatsoever the Romans got, it was not encouragement.

An attempt to parley was made. The deacon Pelagius
—the future pope—a wealthy and influential man who
had been spending his own money freely in helping

Belisarius
to Rome

distress, obtained an interview with Totila. The terms
which Pelagius was commissioned to propose were that,
failing relief by a certain date, Rome should, on three
conditions, be surrendered. The conditions were that
the life and property of the Sicilians should be respected;
that the walls of Rome should be left standing, and that
all Roman slaves among the Goths should be given up.
Totila was informed of them in advance,[1] and did not
think them worth consideration. Without giving Pelagius the opportunity of speaking on the question, the
king rejected all three conditions, and Pelagius returned
without fulfilling his mission.

Totila
and the
Romans

The non-combatant citizens then waited upon the
military commander. They requested him either to give
them sufficient food, allow them to leave the city, or
kill them. He shook his head to all three alternatives:
the first was impossible, the second dangerous, and the
third not to be thought of. If they would be patient,
Belisarius was on the way with rescue.

Hunger increased in Rome. At first it had been possible for rich men to buy grain from the military stores
at a famine price which went into the pockets of the
principal officers; but as the siege continued, this resort
was cut off. When boiled nettles, variegated with dogs
and rats, were the sole remaining food for the ghosts
who remained, Bessas accepted a sum down to allow
them to leave the city. He probably knew what the result
would be. All but a few of the citizens went.

The end of ancient Rome, the city of Romulus and
Augustus, came when the crowd of starving refugees
set out on their travels. The Isaurian and Armenian

The non-
combatants
leave Rome

[1] See the remarks of Bury, *History of the Later Roman Empire*, II. 237–238.

soldiers who watched from the walls saw a sight which was hidden from wiser and greater men. . . . Some of the refugees were killed by the Goths, some captured; many were too weak to go far, and fell and died by the way. So terminated the continuous tradition of ancient Rome.

XI

Belisarius arrived at Portus too late to save all this suffering, but not too late to relieve the garrison. He soon saw that he could not fight the Gothic forces. All he could do was to reprovision the city.

Totila had barred the river with a fortified boom and a chain, no easy matter to break through. Belisarius proceeded to build a floating fire-tower, over-topping all the towers of the boom. The crown of the tower was a boat packed with materials similar to those which had been so effective at Edessa. This fire-tower he towed and floated into position, while the Goths, who did not understand what he was doing, left him alone.

Leaving Antonina at Portus, under the protection of Isaac the Armenian, Belisarius issued his instructions. Isaac was not to move from Portus for any reason of any description whatsoever; this was absolute. A party was detached to fight its way along the bank of the river. Bessas was notified to co-operate. Bessas did nothing of the kind; and events proved him right.

The great push now began. Coming up with his protected ships, crowded with archers, Belisarius dispersed the defenders, hauled up the chain, and advanced against the boom. Totila rushed up reinforcements, and the

Belisarius
at Portus

boom was soon crowded with Goths. While the archers, behind their floating bulwarks, let loose the arrow-storm on the crowded Gothic ranks, the fire-tower was shoved up and rammed into position against a Gothic defence-work. The boat was fired and launched. Crashing down into the defences, it instantly involved them in flames. Two hundred Goths are said to have been burned to death there, and the defenders were cleared from the boom. The obstruction was then pierced and set on fire, and the water-way was clear to Rome.

Belisarius would have been in Rome that afternoon, had not something very strange happened. A courier from Portus arrived with the news that Isaac was a prisoner in the hands of the Goths. The occasion was not favourable for philosophic meditation. Like most men who direct great organizations, Belisarius was probably in the habit of "telescoping" his processes of thought. The capture of Isaac irresistibly suggested the deduction that Portus had been captured by the Goths, **Retreat** and that he was therefore cut off from his base. Without waiting to inspect the intermediate terms, he gave the order for retreat.

Few men, one may imagine, have ever been so horrified at finding their worst apprehensions groundless. Portus was perfectly safe, with Antonina inside. All that had happened was that Isaac had slipped across the river on the look-out for plunder, and had himself been collected by the Goths. Without any substantial cause, Belisarius had allowed himself to be called off in the midst of a critical military operation, and had sacrificed all that he had worked so hard to achieve.

XII

Men who work miracles—that is to say, those who habitually produce excellent results with inadequate means—are frequently dependent for their safety upon their success. To miss one's step in these things may mean a very bad fall. Belisarius suffered such a fall now. In the teeth of every impossibility and every difficulty he had won through—to end in this ridiculous failure. Before many hours were over he was a sick man.[1] Months were to pass before he was again fit for work.

Neither the ingenuity of Belisarius nor the caution of Bessas succeeded in saving Rome. In the city discipline slackened; heart was lost. Two enterprising Isaurians sold their post; and on December 17th a Gothic party was hauled up the wall, the Asinarian Gate was opened, and Totila was admitted into Rome.

Totila takes Rome

The garrison, and the few rich men who still possessed horses, made good their retreat. The remaining civilians, five hundred in number, took refuge in the churches—which they could no longer fill.

Totila, entering St. Peter's church, was confronted by the deacon Pelagius, bearing in his hands the holy scriptures. He heard the deacon's words: "Spare your people, lord."

"No conditions now, Pelagius?" he asked. The deacon replied: "God has made us your servants; so spare your servants, lord."

---

[1] Did Belisarius experience some kind of stroke when the news of the capture of Isaac reached him? Procopius (*History*, VII. xix. 30.) may imply as much. Belisarius had gone through much worry and hard work. His break-down now may have been more than mere disappointment. He died a comparatively young man: he can scarcely have been sixty.

Totila passed the word that Rome had surrendered, and no harm should be done to the inhabitants. Sixty had been killed. The remaining four hundred and forty presumably survived. The Goths gathered what plunder they could find. Unlike many conquerors before and after, they harmed no woman. The king's discipline was rigid.

It was Totila's hope that the war might now end. His power throughout Italy was real and effective. He sent Pelagius to Constantinople with a letter to Justinian. The proposals of Totila, contained in this letter, illustrate the sobriety and the conciliatory temper in which the great Gothic kings so markedly differed from the Frankish. He proposed nothing more than that he should occupy the same position which Theuderic had held, and owe the same allegiance to his imperial overlord. He put forward no such imperial claim as Geilamir had made.

Totila proposes peace terms

If Justinian would not agree to this, Totila proposed to level Rome to the ground and start for Constantinople.

But the emperor declined to discuss the question. Belisarius had full authority to treat: and Totila must apply to him.

So Totila began to level Rome with the ground. He had arranged to burn some of the important buildings, when he received a letter from the sick-bed of Belisarius at Portus. The invalid wrote:

"Just as those who create the beauty of a city are highly thought of, just so those who destroy it are thought fools. Rome is the greatest and most important city in the world; she was made so by a long history, and by the art of many men. Her monuments belong to posterity, who will sit in judgment on the men who injure them. If you win this war, Rome will be your loss. If you lose it, things will go hard with the destroyer of Rome. Meanwhile, your reputation in the eyes of the world is at stake."

Totila took this letter seriously. He read it more than once. He gave instructions that no more harm was to be done to Rome.

In February, leaving a division of his army to watch Belisarius at Portus, Totila himself set out to make a progress through his realm of Italy.

CHAPTER XII

DISSOLUTION OF PARTNERSHIP

I

APRIL had brought the spring before Belisarius, now convalescent, visited Rome to see what the city looked like. It was a strange, a silent and a deserted Rome, on which the Italian sun shone brightly but blankly. The roaring Rome of Marius and Sulla was stilled. Even the quiet decorous Rome of Romulus Augustulus had grown quieter. Most of the tiles were off the Capitoline temple. The gates stood open and valveless. Parts of the wall were down.

Desolation in Rome

For forty days Rome had been empty and uninhabited. Belisarius, looking about, came to the conclusion that the walls could be repaired, and the city made defensible. He had his headquarters transferred from Portus, and forthwith set all the labour he could obtain to the hard work of rebuilding the damaged portion of the walls. Belisarius is the only man in history who restored the walls of both Carthage and Rome. In the emergency he dispensed with mortar and masonry, and was content with rubble walls hastily piled up. In four weeks the walls were sufficient to keep out the foe.

Totila, travelling north, was recalled by the surprising news that Belisarius had reoccupied Rome! He hastened back. The gates were not yet filled with valves, and there was no reason why he should not walk into the city. . . . Organization, and the elaborate process of civilized war, did not count at this juncture. Belisarius hastily picked out his stalwarts, the men whom he knew to be capable of giving and taking punishment, and stationed them in the open gateways. There the Goths found them. Amid the ruins of old Rome, the city of the Antonines and of Augustus, was fought a Homeric combat of the old pre-civilized type, as the Gothic champions sought to batter their way in, and the defenders battered them back. For two days they fought; then they rested for several days, and then the battle was renewed. The king himself was in the thick, for his right-hand man, his standard-bearer, was struck down, and over the body raged a ferocious struggle for standard and standard-bearer. The Goths got the standard and apparently the imperialists got the standard-bearer. . . . By this time the Goths had had enough and they cleared out, followed for some distance by the victorious imperialists, who turned back only when they were tired.

Belisarius accordingly had the new gates finished and erected. He then locked them, and sent the keys to Justinian. The emperor had sought to restore the Roman empire, but apparently he had only restored the Homeric age.

Bitter recriminations followed among the Goths. Why had Totila left Rome open for a man like Belisarius to seize? But it was (as they soon recognized) no use talking. Totila destroyed the bridges across the Tiber, leaving only the Mulvian standing, and established himself at Tibur.

II

This first blow to the prestige of Totila was soon followed by another. The hostages whom Totila had taken at the capture of Rome had been lodged at Capua for safety. The king regarded them as important. While Totila was engaged by Belisarius, John, down in the south, had a brain-wave. Setting out with a fast-moving squadron of cavalry, he beat the Gothic warders, collected the hostages, and was off with them. While the rescued hostages were on the way to Sicily, Totila, hearing the enraging news, set out south with a strong body of Goths. He caught up the unconscious John in Lucania. If he would have waited for morning, the fate of John would have been sealed. The special providence which watched over that very temperamental person was, however, alive to the situation. Totila persisted in making a night attack. About a hundred persons were killed, but John and nine hundred others got away in the darkness, and were soon safe behind the walls of Otranto.

John abducts the hostages

III

Having recaptured and refortified Rome, the next step for Belisarius was to begin a process of recapturing, one after another, the towns of Italy. This had been his plan against Witigis, and it was his plan now, with the difference that instead of turning north, he turned south.

Justinian marked his approval of the work so far achieved by sending, during the autumn of this year

Conquest of Italy recommenced

547, a thousand men of Belisarius' old comitatus,[1] besides some Heruls (whose leader was continually drunk) and a few other details. After strengthening the garrison of Rome from these drafts, Belisarius sailed for the south coast of Italy early in the new year, 548.

It was not merely that luck was adverse; something more dangerous was at work against Belisarius. The discipline and coherence of the troops were crumbling. They were as good as ever, but it was beginning to be difficult to place upon them that reliance which a general needs to feel in his men. All the world seemed to be growing temperamental. The wind would not let Belisarius reach Tarentum. Accordingly, he landed at Croton. There he could not find supplies for man and beast. He sent them, therefore, to relieve Ruscianum, which the Goths were preparing to besiege. In the first skirmish the imperialists beat much greater numbers of Goths, and were so much overcome by the grandeur of their exploit that they acted as if there were no more Goths in Italy—an error which Totila proceeded to correct. The few survivors who escaped from the Gothic counter-attack carried the news to Belisarius, and Belisarius, Antonina and the remaining troops hastily got on board ship and made for Messina.

Disaster at Ruscianum

The reinforcements which soon after landed in Sicily, 2,000 in number, would have meant more, had they not mostly been absorbed in replacing this unnecessary wastage. If Belisarius were to fulfil his aims, he must have larger forces. It was determined now that Antonina should go to Constantinople to see Theodora. Written

[1] This seems to be the meaning of the "more than a thousand doryphoroi and hypaspistae under Valerian": Procopius, *History*, VII. xxvii. 3–4.

reports and requests did not seem to achieve all that was wanted. A personal interview was necessary.

Belisarius accompanied Antonina as far as Otranto, where he saw her off for the east.

IV

The garrison of Ruscianum, blockaded by the Goths, undertook to surrender, if not relieved; but counting on the certain help of Belisarius and John, the commander ignored his promise and held on all the same. Neither Belisarius nor John, however, for all their efforts, could relieve the town. Unable to bring direct help, they attempted to draw off Totila by means of diversions. Belisarius returned to Rome, apparently on his way to the north, while John raided Picenum. Totila was not to be moved by such means. He maintained the siege until Ruscianum fell.

Ruscianum falls

Totila could be genial, and even kindly when it suited him; but he was inexorable towards broken pledges and deceit in malice prepense. Of the commander of Ruscianum he made a horrible example. The garrison was given the choice of entering the Gothic service, or going home. Only eighty elected to go home. The rest threw in their lot with the fortune of Totila.

Meanwhile Belisarius, arriving at Rome, found that the garrison he had left there was in mutiny, had murdered their commander, and had sent to Constantinople to demand their pay, with all arrears up to date, and a free pardon for their mutiny, if they were not to surrender Rome to the Goths. Justinian meekly complied. . . . Belisarius reprovisioned the city and reorganized the garrison. His last days in Italy were approaching, and these were his last actions in the Italian war.

Antonina, reaching Constantinople, had met appalling news. On June 28th 548, Theodora had died.

Death of
Theodora
June 28th
A. D. 548

That the little dark-eyed beauty, with her luxury, her wit, her ardour, her power, should be still for ever was sufficiently memorable in the personal lives of those who knew her. But it was much worse than a personal fact. Theodora, though neither an angel nor an archangel, had been a virtue and a dominion as well as a power. Something strong and splendid faded out of the star of Justinian when she died. . . . Up to this point it had been impossible exactly to distinguish the persons in the imperial partnership. What was really Justinian, and what was Theodora, no one could quite certainly say. With her departure the truth slowly became visible. It was the fierce, the gallant, the youthful spirit which had gone; and by her vacant place sat an old, sad, somewhat unworldly man, who, because he knew too much, often could not make up his mind, and who often forgot what he should have remembered, and put off till tomorrow what he should have done today. The old comedienne had played her part right up to the end. It had been a glorious part; and it was over.

Antonina was suddenly isolated. The power on which she had so long and so confidently relied was gone; she found herself in a world in which the quiet, decorous, but decisive influence of Germanus was for the time being supreme. The very fact that she had been so dependent upon Theodora now fatally labelled Antonina as a member of the opposition. She decided that the safe plan was to withdraw. It was now certain that Belisarius

THE HOUSE OF JUSTINIAN.

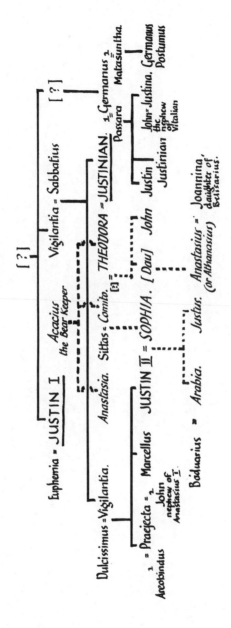

could not hope for adequate support in Italy nor for the means to win the prestige which would attach to the conqueror of Italy. Germanus wanted this prestige, and intended to have it. By far the wisest plan was to get out now. Accordingly, she put in the resignation of Belisarius; and Belisarius, at Rome, found himself re- Belisarius called from the command which had brought him such resigns great vicissitudes of fortune.

Had he failed? It is usual to say so; and yet his skill showed no falling off; he was the same man who had brought two captive kings home to Constantinople. As far as he himself was concerned he might, given the money and his old, trained comitatus, by this time have been riding into Soissons to prepare for the reconquest of Britain. . . .[1] But he had been caught in the current of political change, which had carried him far from these consummations. And like most other men, he was not a free agent.

The return of Belisarius led to the prompt suggestion in Constantinople that Germanus should be the man to succeed him. But before this was brought to pass, some very strange work happened.

V

Belisarius, the man who had suppressed the Nika sedition, had not yet landed in Constantinople when Mar-

---

[1] Mediaeval romance actually attributes this expedition to him. Belisarius in the legendary story returns with the English king as his prisoner. Any one who still wishes to believe in the blindness and beggary of Belisarius in his old age must remember that according to the same authority he conquered England; and one story is as good as the other. (Bury, *History of the Later Roman Empire*, II. 69. f. n. 5.)

cellus, the commander of the imperial guard, made a communication to Justinian. A rapid series of arrests followed, and the senate was soon engaged in trying a complicated case of treason and intended murder in which Germanus himself was involved. Germanus was only discharged from suspicion of complicity by the evidence of Marcellus and several other officers, who answered for it that he had enabled them to obtain full particulars of a plot to assassinate Justinian. . . . Germanus had learnt of it from his son Justin, who had been approached by a certain man named Arsaces. This man Arsaces was the real originator of the conspiracy. The evidence, as it was sifted by the senators, threw an interesting light upon a number of subjects.

Arsaces was an Armenian, whose history was not of the best. He had been detected in correspondence with the Persian government. His sentence, considering the time and the place, had been remarkably mild. He had received a not very severe flogging, and had been shown through Constantinople on a camel. Whether the flogging or camel-ride constituted the iron which ate into the soul of Arsaces, at any rate he schemed revenge.

Naturally he did not propose to achieve it in person. Looking about, he hit upon his kinsman Artabanes as a convenient instrument. The qualifications of Artabanes for conspiracy are worth noting.

Artabanes had once formed a plan for marrying Justinian's niece Praejecta, the daughter of his sister Vigilantia. In furtherance of this ambitious alliance, he began by divorcing his wife as a necessary preliminary. By doing so, however, he had crossed Theodora in two distinct ways. The empress had a great objection to strangers and doubtful persons marrying into the imperial family; and she had an equally strong objection to husbands who treated their wives unfairly. There can seldom have been a more ardent feminist than Theodora. She placed her veto on the marriage with Praejecta; and she insisted upon Artabanes taking back his wife. . . . Artabanes in consequence had not been full of loyal enthusiasm about the emperor and empress. After Theodora's death he divorced his wife again; but Praejecta, being already married, was beyond his reach. . . . This was the man into whose ear Arsaces instilled suggestions. As Arsaces said, it would be quite an easy matter now to bump the old man off. He—Justinian—sat up late at night with a lot of aged persons, sky-pilots most of them, poring over holy books; and all the guardsmen gone to bed. Artabanes heard this with cautious assent. What really swayed him was the assurance of Arsaces that Germanus and his sons were in the business too.

Having secured Artabanes by representing that Germanus was involved, Arsaces next proceeded to get hold of Germanus. The reason he had for supposing it to be possible to do so was that Germanus had a grievance. When Boraides, his brother, died, Boraides, save for a legacy to his daughter, left the whole of his property to Germanus. The will of Boraides was over-ridden by Justinian on the ground that it was unfair to the daughter. . . . In this he was, of course, perfectly right. . . . But Arsaces, smiling politely, was himself probably not altogether free from secret speculations concerning what possible object Boraides could have had in piling so much money upon his brother; and what

[Marginal note: Case of Artabanes]

[Marginal note: Germanus]

possible use Germanus could have had for it if he got it. Justinian may have shared these reflections. . . . And so Arsaces assumed—a subtle touch—that Germanus was much annoyed against Justinian. Why Germanus should have been annoyed was of course one of those things which are best expressed in discreet terms.

Arsaces obtained his access to Germanus through the latter's son Justin. After swearing him to betray what he heard to no one but his father, Arsaces pointed out how badly Justinian treated his relatives and natural heirs. He suggested that when Belisarius returned, matters would be worse. Finally he divulged the fact that a plan was already on foot for the assassination of Justinian.

Justin repeated this to Germanus. It is probable that Germanus, besides being far too wary to snatch at a prize which was sure to come his way in the natural course of events, was also too astute to swallow all the allegations made by Arsaces. He no doubt knew better than Arsaces did the reasons for the return of Belisarius. . . . But it is interesting to observe that Arsaces recognized in Belisarius a man both loyal to the emperor, and also very likely to be his successor.

Remarkable features of the plot

It is interesting, too, to notice that Germanus did not hasten to Justinian with these shocking disclosures. The person to whom he related them was Marcellus, the commander of the guard. . . . This was what Justinian could not understand. Why, he asked, had the matter been concealed from him? Marcellus took the full responsibility for having dissuaded Germanus from telling the emperor. He and some colleagues had investigated the matter, had planned an interview between Germanus and one of the intended assassins, and had overheard the incriminating evidence. The plot was to wait until Belisarius arrived in Constantinople, and then to murder him and Justinian together; because if they slew Justinian first, they might be placing Belisarius on the imperial throne.

And then, when all was safely finished, Germanus was to be emperor.

Such was the plot which Marcellus reported and which the senate investigated.

Had Theodora been alive, the subsequent events might have been lively and unpleasant for some of the parties to this curious affair; but Justinian, after thinking it over, seemed to conclude that all the people who really mattered—such as Marcellus and Germanus—had provided one another with sufficient alibis, and that he could not very well do anything. . . . And neither Justinian nor the modern historian could guess what Marcellus might, could, or would have done, if Belisarius had been a little later in arriving. It was altogether a very remarkable business.

Problem of Marcellus

That Justinian thought it odd, we can see by his actions. The criminals were not even gaoled. After a short interval, Artabanes was set free, and appointed to high military office. If Justinian really believed the evidence of Marcellus and Germanus, his leniency to the men who projected his murder is indeed startling. It is just possible that he entertained private thoughts of his own.

VI

Justinian wanted the Italian war finished; but after all the events that have just been narrated, it is easy to understand that he might feel far more comfortable about the state of affairs with Belisarius in Constantinople and Germanus in Italy. Everything pointed to this exchange as the really happy solution for all purposes.

The news from Italy showed that Totila was steadily gathering the country into his own hands. Belisarius had left Rome early in the year. In late June or early July Totila appeared before Rome.

The siege was tedious, but it was effective. Totila owed most of his success to the fact that he never did anything in a romantic and expensive way when he could do it in a cheap and prosaic one. After testing the walls and finding them too strong to storm, he settled down to a blockade. The garrison sowed the waste land of the city—there was a good deal of it now—with corn, and raised their own supplies. It was January 16th 550 before the old fate of Rome overtook her again. The city was betrayed by members of the garrison. The gate of St. Paul (Porta Ostiensis) was opened, and Totila marched in with his army. . . . The last of the defenders, penned into the mausoleum of Hadrian, were just preparing to sell their lives dearly when Totila, who had a sharp eye, offered them the usual terms of joining him, or of surrendering their equipment and returning home. Practically all joined him.

This time Totila did not abandon Rome, nor attempt to destroy the city. When he had made an offer for the hand of a daughter of the Frankish King Theudebert,

Third siege of Rome

the astute Frank had refused him, on the score that a
fool who did not understand the importance of Rome
would never possess Italy. Totila was ready and willing
to learn and he learnt from this. His efforts now were
directed to restoring Rome.

Sicily was his next objective. But before he went
south he again made those overtures to Justinian which
he had made before. His envoys were not granted an
audience. The emperor had just given Germanus his
commission as commander-in-chief of the expeditionary
force destined for Italy, and it was not worth while
talking of peace.[1]

During the summer and autumn, therefore, Totila
was ravaging Sicily in reprisal for the help which once
the Sicilians had given to Belisarius; while at Sardica
Germanus was organizing a great army. The news of
the invasion of Sicily disturbed the imperial government.
Artabanes was sent to conduct what defence might be
possible, and meanwhile the preparations of Germanus
were pushed on. Justinian granted money rather more
freely than usual, while Germanus sank his own wealth
in the enterprise.

The army intended for Italy was a new one, not
composed of drafts from the imperial standing armies,
but raised from volunteers. Germanus and his sons gathered stalwart highlanders from Thrace and Illyricum
—to this day the home of a tough fighting breed. Many
professional fighting men in private employment re-
signed their posts in order to take service with Germanus.
Among the non-Romans who were engaged for the ex-

Totila in Sicily

---

[1] Germanus received the same status of imperator, strategos autocrator, which
Belisarius had possessed.

pedition occurs a significant name, soon to be famous
—the Langobardi. Their king undertook to supply a
thousand men. A strong Herulian contingent was also
present. It was a powerful army; but it was not an
ancient Roman army. It was such an army as that with
which Agamemnon set out to conquer Ilium: an army
of gods and fighting men. For the time being, Europe
had sunk back into the heroic age from which it sprang.

Germanus
prepares
for Italy

Dangerous as this army was, Germanus had designed
a deeper and yet more dangerous attack upon the minds
of the Goths. This autumn he married Matasuntha, the
widow of King Witigis, and the grand-daughter of King
Theuderic. She was the last heiress of the ancient Amalungs, and her children would in due time by the ancient
tradition and custom of the Goths, have the nearest right
of any human beings to the Gothic kingship. The Goths
could still be stirred by the name of Amalung. The
warmth of their loyalty to Totila sank several degrees
when the news of Matasuntha's marriage became known.

Not only was the policy of Germanus well-calculated,
but the fact that he was able to put it into operation
was the full justification for his appointment in the place
of Belisarius. What was really wanted in Italy was a
pacification which should not be exclusively military,
but one which should appeal to the reason and the tradition of the Goths, and should enable them to accept the
Roman government with a full sense that they were
accepting their own. The fatal fault about Belisarius was
that he was nothing but a soldier. Germanus was able
to introduce into the contest those factors of conciliation which would perfectly heal the scars of war. Indeed,

Marriage of
Germanus
and
Matasuntha

this marriage alliance between the Thracian imperial house and the Gothic Amalungs might yet enable Germanus rightfully to seize the opportunity which Belisarius had rightly rejected, and refound the Roman empire upon the basis of a Gothic aristocracy and a Thracian-Gothic imperial caste. . . . Justinian was old. When Germanus succeeded him, the sacred Amalungs would stand upon the threshold of empire, and the empire would obtain all the benefit of the stability which attached to the northern kingship.

It was a great project. The Goths appreciated it. When in due time Germanus marched into Italy, he might expect to find the whole spiritual atmosphere changed. Many of the Goths would not fight against Matasuntha's husband. Many of the imperialists who had entered the Gothic service would not fight against Justinian's nephew. When Germanus entered Rome, old Rome might suddenly become once more the centre of empire.

VII

Before this could happen, however, certain preliminary operations were necessary. The Persian, the African Delay and the Italian wars had involved a neglect of the Danube frontier that now began to influence the main course of events. The invaders of Illyricum were only savages who made life intolerable to the inhabitants of an agricultural province; they were not dangerous to the empire. They had therefore been neglected as comparatively unimportant. The fighting in Illyricum had been intermittent and ineffective police work. Huns and

Slavs were in the habit of carrying general murder and robbery, accompanied by hideous atrocities, over the face of the land. They had begun to come every year.[1] It made very little difference to the treasury; but it made a great deal of difference to Illyricum, which was slipping steadily down the slope that leads to chaos.

This year, while Germanus was marrying Matasuntha and organizing his army at Sardica, the Sclavenes raided far south, and showed signs of attacking Thessalonica. By the instructions of Justinian, Germanus interrupted his work to divert the intruders into Dalmatia. Having cleared the neighbourhood of them, he returned to Sardica. He had even issued orders that the army should in two days' time begin its march to Italy. But campaigning in the fever-haunted wastes had been too much for him. Before the two days were over, he was sick. Before long he was dead. With him vanished the plans which he had represented.

Death of Germanus September A. D. 550

Matasuntha was left with an unborn child who subsequently came into the world as Germanus Postumus. This child, who never became particularly great or famous, and never shook the world with any surprising exploits, was all that remained of the wonderful scheme for blending the Amalung kingship with the Roman imperial dignity of Justinian.

The name of Germanus is not posted high among the famous names of history. Few have heard of him. Oblivion has rolled over him. Yet he certainly holds a high rank among the splendid might-have-beens.

---

[1] For these Slavonic and Hunnic invasions, see Bury, *History of the Later Roman Empire*, II. 293, ff.

VIII

For a little while, Justinian seemed unable to decide
what next to do: and the struggle waited upon his decision. He might have cut his Italian losses, and postponed the whole question to some successor whose
finances might be in a more fortunate condition than
his own. But he had a duty to the Italian exiles, headed
by Pope Vigilius, and to those in Italy who had suffered
for their imperialistic sympathies. He could not drop
the question merely because he himself was tired of it.
It was his duty to see it through.

There was not another Germanus. No matter whom
he named, the new commander would possess different
qualifications, and would follow different policies. . . .
Justinian finally made an appointment which is almost
as debatable and controversial now as when it was first
made. He appointed the eunuch Narses.

Narses
appointed

If the selection of Germanus had been a stroke of
genius, the appointment of Narses was another such
stroke, though of a different kind. Narses was seventy-
five years old, and he was a man of courts and com-
mittees rather than a man of action. His experience
of war was not very large, nor had he any very great
military sympathies. But he had the gift of making
men work harmoniously together. Most men who knew
him liked him, and he made a good impression upon
strangers. In addition to this, he had a common-sense
and sobriety of temper which made him a reliable man.
In the circumstances of the empire, these were invaluable
gifts to possess. Narses was the kind of man who could
maintain not only amicable but even friendly relations

with colleagues as astonishingly diverse in temper and
tradition as Byzantine Greeks, Persian exiles, brutal
Langobardi, erratic Herulians and temperamental Italian
bishops. He could be depended upon to listen attentively
to all their views and prejudices, and to employ both to
good purpose. . . . Above all, he created in rough and
truculent men the conviction that he was always prepared to pay for those of the company who could not
pay for themselves: and a man of this kind can usually
depend upon being paid for by others when emergency
comes. . . . He was clever enough to possess no particular reputation for cleverness. It pleased his contemporaries to believe that the old fellow was under the special
protection and guidance of the Mother of God. This
was much better than the repute of brains. People admired, but were not jealous.

Narses had first to reach his army. In the unsettled
state of affairs the Sclavenes had been raiding and fighting as near at hand as Hadrianople and a great invasion
of Kotrigur Huns had spread over the peninsula. Narses
waited until the mingled diplomacy and force of the
imperial government had cleared the intruders away.
He set out in June, 551; and it was autumn before he
arrived at Salona, where the army of Germanus was
waiting. To Narses even the army of Germanus did
not seem sufficient. During the autumn and winter he
was busily at work increasing it. He took care to include
in his army a great variety of arms. Whatsoever methods
Totila might resort to, he would find in that army men
who could meet him at the same game, and men who
could meet him with its opposite.

Totila was well informed of all that he had to expect.

Qualifica-
tions of
Narses

He had left Sicily soon after the death of Germanus, and made his way slowly north. While he was preparing for the approach of Narses, the old programme went forward. Ancona was now besieged. The chief new feature was his development of his naval power. Now that he possessed nearly the whole of Italy, he had no difficulty in placing upon the sea a very powerful fleet, which operated along the Adriatic, raiding the coast of Greece, blockading Salona and helping in the siege of Ancona. John at Salona, and Valerian at Ancona answered in kind. There was a good deal of sea-fighting; and although the Greeks had the advantage, nevertheless any such operations as those of Belisarius, when he sailed from Salona round to Rome, had become impossible. One thing Totila's fleet did definitely accomplish —it made sure that Narses should come by land, and that Totila should meet him on definite ground where the Gothic tactics had the best chance of success.

Totila prepares

If the page of history had been torn off at this point; if we did not know any of the rest of the story, Totila's name would bulk very great in men's eyes. In some respects, he had done greater deeds than his predecessor Theuderic. Picking up the Gothic cause when it seemed extinguished for ever, he had reorganized the Gothic power, reconquered Italy, held his ground even against Belisarius himself, and had sought to conciliate the Italians, in accordance with Theuderic's policy. His actions now did not in any way suggest that he anticipated defeat. In spite of the success of Artabanes in recovering Sicily, Totila offset the loss by acquiring Sardinia and Corsica. All this autumn and winter, while Narses was pushing forward his preparations at Salona,

Totila's chances

Totila was at the height of his power and prestige. He had survived Germanus. He might survive Narses. He was perhaps the most powerful single monarch among the northern kings who had settled in the Roman empire.

Only one sign of ill-omen was discernible in the sky. The Frankish kings, who possessed a preternatural intuition as to how the cat would jump, were looking on bland and unimpressed. If anything, they were a little threatening in their courtesies to Justinian. They seemed to think that it was the emperor, not the Gothic king, who needed warning off Frankish territory.

IX

The spring came; and the all-nation army of Narses started from Salona. It was a formidable one. In numbers it was the greatest host which the empire had sent against the Goths. Belisarius had conquered the Africa of Geilamir and the Italy of Witigis with forces of some fifteen to twenty thousand men. The army with which Narses set out from Salona must have numbered some twenty-five thousand all told. But its size was not its only strength. It contained a memorable gathering of fighting men.

Narses sets out

There were four Roman divisions; beginning with the famous comitatus to which Germanus had attracted the best men in the empire. The troops of John we already know from their many deeds in Italy. A third division was commanded by John the Glutton; and the fourth by Dagisthaeus, an experienced veteran of the Lazic and Persian wars. Of these, the men of Germanus and John at least were those famous mailed and mounted bowmen of the type which won the battle of Tricamaron. With them rode a Persian corps, commanded by Kobad, a nephew of Khosru and a grandson of old Kobad, the King of Kings. There was a large body of Huns, and a smaller body of Gepidae under their chief Asbad. Then came two divisions of Heruls, no fewer than 3,000 under King Philemuth, and perhaps nearly as many under a leader named Aruth. Last, and by no means least, came King Edwin [1] of the Langobardi, with his comitatus, some five thousand five hundred strong, mounted knights and esquires all.

The army of Narses

When the army arrived at the head of the Adriatic above Istria, Narses needed to walk warily. He found Franks in possession everywhere: and it was not his object to fight with Franks. To his request for a free passage to Ravenna, a polite refusal was returned, on the ground that they could not dream of allowing a Langobard army to pass through Frankish territory. While Narses was considering this, it was reported to him that the refusal of the Franks was of no importance, since even if they gave permission he could not get south by the trunk road. Teias was at Verona with the Gothic vanguard, and every road was up, and every bridge impassable.

The problem was solved by the daring advice of John, who knew the country well. Instead of going south by the roads, either that to Verona or the coastal road,

---

[1] As few readers of English will realize the sound of such names as "Audoin" and "Alboin," it seems better to write them as "Edwin" and "Aelfwin" which are near enough to the sound and spelling known to our Anglo-Saxon ancestors. It is well to remember that these Langobardi were most of them blue-blooded tribesmen capable of showing their pedigree with any modern German of sixteen quarterings.

John suggested turning off before reaching Altinum, and marching by the sea side. By massing boats at each river-mouth or lagoon in turn, they could get the army over without bridges. . . . Narses, for all that he was a eunuch, and seventy-five years old, was game for the venture, and the plan was adopted.

The army, therefore, was ferried in boats along the great lagoon where Venice now stands. The place was silent and empty enough in those days; and of such persons as may have lived there, we hear nothing. The army then went scrambling on by land, while the boats came round to ferry them over the next water. In this way they got to Ravenna, somewhere about June 6th— and they probably needed a wash and brush-up by the time they got there.

The scramble to Ravenna

Relying on his fleet, Totila had made sure that the army of Narses should not sail into Ravenna by sea; but he had made no provision against it wading in along the shore. Here it was, safe in Ravenna. Narses halted at Ravenna for nine days. Then he pressed on. His aim was to meet and to destroy Totila himself, with the principal force of the Goths, and to this meeting he hastened with all the speed of which his army was capable. At Ariminum the bridge over the river was down. A pontoon bridge was instantly built higher up, and the army crossed.

At this point Narses and his army abruptly disappeared.

X

Totila, in the neighbourhood of Rome, recalled Teias from Verona and advanced north. He heard that Narses had passed Ariminum, but after that there was no news of him. Normally speaking, Totila could rely upon fighting in the neighbourhood of Fanum Fortunae, or even Ariminum: for he held the whole of the great Flaminian highway which ran from Rome to Fanum, and his hold upon it was fixed and confirmed by his possession of the tunnel of Petra Pertusa, the tunnelled rock a little north of Cales. Petra was impregnable. What happened to Belisarius there would not happen to Narses. The head of the road was therefore pretty safe. . . . Teias, arriving from Verona, would come by the route through Hostilia, Bologna, Florence, Arretium and Perusia. Totila would wait for him near Tadinum, which was a convenient spot for any one coming from Perusia to join an army on the Flaminian road. Totila arrived at Tadinum; but almost at once the army of Narses, having left the main road at Ariminum, and marched by a side road to Urbinum,[1] entered the Flaminian highway at Acqualagna, south of Petra, thus turning the position of the tunnelled rock. At Cales, Narses heard of the position of Totila, and at once elected to choose his own ground for fighting. Taking a side road, he established himself somewhere near the castle of Bastia, not far from Fabriano, where some Gaulish barrows marked the scene of a defeat of the Gauls at the hands of Roman troops centuries before.

Totila advances

Narses at once communicated with Totila. He advised him to submit, in the face of such superior force, or, alternatively, to name the time of battle. Totila declined to yield, and named the eighth day.

The armies in contact

[1] For the questions involved here, and the site of the battle, see Bury, *History of the Later Roman Empire*, II. 288, et seq.

It is probable that neither side was taking seriously this concession to convention. Totila moved during the following night, marched towards Fabriano, turned to his left, reached Melano, and pitched camp. At sunrise the imperialists found the Goths lined up a couple of bow-shots away. A battle was obviously imminent.

Narses and his advisers knew what they were about. They had not come all the way from Salona merely to exchange courtesies with Totila. They meant to destroy his army without fail. Their plan was to fight a defensive action if Totila would attack: and it seemed certain that he would. He had nothing to gain by delay. By far the best policy for him was to force an immediate issue. On this Narses calculated.

The Lombards and Heruls, dismounted, formed the centre of the imperialist array. On their right were grouped the imperial troops of Valerian, John the Glutton and Dagisthaeus, armoured and mounted bowmen, faced with a body of 4,000 unmounted archers. On their left, Narses took his own station with the comitatus of Germanus, and a similar facing of foot-archers. Back in the left rear waited the reserve, 500 horsemen, prepared to enter the battle when and where wanted: while a similar body of 1,000 waited well back, ready to make a turning movement to envelope the Gothic right as soon as the word was given.

The arrangements

Totila's forces were the smaller—apparently his strength was as three to five. Hence, though all was ready, his attack was delayed. He was waiting for Teias with the 2,000 horsemen from Verona, and Teias was still on the road. Totila tried to get round the left of the imperialists. Foiled in this, after a brisk skirmish,

he dropped the attempt. In order to pass the time, a few
entertainments were provided. An interesting single
combat between a Goth and an Armenian from Narses'
ranks ended in the triumph of the Armenian. Totila himself—a curious touch—obliged with a little exhibition
horsemanship. He came out in full caparison, glittering
with steel and gold and purple, and showed his paces
and his skill. Soon after mid-day, however, Teias arrived, and the signal was immediately given for lunch.
The Goths went off to their camp. Narses, however, was
taking no risks. He ordered food to be served out to his
army standing in rank.

After lunch the Goths returned, and now the business of the day began. A conference of the leaders had
evidently taken place. The Gothic dispositions were
altered. A deep column of horse, backed by infantry,
now faced the imperial centre. Narses saw that his centre
was to be knocked out by force; and he moved his foot
archers further out to the wings, and brought them
forward like the horns of a shallow crescent.

The Gothic preparations

Word was passed to the Goths to rely upon the spear
only. This order made it perfectly clear that the whole
fortune of the day was to be rested upon the weight of
of a cavalry charge.

So the issue was joined.

CHAPTER XIII

EPILOGUE: THE END OF THE REIGN
OF JUSTINIAN

I

IT was already late in the day when all the marshalling was complete, and the Goths moved. The battle was sharp, but it was short. The Gothic riders, like the Frenchmen at Cressy, came up in a tidal wave of horsemen, who meant to break by main force through all that was in their way. . . . They simultaneously met an immovable obstacle and were struck by an irresistible force. Their charge shattered itself and rolled back in retreat.

Battle of
Taginae
or Busta
Gallorum

Up to the very moment of the Gothic charge, the Langobardi had been an uncertain quantity. Not even Narses could guess whether they would fight, or refuse. Their repute and history are amply sufficient to show that the doubt was not upon their courage but upon their sympathies. Only Narses, we may guess, could have brought them into the field against the Goths at all. . . . What turned the scale, history does not tell us. It may have been prejudice; it may have been pride; it may have been mere ferocity. Whatsoever it was, the Langobardi held their ground with unbending tenacity, and the Gothic charge was repulsed from their solid phalanx.

While the Langobardi and Heruls held firm, the wings wheeled in somewhat upon the flanks of the Goths, and the bowmen, both mounted and on foot, poured in that deadly arrow-storm which had destroyed the Vandals at Tricamaron. It destroyed the Goths now. Held up by the Lombard pikes, and shot down by the Roman arrows, the Goths struggled awhile and were compelled to give back. Their footmen, instead of closing their ranks behind them, ran with them; and all was lost. That it was no trifling punishment which broke the Gothic charge is shown by their casualties. Six thousand men, one third of their whole force, and perhaps half of their Gothic tribesmen, littered the field over which the survivors rode for their lives.

The Gothic charge repulsed

Dusk was at hand. Under cover of it, Totila also rode. The flight was westward, towards the great Flaminian way; and the pursuers were fresh cavalry, who had not been engaged in the battle.[1] Asbad, the leader of the Gepidae, was among them. The story is a famous one how Asbad, galloping in the rout, aimed a blow at a fleeing Goth, and a young squire imprudently rushed in with: "Dog! will you strike your lord?" Asbad knew then whom he had to deal with, and he struck his lance into Totila, being instantly himself struck down by a Goth. The king however, was mortally wounded. His men got him across the Flaminian way to Caprae, and there he died.

Death of Totila. June–July A. D. 552

Teias got away safely; the Goths who escaped the slaughter and the pursuit made for the northern road through Umbria and Etruria, and reassembled at Ticinum. Totila's main treasure was stored there, though some was at Cumae.

---

[1] It is very unlikely that Asbad would have possessed a faster mount than the king of the Goths, and all the story depends on the fact that he was 'overtaking Totila. The king, also, must have been in the thick of the fight, for he was unrecognizable to a man who knew kings when he saw them.

II

That Totila was dead was certain. Some little while after the battle Narses discovered the spot at Caprae where the king was buried, and identified the body. The garments and cap, stained with blood, were despatched to Constantinople in proof of his death.

August,
A. D. 552

The Goths at Ticinum evidently had definite and independent information of their own, for they proceeded to the election of a new king. Teias was chosen. No rival candidates seem to have presented themselves.

A Frankish alliance was the hope and the policy of Teias; but he had not been king many days before he found that the Franks pulled no man's chestnuts out of the fire for him. They had their uses; they warned the imperialists away from Verona, where the Gothic garrison still remained; but they did not propose to help any one but themselves to the conquest of Italy.

Narses was soon in possession of all the fortresses on the Flaminian Way, and in due course he appeared before Rome. The city was held by a few Goths, who before very long surrendered. Unless the new Gothic king could put another army into the field, it was only a question of time before the commanders of the various fortresses, unable to hold out longer, one by one made their own terms with the empire. Teias was no statesman, but he was what neither Totila nor Witigis had been—a sportsman who was prepared to take tremendous risks without flinching. The chances were fifty to one against him. He gambled with his whole heart and soul on the one.

Teias as king

His objective was Cumae, where his brother Aligern was in charge of the other moiety of Totila's treasure.

Before he set out, Teias collected the hostages whom Totila had taken at Rome—three hundred youths from Roman families of standing—and executed them all. In Campania, the senatorial hostages placed there by Totila were similarly slain. If the Goths were to fall, they meant to drag down with them everything they could lay their hands on. Teias set out on his march to Cumae somewhere about the middle of July. By Narses' orders, John was on the watch upon all the Etrurian roads. Teias worked his way by side roads to the Adriatic coast, followed the great coast road southwards, and then apparently took the cross road by Teanum and Luceria, to Beneventum.

From Beneventum the obvious approach to Cumae was by Capua, or alternatively, through Suessula, Neapolis and Puteoli. Teias, however, did not mean to fight his way into Cumae if he could get round the corner at it. He therefore struck south from Beneventum, turned north west again at Salerno, and arrived at Nuceria, overlooking the southern waters of the Bay of Naples. On his left stretched out to sea the Sorrentine peninsula with the rock of Capri beyond it; in front of him, across a steep-banked stream, Vesuvius rose to its plumed summit. Along the shore road which led to Neapolis slept, deep underfoot, Pompeii and Herculaneum, not yet these many centuries to be dug out by archaeologists.

The march for Cumae

It was about the end of August when Teias arrived at Nuceria Alfaterna. All that was available of the Gothic fleet had gathered opposite old Stabiae. The plan of Teias was to embark on these ships, sail across the Bay of Naples, and land in the harbour of Cumae; and he all but achieved this remarkable military feat. Narses, however, when he heard that Teias had not been intercepted in Etruria, had called his best men south to Campania. It is probable, indeed, that his scouts had kept him informed of the route of Teias. At any rate Teias, when he came down to the Bay of Naples, found an imperial army camped on the banks of the river Draco.

To go back was undesirable; to stop still was difficult, and to go forward was impossible. It takes a great deal of brains to be clever in war—more, perhaps, than Teias possessed: and he spent about a month in studying this novel chess-problem, while his fleet kept him provided with supplies. Neither side cared to court defeat by attacking the line of the Draco. Teias was awakened from his thoughts by the arrival of a powerful fleet which Narses had urgently summoned from Sicily. The Gothic fleet, penned in, surrendered. With his supplies now cut off, the position of Teias became serious. Finally he retreated into the mountain which forms the root of the Sorrentine peninsula: the Mount Lactarius. The imperialists at once followed, and blockaded him there— probably with some kind of barricade or entrenchment.

The Goths held up

Teias and the Goths were not attacked in their new position, except by hunger. Their food soon gave out, and no supplies were available. They had been outmanœuvred and outwitted by a keener intelligence. Only one resource was possible—to sally out, and try whether it were possible to smash the cordon.

III

Procopius did not himself witness the battle of Mount Lactarius. His narrative is from the description of informants who may or may not have been reliable, but who were certainly deeply impressed by what they saw.

Abandoning their horses, the Goths fought [1] on foot in a solid phalanx. The imperial troops were taken by surprise, and had no opportunity for organised tactics; and it is probable that the ground rendered all tactics difficult, and cavalry tactics impossible. The army of the Goths was led by Teias in person, backed by some of his most trustworthy men. For a third of the day he fought, protected by his huge shield, from behind which he struck down his opponents by means of his long stabbing spear. When his shield was over-weighted with arrows, he called the name of a squire, who brought him a fresh shield. . . . At last, with twelve spears stuck on the shield he was using, the change of shields was bungled, and he was shot through the chest while making the exchange.

Battle of Mount Lactarius Oct. 1st 552

The head of Teias was stuck upon a spear and looked down upon the subsequent events.

Taking no heed of their lord's death, the comitatus of Teias fought on till dark. The next day they went on fighting. Only in the evening of the second day, when probably most or even all of the comitatus had fallen, and the only men left were the squires, servants and supernumeraries, did the Goths propose terms. They of-

[1] The battle of Mount Lactarius is not perfectly explained by Procopius. See Bury's *History of the Later Roman Empire*, II. 273, f.n. 2, where he puts forward Delbruck's suggestion that the Romans had constructed fortifications which needed to be attacked and defended on foot. . . . But as the Goths were forced from their position by famine, it is possible that their horses were not in condition to face a fight, and may even have been eaten. The suddenness of the Gothic attack was meant to prevent the imperialists from mounting. The ground may have been unsuitable for horses in any case.

fered to stop fighting if they might leave Italy with their movable property.

John advised that these terms should be accepted, and Narses approved. After the Goths had taken an oath never again to fight against the empire, they were allowed to disperse. With their surrender the last organized field force of the Goths was extinguished, and the long-drawn out struggle was at an end.

End of the battle

Unless another field force could in some way be invoked, the surrender of the Italian fortresses was certain. The Franks had declined to assist Teias, and even now they were particular to keep officially and formally on amicable terms with Justinian. But they had so little liking for a proud and victorious empire as their Italian neighbour, that the war which they would not officially approve they informally winked at. Two brothers, Leutharis and Buccelin, of the Alamanni, were allowed to fit out what later ages would have called a filibustering expedition. They raised an army of some 75,000 men. Their object was to plunder Italy rather than to defeat Narses: but as long as their help was a possibility the hopes of the Goths were not absolutely extinct. Cumae therefore, still held out. They entered Italy in the spring following the death of Teias: the spring of 553.

Narses detached a force to watch Cumae, and himself proceeded north. Sending John and Valerian to hold the line of the Padus, Narses devoted his own energies to obtaining the surrender of the Gothic fortresses. In this he was very successful. The most obstinate case, Lucca, surrendered in the autumn. Aligern, the commander at Cumae, came to Ravenna in person to yield up the city. He had given up hope. The exception to this tale of uni-

Leutharis and Buccelin in Italy

form success was the case of the Franks, who had forced the crossings of the Padus and taken Parma; in consequence of which John and Valerian fell back to Faventia, where they covered Ravenna and Ariminum.

Upon the whole, Narses was a humane man. He must have thought matters out during the winter, for when the campaigning season returned, he issued orders for the reconcentration of his own field army at Rome. Although the fortresses would be unaffected, the civil population would be completely exposed to the tender mercies of the Franks; and the only reason which Narses can have had for a measure so damaging to innocent people is a wish to bring the Franks to a definite action. By far the worst prospect was that of a dragged-out war. Almost any expedient was justifiable which would bring a swift development and a decided end.

Although he had to wait for the fulfilment of this wish, in the end he obtained it. The invaders parted their forces. The smaller body after ravaging Apulia and Calabria, returned north laden with booty, most of which it lost to a surprise raid by the garrison of Pisaurum. At Ceneta in Venetia plague broke out and Leutharis was one of its victims.

A different fate befell the other portion. Buccelin led it as far as the straits of Messina. On his return he listened to the persuasions of Gothic advisers, who promised him the kingship of the Goths if he would expel the imperialists; and, confident in his power to conquer, he accepted the proposition.

Destruction of the invaders

The news that Buccelin had "dug in" at Casilinum on the Volturnus brought Narses instantly from Rome. The two armies were not dissimilar in numbers, though

the Franks had the more men.[1] At Capua the story of
Tricamaron and Taginae was repeated. The Franks
planned to smash the Roman centre by sheer force.
Narses refused his centre, advanced his wings of mounted
bowmen and shot the Franks down *en masse*. It was said
that only five Franks escaped. The casualties among the
imperialists numbered eighty.

This time it was the end. The Goths had no more kick
left in them. The Franks did not repeat their invasion
of Italy, and at some time during the next few years
they abandoned their conquests between the Alps and
the Padus. Their purpose had been sufficiently fulfilled.
They had finally and for ever destroyed any idea that
may have lingered among the imperialists of reconquering Gaul. From this time forward Gaul was unquestion-
ably Frankish.[2]

IV

In the August after the defeat of the Franks, Narses
received from Constantinople the new constitution for
Italy. He spent thirteen more years in the peninsula, and
he saw out the reign of Justinian. He was a good ruler,
and on the whole a wise and well-disposed man.

**Settlement
of Italy**

---

[1] Narses had 18,000. The figure 30,000 given by Agathias for Buccelin's army
is doubted by Bury, (*History of the Later Roman Empire,* II. 279, f.n. 1.) Between 20,000 and 25,000 would be nearer the probability.

[2] The independence of Gaul of course involved that of Britain. The case of
Spain is curious. A portion of Spain was actually reconquered by Liberius in
the year 550. Baetica remained part of the empire for more than a couple of
generations. But any idea of reconquering the empire, and restoring its old boundaries, came to an end with Justinian. When the Franks themselves took up the
idea, times had so changed (partly through Frankish agency) that their policy
had a new meaning, and implied a new world.

A kind of lethargy was stealing over the world. We can hardly call it peace. Men went on struggling; but the vital energy which had once inspired them was dying out; the struggle seemed to become more and more aimless, or to be diverted to fresh aims. The reconquest of Africa, Italy and part of Spain had been accomplished; the great Corpus of Roman Law had been drawn up: but although these were great things, and although Justinian's legal activities have been enough by themselves to make his name immortal, we must not forget that they were all side-issues. The great project, the plan of campaign, the ambition of Justinian's youth, the work of his life—the restoration of the Roman empire—to which all these things had been subsidiary; this was failing. He had faced without flinching all the difficulties thrown in his way by God and man; through fire, earth-   Upshot
quake, war, pestilence and human hatred he had pursued a firm and unfaltering way; now his power was slowly ebbing, with the work undone. . . . No one can say that the Roman empire, the world-state, slipped out of existence accidentally or unobtrusively. Its fight to come back had been a long and a magnificent fight. . . . But those men, like the historian Procopius—and he was only the mouthpiece of a party—who saw the fruits of that struggle, and the human life and happiness destroyed in the process, recoiled from it with an almost hysterical horror. To their eyes, the great man who had guided that contest was a devil gloating over the agonies of a ruined world. . . . And still he lived and kept on his path; he had not given up yet.

V

It was in the year before the destruction of Buccelin and his army that the silk-worm was brought to the west; and in that same year Procopius finished his history.

The struggle with Persia had throughout been an economic one—the first stages of a contest which, much

later, drove the western nations to the exploration of the Cape route to the Indies, to the discovery of America and the circumnavigation of the globe. During this earlier period the silk trade played a principal part, and the economic side of Justinian's reign might almost be written in terms of the struggle for silk. Most of the fighting with Persia on the Mesopotamian frontier had been an attempt to obtain military advantages with which to bargain for commercial ones. Success in this respect had not been great. Persia's complete control of the silk routes from China, the source of the raw material, gave her an unshakeable position as a monopolist power.[1] None of the fighting in Mesopotamia succeeded in modifying this fact.

An interesting—if ironic—book might be written on the part played by short-sighted policy in creating the results it attempts to avoid. Persia might in the long run have found it the wiser plan to use her advantages with moderation; for her monopoly was so serious a matter for western merchants that it drove them to expedients

[1] Diehl, *Justinien*, pp. 536–537. The map facing p. 320 will show the ease with which Persia could control the routes feeding not only the markets at Merv, Balkh, etc. but the north-west Indian markets also.

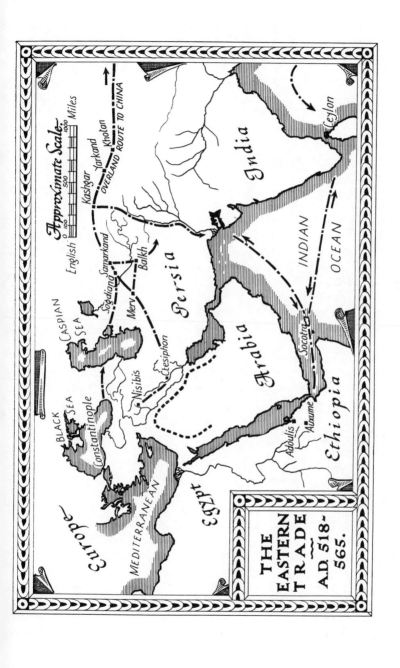

THE
EASTERN
TRADE
A.D. 518–
565.

and experiments some of which produced the very last results which the Persians would have wished to see.

Early in the reign of Justinian the merchants of Constantinople, helped by the imperial government, developed closer relations with the Arab and Ethiopian kingdoms at the southern end of the Red Sea. They were able to regain some of the direct touch with India which their predecessors had once possessed. The great port of Adulis was a market both for Indian and African products, and the operations of Roman capital, and the journeys of Roman commercial representatives, penetrated into both countries.[1]

The Persian monopoly

All efforts, however, to break the Persian silk monopoly through a combination of Roman capital and Ethiopian agency were fruitless. The Persian mercantile interests were too firmly entrenched to be dislodged. After the peace with Persia in 532, the old state of things continued. Somewhat similar conditions existed on the northern border of Persia. In addition to the military danger which Justinian had every reason to fear from a Persian occupation of Colchis, he needed free access to that part of the world because through Colchis it was possible to reach Sogdiana without touching Persian soil. A vain passion for ruling the rocks of the Caucasus was hardly the motive for the money and the men and the trouble he spent on his Lazic wars. A possible access to the Chinese silk market was in his mind.

Justinian's attention to the commercial interests of

[1] Diehl, *Justinien*, p. 535. Merchants of the empire seem to have employed Ethiopian ships and seamen as more suited to the climate.

the empire in this region did not lead to any great development during his own reign. The connection with Turkestan was developed by Justin II. But it led indirectly to an expansion of Roman trade with the great pastoral steppes north of the Black Sea, and an increasing penetration of those countries by Roman influence and Roman ideas: roads, methods of communication and geographical knowledge became more familiar—a result which heralded the vast changes which during the next few centuries were to transform eastern Europe.

Spread
of trade

As long as the Persian silk monopoly remained unbroken, however, the industry and trade of the empire were not in a settled or satisfactory condition. The connection between events is often noteworthy. Khosru's uneasiness about the political results of the conquest of Italy led him (as we have seen) to renew the war in 540; and the closing of the Persian border, which naturally followed, led to an immediate rise in the price of raw silk. At the emperor's direction, the ministers concerned fixed a maximum price at which the manufactured silk could be sold to the public. As he could not control the price of the raw material, the margin of profit promptly disappeared, silk was driven off the market altogether, and the industry stopped. . . . Peter Barsymes, the secretary of the public treasury, thereupon came to the rescue by taking over some of the ruined businesses. There was already a government silk manufacture. Peter transformed the whole silk industry into a government monopoly. This certainly saved the work-people and maintained the work.

But in that year when Leutharis and Buccelin invaded Italy, a proposal was made which was of historic importance. Two monks of Khotan [1] undertook to procure silk-worms' eggs, and to make the experiment of rearing the silk-worms upon Roman soil. Backed by the imperial treasury, they carried out the task. The eggs were smuggled from the Chinese border concealed in a hollow cane; the worms were hatched according to the correct methods, and the production of silk was established in Syria.

Silk-worms brought to Syria A. D. 553

The supply of home-grown silk, so begun, was not at first sufficient to provide for the necessities of the industry in the Roman empire. But even although many years had to pass before the demand could be met by home-grown silk, it had now become certain that in due course the Persian monopoly would be broken, and that comparatively cheap raw material would be available in the west.

VI

Theodora had left behind her one legacy of importance; and that was her conviction that voluntary religious reunion was indispensable to the empire. Justinian continued to work at this object after her death, as if he felt that it was one way of honouring her memory. The year which saw the silk-worm introduced into the empire saw also the second Council of Constantinople, which is reckoned the fifth oecumenical council.

Second Council of Constantinople

It might possibly have been wiser to leave matters alone; but Justinian was not a man to flinch from diffi-

---

[1] "Serinda" (Procopius, *History*, VIII. xvii. 1–8) Khotan is usually supposed to be the place intended. Cochin-China, which has been suggested, seems unlikely. Procopius only tells us that the place in question was "above" or topmost of the Indians. Warmington and Cary, in *The Ancient Explorers* (1929) seem to accept the monks as coming from China itself.

cult enterprises. The progress made with the conquest of Italy seemed to call for progress in the task of moral reunion. The task might have been a difficult one, even if the issues had been placed before all the parties in their baldest and most obvious form. It became almost impossible when they were studied under the disguised aspect of theological questions. Whether old Rome was to retain her ancient place and prestige in the empire, was a question worth discussion, though hard to answer. But the main form in which the problem was tabled for discussion was whether the works of Theodore of Mopsuestia should be condemned by the church.

The opinions of Theodore of Mopsuestia are fully as well worth the time and attention of mankind as crossword puzzles and missing-word competitions: and study devoted to his theological works is probably not always wasted. The modern reader, however, who studied those works in order to discover a key to the proceedings of the Council of Constantinople, would be committed to a labyrinth which could not possibly have any issue. And the explanation of this strange fact is that the works and doctrines of Theodore were only an excuse for the Council—not the reason for it.

We shall, accordingly, search in vain through the works of Theodore for an explanation why, during the controversy which led up to the Council, the pope and the archbishop of Milan were involved in physical violence with the police. Neither the preliminaries of the Council nor the Council itself would have taken the form they did, had Theodore been their real subject of discussion. The theme which they really did meet to argue was, Who ought to be the fount of authority in the

Subject of discussion

Roman world? And this theme they certainly did discuss.

When the letters of convocation were issued to the bishops, invitations were restricted to those of the eastern provinces of the empire. The Council was opened [1] by the reading of a communication from Justinian in which he stated the subjects supposed to be under consideration. As any other subjects would have done just as well, we need pay no further attention to them.

The
Council
meets
May 5th
A. D. 553

The pope, although he was in Constantinople, had been as careful as the emperor to avoid being present at the Council. Informed of the agenda, he replied that he would issue a judgment in writing. As soon as it was ready, the emperor sent Belisarius formally to call upon the pope, and to communicate his refusal to receive the document. It was therefore sent to the emperor by messenger. Justinian sent it back. He did not intend to receive any papal judgments of this description.

This much being settled, the next step was to carry the war into the enemy's camp. Justinian submitted to the Council a fully documented report of the pope's changes of opinion, and general indecision and untrustworthiness. It was accompanied by an official edict with the force of law, deposing the pope.

The proceedings of the Council, as approved by Justinian, were then formally passed, and the Council terminated.

---

[1] The view here taken of the Council is confirmed by the fact that the serious theological work, the canons dealing with Origenistic heresies, was done at meetings before the formal opening of the Council on May 5th. (Bury, *History of the Later Roman Empire*, II. 389, f.n. 2.) A good short description of Justinian's ecclesiastical policy will be found in Vasiliev's *History of the Byzantine Empire*, I, 181–189.

Justinian and Pope Vigilius both of them lived many centuries before the births of Gregory VII or Innocent III. Neither of them had heard of any long tradition of Roman ecclesiastical authority, which at this point had scarcely begun. They were therefore not in any way influenced by preconceived ideas concerning these matters. Their actions sprang direct from the pressure of contemporary needs.

Had the proceedings of the Council produced the results for which Justinian hoped, the trouble he took over it would have been rewarded; but so far from this being the case, he quarrelled with the Catholic west without healing the breach with those Monophysites of the east whom it had been his purpose to conciliate. The

Conflict of east and west

pope, sick, and alarmed at his own apparent isolation, apologized and recanted; but his fellow-churchmen of western Europe were far from endorsing either his recantation or his apology. Whether their views concerning Theodore of Mopsuestia were always based upon remarkably close acquaintance with his works may be very much doubted; but they were quite clear that an emperor at Constantinople was not competent to settle a disputed question: and it was precisely this competence of the emperor which was the issue. If any authority could solve doubt and soothe dissension, apparently it was not he. Every one seemed to agree on this point. The Monophysites of the east and the Catholics of the west might dissent from one another's theological opinions— but they were at one upon the principle that there was no authority which could cover alike the Greek east and the Roman west.

VII

The second Council of Constantinople thus represented the critical decision which determined the final
dissolution of the Roman empire as a world-state. If there
were no longer to be any universal authority to which
all men could assent, then the empire itself was surrendering its function. It had first arisen through its
power of commanding, by one means or another, the
assent of all men everywhere. When it lost this power,
its end was at hand. . . . Within a century, the Monophysite lands had become Muslim, and the kingdoms
of the west were forming a new comity of nations on
the basis of a common Catholicism. . . . Justinian had
set out to restore the ancient limits of the empire. This
was the result.

A critical decision

War, comet and plague had heralded the fateful years
of decision; they went out in earthquake. While Narses
was wiping out Buccelin, and the bishops were still talking about their visit to Constantinople, a series of shocks
did disastrous damage throughout Asia Minor. At
Cyzicus the church collapsed during the time of service,
and fell on the worshippers. Three years later, a great
earthquake shook Constantinople. In that year—A. D.
557—the long drawn out Lazic war came to an end,
favourably for Justinian. He had kept Persia out of the
Euxine. The formal peace was not concluded until five
years later, in 562: but when it came, it settled the Lazic
question in favour of the empire. So the wars were
wound up.

As Justinian began to grow very old, and one after
another his great tasks were successfully or unsuccess-

fully finished, there came a quality of incoherence over
the story of his remaining years. He was slipping into
those days in which the man who once could work his
subordinates to exhaustion is more and more often found
by them quietly dozing over his own desk. The dome of
Sancta Sophia gave them all something to think about in
the year 558, by falling. Anthemius was dead; but his
colleague and successor did a few interesting and ingenious things, and put the dome back; and they enjoyed a solemn service of dedication. And in the same year
Constantinople had alarums and excursions of another
sort. The Kotrigur Huns, under their King Zabergan,
slipped past all the Illyrian castles, and raided up to the
very gates of the great city. Wives clung to their husbands, tradesmen buried their safes in convenient places,
and the elderly Belisarius was hastily summoned to save
his native country. He was still the same old Belisarius,
the artful dodger whose gifts as a military improvisator
were perhaps second only to those of Hannibal. Having
next to no army, and no means of fighting, he rigged up
a fake army which answered all the necessary purposes
equally well.

The last campaign of Belisarius illustrates to perfection
his peculiar gifts. He had three hundred veterans of the
Italian wars, a large mass of useless amateur soldiers, and
a mob of peasant refugees who would be only too glad to
kick a Hun to death, but who were not otherwise qualified
for warfare. No one was better acquainted than Belisarius with the Hunnic tactics, which he had himself exploited a hundred times with deadly effect. What he had
to do now was to invent a method of circumventing the

tactics which had once made him an unbeatable commander.

He was perfectly successful in doing so. He so manœuvred and laid his dispositions that he induced a large body of Huns to ride straight upon a limited front which was held by his veterans. Before the Huns closed, they were attacked by concealed wings of javelin men and slingers. The result was that the Huns instinctively closed their ranks, and became jammed into a mass in which there was no room for them to use their bows. They were then stampeded by the well-judged use of a stage army in the background, which proceeded to enact a suitable demonstration of raging warfare "off." Before the wretched Huns could reach what they imagined to be safety, four hundred had been killed, without the loss of a single life in Belisarius' comic opera army. They abandoned their camp and departed in full retreat under the impression that they were being pursued by immense numbers of Roman troops.

Battle of Chettus A. D. 558

The little battle of Chettus exercised a great moral effect. It was largely instrumental in clearing the Huns from the neighbourhood of Constantinople, and in inducing them to return home. But its chief point of interest to posterity is the justification it affords of the military genius of Belisarius. It proved that he could defeat the tactics which he had used so often to defeat others.

Justinian ransomed the captives carried off by the Huns. He then wrote to Sandichl, the king of the rival Utugur Huns, pointing out that the Kotrigurs possessed a large amount of money which ought to belong to Sandichl. The latter appreciated the point and lost no time in transferring it to his own strong-box, wiping out most of the Kotrigur Huns in the process. Nobody wept over them, and the world was not noticeably poorer for their loss.

VIII

The majority of men, in all ages, live and die without passing definite judgment on their leaders. Justinian indeed had never been the type of man who arouses popular enthusiasm. His virtues were not those which are loved by the ordinary man: his faults were strange and recondite. For the most part the verdicts which live are passed by a small group of educated men: or at any rate, by men who have the gift of words. Procopius, like Tacitus, had the power of determining the opinions of posterity.

The year in which the treaty with Persia was signed, and in which the seal was set to the emperor's success in Lazica, had other claims to be memorable. A certain Procopius was prefect of Constantinople, and it is possible that he was the historian.

Procopius
and
Justinian

After leaving the household of Belisarius he had evidently obtained employment from the emperor, who appreciated his historical value and his literary style. His work on the Buildings of Justinian was completed in the year 560. It is a general survey of the emperor's architectural activities, and it still remains a work of the first importance. . . . Procopius, in his history, had been non-committal respecting the character and policy of Justinian. In his work on the Buildings, he lays on his loyal eulogiums with marked fervour. He had his reward, and two years later reached the proud status of prefect.

He did not, however, burn the manuscript of the *Anecdota,* which he had carefully compiled as an appendix to his History. While he was submitting to Justinian his fervid flatteries in the *Buildings,* that manuscript must have been locked in some safe hiding place, not to see the light of general publicity for some eleven centuries or so. . . . While the aged emperor was laboriously attending to the diploma by which Procopius became a prefect, the would-be prefect may have been re-reading and retouching his account of the Demon Emperor and the Harlot Empress, and inserting a few more lurid tales of their horrid iniquities.

Verdict of the *Anecdota*

It was not altogether an accident that the historian dared not publish a book containing such allegations. A large number of his contemporaries would have been as much astonished to read them as we are. Many persons, well acquainted with Justinian, would have remarked that they had never noticed any tendency on his part to walk about without a head. As for the friends of Theodora—they would instantly have burned the book. But ungrateful, unreasonable and incredible as Procopius was, he did in his unreason reflect a wide-spread discontent, a deep disillusion. He succeeded in expressing, in a symbolical form, truths the direct expression of which escaped him.

They escaped him, because they were too subtle for Procopius—perhaps too subtle for any man of his era. There are certain conditions in which force is a remedy. In some circumstances war can repress disunion and rebellion, and reunite the State. . . . But Justinian had been fundamentally wrong in supposing that by war he could reunite the Roman empire. Its disunion was past the point at which force was a remedy. It needed patience, time, commerce, the mutual accommodation and interplay of friendly contact, to restore and maintain a unity which in earlier ages had first been created by just such means. War only intensified the disunion which Justinian set out to cure. . . . And Justinian had been fundamentally wrong in persisting with his policy in the teeth of all the reasons against it. Heaven and earth had cried out to him; but he would not hear. . . . And because he did what he did, and thought as he thought, the gift of political unity was withdrawn from Europe, which has never had it since. . . . But Procopius could not say all this.

The condemnation of Justinian

Hence, two portraits have descended to us: one of the Demon Emperor of Procopius, and another of that great and august man, something of whose wisdom and large-mindedness is traditionally enshrined in the very name "Justinian." . . . But they were one and the same man.

IX

Every one was so ready to see Justinian gone, that a few persons thought it might be well to hurry him off. A conspiracy by a group of obscure individuals, who designed to murder the emperor during one of those quiet hours when he was alone, was detected and suppressed. No one would have thought it particularly important had not the confessions of the conspirators involved two of the chief servants of Belisarius; his steward

The last plot

Paulus, and another. These were arrested, and, put to the question, asserted that they had acted under the direction of their master.

A meeting of the senate was convoked for the fifth of December, and on that day Justinian laid before the senators the confessions of the conspirators. Exactly what they were, and how they implicated Belisarius, we do not know. When he heard the charges made against him, he was much cast down. Ordered to dismiss his retainers, and to place himself under arrest, he did so. There had in all probability been some indiscretion on his part, which gave a certain face to the charges; but his history, and his character, and the readiness with which he obeyed the disciplinary measures imposed upon him, mollified Justinian, and removed the vexation he had felt. In July, after some seven months' disgrace, Belisarius was once more received at court, and the incident closed.

Belisarius and Justinian reconciled July 19th A. D. 563

Belisarius lived about a year and three quarters after this last adventure. He died in March, in the year A. D. 565, in the full possession of his honours and his property, and the friendship of Justinian. He cannot have been much more than fifty-seven or fifty-eight years old; and he may even have been younger. . . . He is almost the one human being of whom Procopius drew a wholly favourable portrait: a tall, handsome man, a skilful and chivalrous soldier, a faithful husband, a leader beloved by his followers and all who knew him: [1] a man who was never seen drunk, and never assumed any airs of superiority. . . . It is probable that Antonina had predeceased him,[2] for after his death his property went into the im-

---

[1] The description of Belisarius is in Procopius, VII. i. 5–21.

[2] For the rather tenuous evidence to the contrary, see Hodgkin, *Italy and her Invaders*, IV. 543, f.n.

perial treasury, and was administered by the treasury offices which were installed in the palace of Marina.

X

Death of Justinian

With the death of Belisarius, Justinian himself seemed to feel that his last personal link with the world was snapped. Eight months later, on November 14th 565, Petrus Sabbatius, the Thracian peasant, the great emperor JUSTINIAN, followed the mighty band of friends who had made his reign so memorable. He was eighty-three years old.

His nephew Justin, the son of his sister Vigilantia, was his natural heir. While Justinian lived, he had held on firmly to supreme power, and Justin held only the comparatively humble post of Curopalates, and the dignity of Patrician. But he had married Theodora's niece Sophia, a woman of ability, the daughter of Sittas and Comito; and he had been kept near the emperor's person, where he could make those intimate acquaintances which would enable him to secure in due course the support of the necessary allies. Justin became the new emperor without opposition or trouble, and the new empress, Sophia, cast over the coffin of Justinian a pall of imperial purple, embroidered in gold thread with the series of his labours. . . . It was a magnificent theme for the artist. Imagination likes to dwell over the scenes that should have followed one another round the border—Geilamir bowing before the imperial thrones, and Witigis riding through the streets of Constantinople, and Khosru turning away baffled from Edessa, and Totila galloping for his life; and castles being built in Africa, and silk-worms being reared in Syria, and ships sailing the Indian seas. But no matter what went round the border, nearly every man who had to guess at the subject of the great centre-piece would imagine that it contained a picture of Justinian enthroned, ordering the compilation of the Corpus of Roman Civil Law. For all the other things were the romantic adventures of Justinian; but this was his solid success.

His work

XI

Procopius, concluding his life's labours, had remarked that the truth would be known when the Demon died, or disappeared in a stench of brimstone. The Demon was dead, but no remarkable revelations seem to have come to light. His treasury was not so full as it might have been; but this was its usual state.

The only truth that came to light came slowly and by degrees. It was the fact that the Roman empire was no longer a world-state, and the world was no longer the world of Augustus. . . . Procopius still wrote the language of Thucydides: but the material of his history was the world of Froissart.

INDEX

Enter Justinian

Exit Justinian